BORN BAD

BORN BAD

ORIGINAL SIN AND THE MAKING OF THE WESTERN WORLD

JAMES BOYCE

COUNTERPOINT
BERKELEY

Library of Congress Cataloging-in-Publication Data
Boyce, James, 1964-
Born bad : a novel / James Boyce.
pages cm
Includes bibliographical references.
ISBN 978-1-61902-498-4
1. Sin, Original. I. Title.

BT720.B69 2015
233'.14--dc23

2014044899

COUNTERPOINT
2560 Ninth Street, Suite 318
Berkeley, CA 94710
www.counterpointpress.com

Printed in the United States of America
Distributed by Publishers Group West

10 9 8 7 6 5 4 3 2 1

To my parents,
Peter and Lorinne Boyce

In gratitude
ॐ

I am confounded, I am confounded,
poore silly wretch that I am, I am confounded,
and my minde is distracted, my tongue is
confounded, and my whole nature corrupted ...
—GEOFFREY GOODMAN, *The Fall of Man; or,*
The Corruption of Nature, 1616[1]

He did not need man's testimony about man,
for he knew what was in a man.
—JOHN 2:25

Original sin: The view which holds that the sin which caused Adam's fall and expulsion from paradise is transmitted from generation to generation, so that all descendants of Adam must be regarded as being of a 'perverted' or 'depraved' nature.
—MARTIN LUTHER KING, SERMON NOTES

BORN BAD

ORIGINAL SIN
IN CHRISTENDOM

PREFACE

But for this mystery [of original sin], the most incomprehensible of all, we remain incomprehensible to ourselves.

—BLAISE PASCAL

WHAT IS WRONG WITH ME? This question has haunted the West for fifteen hundred years, but until recently it came with an answer – which was called original sin. Western people believed they were 'born bad' because they had inherited the sin of the first humans. Their understanding of themselves was shaped, as it has been in almost all cultures, by an overarching story of creation.

Adam and Eve is an ancient myth whose origins are lost in the campfires of prehistory, making the Western interpretation of the story a comparatively recent innovation. The West shared the same primal parents as now vanished tribes, Jews, Muslims and Eastern (Orthodox) Christians, but it stood alone in seeing the eating of the forbidden fruit in the Garden of Eden as the *original* sin – not only the first sin of human history, but also one that subsequently became innate to the human condition. Only in this version of creation did a decision to disobey God in Paradise become a sin that was inherited by all.[2]

The articulation of original sin and the making of the Western world were enmeshed. The doctrine, like the West itself, was a

3

product of the tumultuous breakup of the Latin-speaking part of the Roman Empire. It underpinned the distinctive religion formulated by the Catholic Church as a Christian culture was built out of the imperial ruins. The creation story was the spiritual foundation on which the Western world was made, directing how people understood the divine, each other, the natural world and, above all, themselves.

Original sin is not part of the wider Judeo-Christian tradition. For Jews and Eastern Christians, the doctrine's divorce of sin from morality was incomprehensible. It was not just the modern mind that found it difficult to imagine how Adam's sin could become everyone's, or to conceive of a God who would condemn otherwise innocent people to hell because of it. In no other religion were people understood to be *born* bad; in no other were they conceived with a permanently corrupted nature that faced the wrath and judgement of God.[3] The deity of the West is unique in judging people before they commit a moral act. Those who first fought against the doctrine, in the fifth century, argued that a newborn baby could not be regarded as a sinner. They lost the debate.

An alternative tradition, inherited from Judaism and sustained by Eastern Christianity, recognised that all human beings sinned but saw sin as freely chosen behaviour which did not corrupt the essential goodness of created nature. This perspective was never totally extinguished in the West, but the dominant view was that human beings were born sinners, subject to the just wrath of God not only because of *what they did*, but *who they were*.

Original sin makes so little rational or ethical sense that it is not surprising that even the churches now prefer to pretend that the West's Christian inheritance is centred on good behaviour rather than inescapable corruption. But the doctrine is much more than the idiosyncratic teaching of a bygone age. In 1934 Carl Jung observed: 'Christianity is our world ... Our whole science, everything that passes through our head, has inevitably gone through this

4

history.' Jung exaggerated in claiming that 'the age of rational enlightenment has eradicated nothing', but he was right to be frustrated at the assumption that the influence of Christian ideas concluded when people rejected the Christian religion.[4] This influence is most obvious in the distinctive discontent of modern people – the feelings of guilt and inadequacy associated not with *doing* wrong but with *being* wrong. This angst is as evident in the anxieties of contemporary consumers as it was among ancient believers.

Because most people since the start of the scientific age have preferred to reject or forget their culture's strange spirituality, it has become a near-impossible task to untangle the threads that connect a secular mindset to ancestral religion. Nevertheless, an attempt must be made, because no religious inheritance can be banished by such feeble weapons as amnesia or scorn. Indeed, disdained beliefs readily metamorphose into new dogmas, as fewer people recognise their continuity with older ways of thought.

Perhaps no culture in human history has been as dismissive of religion as the twenty-first-century West, but the question discussed in the second part of this book is whether that has freed people from the ingrained suppositions of the religious tradition discussed in the first part. The fact that the question cannot be definitively answered does not meant that it should not be asked. The alternative is to believe that any continuity between original sin's perspective on human nature and that of the philosophies which define modernity is mere coincidence. Even if that is true, it should be argued rather than assumed.

Western people are increasingly ready to respect creation myths. It is now widely understood that the point of such allegories is not to document a literal, historical truth; rather, they represent internalised lore which helps people place themselves in the cosmos. They provide a foundation to the framework that shapes consciousness itself. But this anthropological wisdom, so sound in its application to other cultures, seems to be suspended when the thinker turns to home. Even those who courageously endeavour to understand themselves and mend their relationships with other people and the natural world often remain ignorant or scornful of the story that shaped them.

The purpose of this book is neither to defend nor condemn the Western creation story, but to show that its influence was not ended by science and secularism. I do not wish to join the ancient argument about the truth of original sin's insights, but I hope to demonstrate that, for better or for worse, the doctrine has always been central to the Western experience of what it means to be human. Without some knowledge of this mystery, the danger is that we will be, as Pascal suggested, 'incomprehensible to ourselves'.

It is because understanding should precede judgement that our first task is not to decide on either the truth or the worth of original sin, but to sit at the feet of our ancestors and listen carefully to what it meant to them.

1

THE FATHER OF ORIGINAL SIN

We do not say that God is the author of evil, and yet we can correctly say that human beings are born evil as a result of the bond of original sin with God alone as their creator.

—ST AUGUSTINE[5]

ST AUGUSTINE (354–430) IS THE FATHER of Western Christianity. He completed for religion in the West what St Paul had begun for the faith as a whole: the creation of a cohesive and binding set of teachings from diverse and disputed traditions.[6] He was also a faithful lover and doting father, who famously struggled with sex. Much of Augustine's extraordinary theological output of some ninety books and eight thousand sermons (distributed by relays of stenographers and teams of copyists across the Roman Empire) was highly original, but his struggle to achieve celibacy, as he documented in his autobiography, *Confessions*, was standard fare in the saintly struggle. What was distinctive in Augustine's account was that he blamed himself, rather than the seductive temptations of the Devil, for his plight. Appropriately enough for the author of the creation story of a culture which would become focused on individual experience, lust led him to search *within* to understand sin's inexorable grip, and from this intensely personal journey emerged an explanation for *everyone's* desire to sin.

Augustine's extended effort to achieve chastity has been satirised for centuries. It is usually assumed that before he became a repressed celibate, Augustine led a life of debauchery. In fact, his family life, both as a child and after he became a father himself, was unremarkable. Augustine recorded his life journey not because he thought it unusual – the standard autobiographical motivation – but because he believed it represented the universal human condition.

Although Augustine's father, who died while his son was still in his early teens, had not been a practising Christian, the young man was brought up a Catholic by his mother, Monica. In his late teens, he formed a faithful long-term relationship with a young Catholic woman from a neighbouring town, and their son, Adeodatus (meaning 'gift of God'), was born in 372. Augustine records that he 'lived with only one woman and kept faith with her bed' during the fifteen years they were together.[7] He ended the relationship only when his family arranged his engagement to a girl of higher social standing.

The two-year wait until his new fiancée reached the legal marriageable age (which was twelve) was a critical period in Augustine's self-discovery. An old translation of *Confessions* well captures his inner torment:

> [She] who was wont to be his bed-fellow, being torn from my side as an impediment to my marriage, my heart that cleaved to her was broken and wounded until it bled. To Africa then returned she, vowing to thee that she would never know man more, and leaving with me the son whom I had begotten of her. But I, miserable man, unable to imitate the woman, and being impatient of the two years delay after which I should receive her whom I desired [for marriage], and being less a lover of marriage than a slave to lust, did procure yet another – though not a wife – by whom that disease of the soul, as strong or even stronger than before, might be sustained.[8]

It was in the ashes of a broken relationship, seeking consolation in sex which comforted the body but tortured the soul, that Augustine embarked on the confrontation with his inner self that would provide the template for the authentic Western spiritual search. 'Depressed and even overwhelmed', he began to 'search after the cause of evil' by entering 'into the very innermost part of my soul', lamenting: 'What torments did my heart endure in that travail, what sighs were those, O my God!'[9]

At the core of his bodily being, Augustine found not the evil that the Manicheans and the Platonists stressed, but evidence of the enduring love of the creator God.[10] Augustine discerned, 'even beyond my soul and mind itself, the unchangeable light of the Lord', and that all creatures 'have a being because they are of thee'. He argued that 'the Catholic truth was distinguished from the false doctrine of Plotinus, in respect of the phrase *the Word was made flesh*'.

But if goodness was the essential substance of the body, whence came its attraction to sin? How could Augustine reconcile benevolent creation with his determination 'to will that which is evil, and not to will that which is good'? The critical question was this: 'Who placed this [evil] power in me, and who engrafted upon my stock this branch of bitterness, seeing that I was wholly made by my God, most sweet?' Augustine believed that the Devil could not be the *origin* of evil, since even he was made by the 'good Creator'.[11]

It was through the Bible, and 'above all others ... thy Apostle Paul', that Augustine learnt that 'the flesh lusteth against the spirit, and the spirit against the flesh'. He came to believe that accepting this reality, through 'tears of confession, and ... a troubled spirit, [and] a broken and contrite heart', was the essential first step towards salvation.[12]

The purpose of *Confessions* was to document how Augustine came to accept the truth of the human condition. It was not intended to illustrate the author's growing piety or the evil of sexual desire, but to highlight the insurmountable depravity that must be accepted

9

before grace, the unearned gift of God's forgiveness, could be received. Augustine's point was that the desire to sin could not be banished by human effort.

To illustrate this, *Confessions* places surprising emphasis on a seemingly harmless adolescent prank. As a youth, Augustine once stole pears from an orchard; even though he had no need of the pears, already having his own, and never ate them, he nevertheless enjoyed the sin: 'What an abomination! What a parody of life! What abysmal death! Could I enjoy doing wrong for no other reason than that it was wrong?'[13] Observing the supposedly wilful greed of babies revealed the same truth: the basic human desire, from the very first, was to sin. No human being could free themselves from this perversity, which infected every aspect of human nature.

Augustine chose Christ and celibacy in the Easter of 387, and shared his baptism with Adeodatus. The boy whom his father had called 'the child of my sin' was now also a child of grace. Father and son shared the grief of Monica's death later the same year, and eventually lived together as members of the scholarly community Augustine formed in North Africa. Adeodatus was central to the learned discussions that took place there, but died in 389 or 390, before he was even eighteen years old.[14] The loyalty and love Augustine showed to his son and had long maintained for the child's mother was glossed over by the church for centuries; this was not proper behaviour for a saint.

In 391, at the age of thirty-seven, Augustine became a priest in the North African town of Hippo, and in 395 was made bishop. It was not until the early fifth century, while immersed in a study of Genesis, that he expounded the doctrine which he had begun to set out in *Confessions*. Having limited Greek, Augustine adopted the mistranslation of Paul used in the fourth-century Latin Bible known as the Vulgate, which stated that 'all men had sinned in Adam', and he became ever more concerned to stress how much the original sin in the Garden of Eden had permanently corrupted human nature.

Augustine drew heavily on custom, theology and tradition to buttress his case.[15] He accepted that original sin was not fully expounded in the Bible, but was adamant that unless it was accepted, even good Christians would be tempted to seek salvation through holy living and end up in hell.[16] Before they could be saved, he argued, a person must admit that they were wholly incapable of reforming themselves, so that they would rely only on the mercy of God: 'One hope, one trust, one firm promise – your mercy.'[17]

The obvious difficulty in Augustine's account was how the transmission of sin occurred. This was to remain the subject of confused controversy for centuries to come – in fact, it would never be resolved – but Augustine kept his answer simple: semen was the culprit. Original sin, and the guilt and just judgement of God which followed from it, was physically transmitted via sexual intercourse to every human being. Only Jesus 'alone of those who are born of a woman is holy ... by reason of the novelty of His immaculate birth', whereby the Holy Spirit 'infused immaculate seed into [Mary's] unviolated womb'.[18]

Despite his grim view of human nature, Augustine did not despise the body, as many of his opponents suggested. Indeed, he was critical of the ascetics who were 'waging war on their body as if it were a natural enemy'; he believed that they were blind both to God's goodness and to the necessity of relying on grace alone.[19] For Augustine, God had not made the slightest error in his creation of human beings, but evil desires, 'after establishing themselves in the stock of our ancestors, have become naturally ingrained'.[20] He was convinced that everyone was hopelessly and innately subject to desires that could never be overcome by human will. At the core of each person was not an incorruptible divinity, as some Eastern theologians suggested, but a putrid lust which continuously contaminated the whole being. To his optimistic opponents he pointed out that even when sexual intercourse was prohibited and lustful thoughts were vanquished, random erections and night-time emissions remained.

11

Augustine knew that original sin was an idea well suited to the times. Many pagans remained in the Roman Empire, and teachings that explained why even the most moral of them was destined for hell encouraged precautionary Catholic baptisms. Moreover, Catholicism did not enjoy an ecclesiastical monopoly even in the Latin-speaking West.[21] One of its rival churches, that of the Donatists, which was particularly strong in North Africa, sought to preserve its purity by avoiding any compromise with the world and its sinful ways. This ensured Augustine's assertion that the church was a community of fellow sinners would be tested in the fires of public debate. And when Augustine wearied of argument, original sin provided a justification for the forceful suppression of such dissidents. Because people were not rational beings who could freely choose good, *disciplina* – 'an active process of corrective punishment' – had to be employed against Christians as readily as pagans. Augustine believed that the law must be imposed on his fellow believers: 'Take away the barriers created by the laws! Men's brazen capacity to do harm, their urge to self-indulgence would rage to the full.'[22]

Augustine's argument with the doomed Donatists was largely over by the time his doctrine of original sin found its final, extreme form. Whereas in his earlier writings he had held on to a notion of free will, in the last decades of his life, he came to believe that human beings were so corrupted that they could not even *choose* to embrace the mercy of God: those who appeared to have chosen to be saved had, in reality, already been predestined by God for salvation.[23] For Augustine, this was a paradoxical source of hope: whatever happened in this fallen world, God had already set apart those who were to be saved. But the comfort this gave baptised believers came at a considerable cost to everyone else, 'that mass [of people] which will certainly be damned'.[24]

When Augustine was born, the Roman Empire was enjoying renewed prosperity, but by the time he died, in 430, the Vandals were besieging his home in Hippo. Although the growing power of the barbarians corresponded with Augustine's increasingly bleak prognosis of the human condition, their rampages were not solely to blame for this. His most forlorn descriptions of human nature were formulated during a ferocious public debate that began when a group of intellectual ascetics from Rome sought refuge in North Africa following the sack of Rome in 410. It was within the furnace of a culture war that Augustine's most cherished doctrine would be refined and tempered, and would ultimately receive papal and imperial sanction.

2

THE CONTEST FOR
THE WESTERN SOUL

IT WAS NOT UNTIL THE LATE FOURTH CENTURY that most of the wealthy citizens of Rome became Christian. Few elite converts were as willing to give up their privileges as the persecuted generations of believers, and prophets who challenged the comfort and complacency of the church soon emerged. Foremost among these was Pelagius, a holy man originally from Celtic Britain, who asserted that for Christians to be saved, they had to overcome the temptation to sin and start following the teachings of Jesus. It was this seemingly straightforward instruction which brought Pelagius and his followers into conflict with Augustine, and helped refine the very teaching they disdained. The doctrine of original sin became ever more extreme during the course of Augustine's long fight with the Pelagians, and, fatefully, the church was forced to decide which teaching would become dogma and which heresy.

Few of Pelagius' writings survived their later condemnation, but much of what he believed was preserved by Augustine, who favoured point-by-point rebuttals of his opponents' texts. One piece of Pelagius' writing not burnt out of existence was a letter to a young noblewoman on how to live a Christian life.[25] In his *Letter to Demetrias*, Pelagius wrote: 'Whenever I give moral instruction, I first try to demonstrate the inherent power and quality of human nature. I try to show the wonderful virtues which all human beings can acquire.'[26]

He explained why this was the foundation of his teaching:

> When he created the world, God declared that everything he
> had made was good. So if every tree and animal, insect and
> plant is good, how much better is man himself! God made man
> in his own image; and so he intends each of us to be like him ...
> Day by day, hour by hour, we have to reach decisions; and in
> each decision, we can choose good or evil. The freedom to
> choose makes us like God: if we choose evil, that freedom
> becomes a curse; if we choose good, it becomes our greatest
> blessing ...[27]

Unsurprisingly, Pelagius read the story of Adam and Eve very differently from Augustine:

> When Adam and Eve ate from the tree of knowledge they were
> exercising their freedom of choice ... Before eating the fruit
> they did not know the difference between good and evil; thus
> they did not possess the knowledge which enables human
> beings to exercise freedom of choice. By eating the fruit they
> acquired this knowledge, and from that moment onwards they
> were free. Thus the story of their banishment from Eden is in
> truth the story of how the human race gained its freedom: by
> eating fruit from the tree of knowledge, Adam and Eve became
> mature human beings, responsible to God for their actions.[28]

It is sometimes claimed that Pelagius reduced the Christian faith to
a set of impossibly high moral standards which most people could
never live up to, and that it was the reality-accepting Augustine,
with his lower expectations of humanity, who provided ordinary
believers with a meaningful religion. While there is some truth to
this, Pelagius was no ascetic-extremist. He maintained that, 'contrary to what some religious leaders teach, perfection is not the

denial of pleasure, but the enhancement of it', arguing that those who seek perfection acquire 'more and more pleasure from less and less'. Even the practice of celibacy, which both sides in the controversy assumed to be a virtue, only arose because 'the perfect person sees beauty in every human being'. Forgotten in the stereotype of Pelagianism is the Celt's assertion that 'the world would be a most wonderful place if everyone was loving and generous, yet no one sought perfection', which he described as 'a spiritual luxury, not a necessity'.[29]

In early fifth-century Rome, this teaching was challenging but not heretical.[30] Indeed, until 410 there was nothing to suggest that the differences between Pelagius and Augustine, both of whom could claim to be within the diverse Catholic tradition, would erupt into a culture-changing controversy. But among those who fled to the relative safety of North Africa after Rome was besieged by the Goths was one of Pelagius' more enthusiastic followers, Caelestius, who lacked his teacher's diplomatic touch.[31] When Pelagius moved on to Palestine, Caelestius stayed in Africa, teaching the people that since all humans were created good, newborn babies must be innocent of sin. This teaching enraged Augustine and other local bishops.

A church council was convened in Carthage, at which Caelestius was condemned. But a subsequent synod in Palestine in 415, at which Eastern bishops held more sway, exonerated both him and Pelagius.

Augustine was not present at either congress but countered the public challenge to original sin in a series of writings, culminating in *A Treatise on the Grace of Christ, and On Original Sin Written Against Pelagius and Caelestius in the Year 418*.[32] Augustine maintained that unbaptised babies were 'rightly punished' because they belong 'to the mass of perdition ... born of Adam, condemned under the bond of the ancient debt'. The Bishop of Hippo quoted Job: 'No one is pure from uncleanness ... not even the infant, whose life is but that of a single day upon the earth'.[33]

Augustine did not rely on theological argument alone. With the support of well-placed lobbyists in the imperial court, he sought the intervention of emperor and pope. The issue was presented as one of authority: Pelagius was described as the leader of a secret movement that taught people how to save themselves without needing to rely on the sacraments of the church.

Pope Innocent, who died in March 417, was not persuaded. Nor, at first, was his replacement, Zosimus, but late in 417 the emperor intervened after riots broke out in Rome between the two sides of the controversy. Neither the cause nor details of these street fights are clear, but it is probable that public proclamations by the intemperate Caelestius contributed to the disorder. On 30 April 418, the emperor ordered that Pelagius and Caelestius be expelled from the city. Zosimus then belatedly condemned the newly defined 'heresy', and excommunicated and exiled eighteen Italian bishops who refused to endorse the official condemnation.[34]

It is not clear what happened to Pelagius after this. The dearth of news suggests that he died soon after, or perhaps returned home to Britain, which was no longer part of the shrinking empire. But his absence only intensified the public debate, because in one of the young Italian bishops in exile, Julian of Eclanum, the Pelagians found a man with the zeal, intelligence and eloquence to match the now ageing Bishop of Hippo.[35]

Neither Julian nor Augustine believed he could change the mind of his opponent. The intended audience for their decade-long public dispute was the educated public, which in turn influenced the judgements of emperor and pope.[36] It is not surprising, therefore, that their writings focused on two major concerns of the elite of the Roman Empire: the status of their offspring and the legitimacy of sex.

Julian thought that pronouncing newborn babies guilty of sin and deserving of punishment turned God into a monster:

Tell me then, tell me: who is this person who inflicts punishment on innocent creatures ... You answer: God. God, you say! God! ... He is the persecutor of new-born children: He it is who sends tiny babies to eternal flames ... It would be right and proper to treat you as beneath argument: you have come so far from religious feeling, from civilized thinking, so far, indeed, from mere common sense, in that you think that your Lord God is capable of committing a crime against justice such as is hardly conceivable even among the barbarians.

Augustine acknowledged that sending infants to hell was a sensitive matter, but God's ways were 'inscrutable' and 'unsearchable'. He asked: 'Who will be so bold as to say that Christ is not the saviour and redeemer of infants? But from what does he save them, if they do not have the disease of original sin?'[37] He called for babies to come 'to Pelagius for praise, but to Christ for salvation'.[38]

What of sexual desire? For Julian, it was a sin to have sex contrary to God's laws (that is, outside marriage), but within marriage sex was part of the goodness of created nature:

God ... made bodies; God distinguished the sex of the bodies; God made the genital organs; God implanted the longing in order that these bodies would be united; God also gave the power to the seeds ... God made the sexual desire of human beings, just as he made that of animals. But God put irrepressible instincts in the animals, while setting a limit for rational human beings ... God, therefore, blames not the limit, not the genus, but its excess, which arises from the insolence of the free will and brings accusations, not against the state of nature, but against the merit of the agent.[39]

Augustine accused his opponent of encouraging husbands and wives to engage in unlimited sex:

So you would not have married couples restrain that evil – I refer, of course, to your favourite good? So you would have them jump into bed whenever they like, whenever they feel tickled by desire. Far be it from them to postpone this itch till bedtime: let's have your *legitimate union of bodies* whenever your *natural good* is excited. If this is the sort of married life you lead, don't drag up your experience in debate ...'

Augustine called on 'Christian spouses' to 'practice self-control in order to have time for prayer, and when they return to the marriage act on account of their lack of self-control, let them remember to say to God for this reason too: *Forgive us our debts*.[40]

Julian retorted that the evils that so concerned 'old Augustine' might be 'more products of your memory than of your mind', and argued that modesty did not arise from some original sin but from custom. Even the wearing of clothes, Julian pointed out, was not universal: 'In fact, among certain peoples, not merely the young folk and those joined in sexual liaisons ... all people of both sexes are unclothed, and they have intercourse without looking for privacy ... the Scots and ... neighbouring peoples do this.' Augustine countered that Julian should look at 'human beings, not of some nation, such as the Scots, but the parents of all the nations ... See them [Adam and Eve], before the sin revealing their freedom, but after the sin teaching modesty ...'[41]

Julian's confidence in the goodness of created nature was such that he asserted that even Jesus experienced lust, because 'if something is clipped from the fullness of his substance, all the beauties of his moral conduct perish'. Augustine was outraged: 'You ought to have ... trembled in fear ... to have said that part of his holy body became erect for some forbidden uses against his holy choice' and poured forth 'useless seeds'. The only way Augustine could see to avoid this blasphemy was for the 'perfect man' to have been 'born of the Holy Spirit and the Virgin Mary', and thus be free from every inheritance of original sin, including sexual desire.[42]

Ultimately, their differences boiled down to contrasting views of creation. Was the world still essentially as God had created it, or had it been distorted forever by original sin? 'You ask me why I would not consent to the idea that there is a sin that is part of human nature?' Julian thundered to Augustine. 'I answer: it is improbable, it is untrue; it is unjust and impious; it makes it seem as if the Devil were the maker of men.'[43] Julian condemned the extreme contrast Augustine drew between human nature before and after the Fall, accusing Augustine as having 'extolled with great praises and blackened with even greater accusations one and the same thing, namely, human nature.' Julian would have none of what he referred to as 'natural sin', seeing birth, sex and death as God's handiwork. He saw Adam and Eve as a story not of paradise lost, but of one man's mistake.[44]

Augustine replied that if human beings were how God had intended them to be, then *this* life must be 'Paradise', and he called on Julian to cease associating God's handiwork 'with human beings born with defective minds and bodies in order that you may ... deny original sin with your eyes closed and your mouth impudently open'. For Augustine, whatever beauties remained, 'the earth was cursed ... on account of the punishment of the man'.[45] Every part of the natural order had been damaged: people were born in sin, reproduced in sin, and died because of sin.

The only matter on which the protagonists seemed to agree was that their dispute could not be resolved through compromise. Human beings were either born good and innocent, or bad and guilty; Adam's sin was either a wrong choice that affected him alone, or it had changed human nature forever; the world either remained as God had created it, or it had been forever distorted by the Fall. When on 28 August 430 Augustine died, he had been hard at work on the sixth volume of his series *Against Julian*. Right to the end, the Bishop of Hippo held fast to his vision of paradise, in which there was no suffering, no death and no involuntary erections, and where no troubled teen would wilfully steal pears.

Augustine is often presented as the pessimist in this debate, but to him no account of reality was more forlorn than the earth-bound 'paradise of the Pelagians', which he believed conferred divine blessing on the world as it was. It is unsurprising that, as the Vandals plundered Hippo and the barbarians claimed an empire, many others in the battered West also took greater solace from Augustine's focus on a heavenly afterlife than from the meditations on the glory of creation which still issued from the comparatively secure citadels of the East.

Yet even after the final confirmation of Augustine's apparent triumph, with the condemnation of Julian by a church council in Ephesus in 431, original sin's emphasis on the powerlessness of the human will remained problematic for many faithful Catholics. Could missionaries realistically deny people's capacity to choose Christ? Could those seeking to convert and civilise the barbarian tribes really be expected to put their faith in God's grace alone?

3

THE CHALLENGE OF THE CELTS

As the Roman Empire retreated and then collapsed in Western Europe, the church stranded within barbarian lands sought to soften the edges of original sin. Monk-missionaries based their work on Paul's injunction that God 'desires all men to be saved', and it was a foundation of their endeavour that all people had the capacity to choose God and live morally upright lives.[46] The notion that human beings were so lost that they could not decide to follow Christ unless already chosen by God might have given strength to besieged believers, but it had the potential to paralyse any missionary effort. What the Western church needed was not a theology that revealed how the elect would be preserved, but one that showed how the heathen might be saved.

A local monk, Hilarius of Arles, wrote to the Bishop of Hippo summarising how original sin was seen in the monasteries of southern Gaul:

> ... all the effectiveness of preaching is excluded if one says that nothing has remained in human beings which preaching can rouse ... For they maintain ... the words of Scripture, Believe, and you will be saved ... [and] they think no nature has been so corrupted or destroyed that one should not or cannot will to be healed ...[47]

A particularly influential critic of original sin was John Cassian, who came to Gaul after an extended sojourn with the Desert Fathers – hermits who sought to escape the evils of the world by living a life of penance and prayer in remote regions of Egypt, Palestine and Syria. Cassian's *Conferences* (426–429) comprised twenty-four imagined dialogues with the Fathers. Using the voice of Abbot Germanos of Panephysis, whom he had visited in the Nile Delta some forty years before, Cassian asserted that 'in the words of the Apostle it is very clearly stated that after Adam's sin the human race did not lose the knowledge of the good'. He provocatively concluded: 'Anyone who denies that nature is to be proclaimed in its good qualities, simply does not know that the Author of nature is the same as the Author of grace.[48]

In 529 the persistence of such semi-Pelagian dissent (as it has become known) led to a meeting of bishops at Orange, in Gaul, to clarify the doctrine of original sin. The outcome was to affirm Augustine's essential teaching: 'Through the sin of the first man, free will had been bent and weakened in such a manner that consequently no one can love God as he ought, or believe in God, or do good because of God unless assisted by the prevenient grace of God's mercy.' However, predestination was rejected on the basis that although the capacity of human beings to choose good had been severely weakened by original sin, 'all the baptized with Christ's help and cooperation can and have a duty to fulfil what things belong to the soul's salvation if they are willing to work at it'.

The findings of Orange were ratified by Rome, and in broad terms this has remained the Roman Catholic position ever since.[49] Once due consideration was given to the value of missionary effort and moral endeavour, through the rejection of predestination and an affirmation that all human beings retained a limited capacity to choose good, original sin, it seemed, had triumphed irrevocably.

The problem for the popes was that consistent dogma did not guarantee consistent practice. The church's capacity to impose its doctrine across the disparate West was still limited, particularly in the British Isles, where a century and a half of comparative isolation following the withdrawal of the Roman legions had allowed an alternative Christian tradition to flourish.

Celtic Christianity, which was influenced by the Desert Fathers, represented a stark alternative to Augustinian orthodoxy. In the Book of Kells, which dates from as late as the 800s, pictures of plants, animals and human faces are intricately interwoven into the Biblical text. What is being represented is the Celtic belief that God is revealed in creation *and* in the scriptures – both are 'the word' of God.[50] Evil was real and the temptation to sin ever-present, but this was understood to be the fault of the Devil and his demons; it was not due to any original distortion of God's creation. The Gospel of John, beloved by the Celts, records that when Nicodemus, a member of the Jewish ruling council, approached Jesus at night, he was told, 'No one can *see* the kingdom of God unless he is born again.'[51] Entry to the kingdom meant seeing the divine presence in this world as much as passing into a distant paradise.

Such was the vigour of Celtic Christianity that when a second Augustine landed in England in 597, as the head of a mission sent by Pope Gregory, he came not, as legend would have it, primarily to convert the heathen Angles, but to ensure the obedience of the local church to Rome. Indeed, in the very year that Augustine arrived in Britain, an Irish nobleman, St Columba, died in the famous monastery he had established on the isle of Iona, off the west coast of Scotland, whence missionaries had long been sent into the pagan regions of Britain.[52]

The Venerable Bede, whose seventh-century *Ecclesiastical History of the English Nation* celebrates the arrival of Roman authority, documents the vigour and independence of the native church. The British bishops told the newly arrived Augustine that they 'rather preferred their own traditions to the universal practice of Churches'. The pope's emissary was prepared to accept that 'in many things you act contrary to our custom', so long as 'in these three things you are willing to be ruled by me – to keep Easter at its proper time; to fulfil the ministration of baptizing ... [and] to preach the Word of the Lord together with us to the nation of the Angles'.

The injunction to baptise infants was necessary because the Celts did not see a newborn as a sinner in need of forgiveness. St Patrick, who was brought up in the Celtic church of Britain, recalled that he was not baptised until he was an adult, even though his father was a deacon and his grandfather a priest.[53] The favoured ceremony simply blessed the new life which reflected the glory of its creator – an image of the divine that would be obscured but never extinguished by the inevitability of sin.

Such theology suggests that it is no coincidence that Pelagius was British. Michael Herren and Shirley Brown, historians of Celtic Christianity, even raise the possibility that during the fifth century there may have been an organised Pelagian church in Britain, led by the bishops who had been expelled from Rome in 418, possibly even including Pelagius himself.[54] Bede, too, was in no doubt about his influence:

Pelagius, a Briton, dispersed far and wide the poison of his perfidy against the aid of grace from above ... to whom St. Augustine, as well as the rest of the orthodox fathers, replied with many thousands of Catholic opinions, yet were not able to correct their madness; but, what is more grievous, their madness being inveighed against, was more inclined to increase by contradicting, than be purged by favouring, the truth: which Prosper the Rhetorician well expresses in heroic verses, when he says: –

A writer 'gainst Augustine snakelike glides,
And in his breast a gnawing rancour hides.
Whoe'er induced this snakeling vile to lift
Its head from out its cavern's darksome rift?

Either the sea-girt Britons it maintain,
Or else it battens on Campania's plain.[55]

Bede records four Roman missions to Britain to counter 'the Pelagian perversity'. These were 'directed to the common people, for the correcting of the perversity, and by the judgement of all, the authors of the perversion, who were expelled from the island ... [so] that both the region might obtain release, and they correction'.[56]

According to Bede, Pope Honorius 'sent a letter to the nation of the Scots ... earnestly exhorting them not to esteem their own small number ... wiser than the Churches of Christ, ancient and modern'.[57] In December 640, Pope John appealed once more to the Scots to abandon their support for the teachings of Pelagius:

We ... understand that the venom of the Pelagian heresy is revising afresh among you; wherefore we by all means exhort that the venomous wickedness of this superstition be removed from your minds. For it ought not to escape your recollection, how this execrable heresy has been condemned, in as much as it has not been abolished for these two hundred years, but is also daily condemned by us as buried in a perpetual anathema; and we exhort you not to let the ashes of those whose weapons have been burnt, be stirred up among you. For who would not execrate the proud and impious suggestion of those who say that man can exist without sin of his own free-will, and not by the grace of God ... men, being born in original sin, are known to bear testimony to the prevarication of Adam, even whilst they are without actual sin; according to the saying of the prophet, 'Behold I was shapen in iniquities, and in sins hath my mother conceived me'.[58]

Sayings and writings of the Celtic saints confirm their Pelagian tendencies. In Adomnán's *Life of St Columba* are two stories of pagans who 'preserved natural goodness' throughout their lives. Columba, an influential Irish monk and missionary, believed that the 'grand distinction for man is [his] likeness [to] God', and that 'whatever virtues God sowed in us in our original state, He taught us in his commandments to restore the same to Him'.[59] In the so-called *Alphabet of Piety*, written in Old Irish probably in the early seventh century, salvation is open to 'Anyone … who shall fear God and who shall love Him and who shall fulfil His will and His commandment'.[60]

For this Christian tradition, the true nature of the human being, made in the image of God, was captured in the innocent face of a newborn baby. Divine judgement related only to freely chosen sin. Whereas Augustine saw people as judged by God for who they were, the Celts concentrated on what they had done.

The Roman and Celtic churches confronted each other at the Synod of Whitby in 664. Oswy, the devout King of Northumberland, called this meeting to determine if Rome had the authority to impose its doctrine and customs. It seems to have been anxiety for his own salvation that led the king to find in favour of the institution that claimed its authority from St Peter. 'When I come to the doors of the kingdom of heaven,' he wrote, 'there may be no one to unlock them for me, if he is averse who is proved to have the keys.'[61] The Celts' beloved St John, the man who had leaned intimately against Jesus during the last supper, lacked Peter's fearsome power.

Nevertheless, the Celtic church did not disappear when Catholic custom was imposed in Oswy's kingdom. In 688 Adomnán, the Abbot of Iona, deferred to Roman authority; on returning to the monastery with a tonsure as a symbol of his submission, however, he was rejected by his monks, who insisted on keeping their own hairstyle and the alternative tradition it signified. Iona was to maintain its autonomy for nearly 200 years, with the last independent abbot dying in 860, and the Vikings, not the Vatican, ultimately bringing on the end.[62]

In the centuries to come, the assertion of Roman authority would be completed and Celtic Christianity largely brought into line with Catholic orthodoxy. Nevertheless, it is possible to see a Pelagian thread running through the history of British and Irish Christianity, and not just in remote Celtic lands such as the western isles of Scotland, where the Celtic tradition was long sustained in local songs, stories and prayers.[63] One of the twentieth century's most famous theologians, Karl Barth, believed the British to be 'incurably Pelagian'. As we shall see, the history of Christianity in Britain provides much evidence to support his view.

4

SCHOLARS AND SINNERS

In the centuries after the Council of Orange, the Catholic Church slowly constructed Christendom out of the ruins of the Roman Empire. While this period was no 'Dark Ages', a doctrine that justified an autocratic church asserting absolute authority over a sinful people was well suited to turbulent times. But once church power had secured social order, and Western thought had been reconnected to the wisdom of the Roman and Greek worlds, the case for original sin was not so obvious. Could the doctrine coexist with medieval order and classical scrutiny?

When St Francis of Assisi (1181–1226) wandered through the towns and villages of Umbria proclaiming that 'nothing separates us' from the God who is 'indescribable and ineffable', he was not setting out to question the totality of the Fall. Yet in celebrating 'Brother Sun', 'Sister Moon' and God's loving presence among 'those who beg by the wayside', Francis critiqued the orthodoxy of original sin more effectively than any of the brilliant intellects of his age. Francis did not deny that 'our lower nature is opposed to every good' or that 'we have nothing which we have not received' from God, but his life and teaching had more in common with a Celtic monk's than with a conventional cleric's.[64]

The life of St Francis reflected not only the relative peace of the Middle Ages, but also Catholicism's sometimes surprising tolerance of diversity. The writings of Augustine, which had assumed a quasi-scriptural status, were so voluminous and varied over his long life that they underpinned this heterogeneity as much as challenged it. The Bishop of Hippo's carefully preserved and sometimes contradictory canon supported both the new ideas and the resistance mounted to them. Nevertheless, the church hierarchy understood that the only reason that everyone needed a Catholic baptism was still because *everyone*, no matter how Godly or chaste, had inherited the sin of Adam and was therefore destined for hell. Since the church's justification of its monopoly on salvation relied wholly on the concept of original sin, belief in the doctrine remained non-negotiable, and few people were prepared to risk the charge of heresy that was likely to follow a public challenge to its truth.

Probably the best-known scholarly dissenter was Peter Abelard (1079–1142), who is mainly remembered today for his tragic relationship with his pupil, Heloise (a courageous and original thinker in her own right), an affair which ended in confinement to a convent for one party and castration for the other.[65] Like the Celtic saints and Eastern theologians, Abelard believed that redemption was associated with being 'awakened in our hearts' to God's love, which was *always* and *already* present.[66] Perhaps with the joys of his forcibly interrupted union with Heloise in mind, Abelard even dared to suggest that, of itself, 'no natural physical delight can be accounted a sin'.[67]

Bernard of Clairvaux (1090–1153), an intellectual warrior and the energetic founder of the Cistercian order, confronted Abelard through a dual strategy of public debate and political intrigue that was reminiscent of Augustine's tactics against Pelagius. He wrote to Rome of Abelard's 'crop of sacrileges and errors'; Abelard was duly condemned for nineteen propositions found in his work, including *Quod non traximus culpam ex Adam, sed poenam tantum* ('That we do not get guilt from Adam, but only punishment').[68] That this proposition was based on a literal reading of the Bible (which speaks of mortality, labour pains and toil as the consequences of the Fall) proved to be no defence.

The vigour of Rome's response reveals that the threat posed by the old Christian tradition to which Abelard gave voice was still seen as a serious one. It is not true that the medieval mind placidly accepted what the modern one cannot: that a loving God would punish people for a sin they had not themselves committed.

In the Middle Ages, for God's response to humanity to be just, it needed to become law. Anselm (c. 1033–1109) first developed the legal justification of original sin.[69] In logic which still makes surprising sense to many people, this creative Archbishop of Canterbury argued that the remission of sins is only possible 'if complete satisfaction has been made':

> But [because of original sin] human nature by itself did not have this payment. And without the required satisfaction human nature could not be reconciled ... Therefore Divine Goodness gave assistance. The Son of God assumed a human nature into His own person ... And since He owed nothing for Himself, He paid this sum for others who did not have what they were indebted to pay.[70]

Anselm spoke of his own 'darkness' and 'unbearable inner burden' to justify the truth of original sin, but his legalism also exemplified the detached spirituality of the scholastics.[71] Parodied by later humanist and Protestant reformers, scholasticism was nonetheless a sophisticated system of belief, premised on the assumption that there was a unified explanation for everything which ultimately went back to God.

Pre-eminent among the scholastics was a knight's son from southern Italy, Thomas Aquinas (c. 1225–1274), who, after he joined the newly established Order of Preachers (commonly known as the Dominicans) in 1244, wrote brilliant philosophy with prodigious efficiency. The standard English edition of his major work, *Summa Theologiae* (meaning *The Sum Total of Theology*, often known as the

Summa Theologica), runs to sixty-one volumes.[72] Influenced by Aristotle and Arabic thinkers, Aquinas, while never denying Augustine, sought to integrate reason with faith, and thus to construct an integrated Catholic world view built on solid classical foundations. This was no easy task, given he was dealing with a disparate and often unreasonable tradition still grounded in the doctrine of original sin.

Aquinas' approach was to deny that anything of itself can be innately bad because everything has been created by God. He explained evil, including the consequences of original sin, in terms of *privation*, or the absence of the goodness that a created thing should have. This was particularly true of God's supreme act of creation, human beings: 'The stain of sin does not impose a nature on the soul, but only the privation of grace.'[73] In other words, evil within people exists in the same way that blindness exists: as the absence of sight, rather than as an active force or substance in its own right.[74] People shared in original sin not because they personally *inherited* an actual sin, but because all human beings shared in the privations inherent to the human condition.[75]

The expansive genius of Aquinas ensured that the doctrine of original sin received its most considered intellectual scrutiny yet, but in the process it became more of a philosophical proposition about human nature than a terrifying religious truth.[76] In retrospect, his explanation of original sin might even be said to have begun the doctrine's slow transition into the secular world.

Aquinas never finished the *Summa*. After returning from the University of Paris to live in Naples in 1272 (close to the town of Roccasecca, where he grew up) and beginning work on the third part of his magnum opus, he suddenly abandoned the project in December 1273. He reported that he had experienced a mystical vision, and that his own writing, compared with what he had witnessed, was as insignificant as straw.[77] He died the following year, but his influence grew over the centuries. After the early doubters passed away, Aquinas was canonised in 1323 and recognised as a doctor (or official teacher) of the church in 1567.

During the fourteenth and fifteenth centuries, scholasticism was gradually superseded by the so-called *via moderna*, or 'modern system'. The theology developed by William of Ockham and his colleagues was closer to Pelagius than Augustine in the value it ascribed to human effort to achieve salvation. It only escaped this damning charge by acknowledging that while human virtue was in reality worthless, God in his mercy ascribed value to human effort anyway; in the oft-quoted words of Gabriel Biel, God allows a human being 'to do that which is in oneself'. The implications of this pragmatic theology were radical: even pagans – or at least those who had no opportunity to be baptised – might gain salvation.[78]

The reinterpretation of original sin was taken still further during the later Middle Ages by humanist scholars, who embraced the classical understanding of the human as a microcosm of the divine. By joining in the celebration of man in Renaissance art (rib-derived women remained a secondary image of the creator), they and the popes who sponsored or protected them effectively rejected the teachings of Augustine.

In 1486 the 23-year-old Pico della Mirandola announced his intention to define nine hundred theses derived from Greek, Latin, Hebrew and Arabic writers, and to invite scholars from all over Europe to Rome for a public disputation on his *Oration on the Dignity of Man*. Pico was seeking to compose a new creation story for the Western world: God created the earth as a sacred temple, and created man to reflect, admire and love its grandeur. Adam was not just another dimension of creation, because he was 'confined by no limits' and was told by his creator to 'determine for yourself your own nature, in accordance with your own free will'.

This went too far for Pope Innocent VIII, who forbade the international gathering. A papal commission duly condemned several of Pico's propositions, but it was indicative of the mood in Rome that the public expression of such heretical sentiments was tolerated at all.[79]

The openness of some popes to the new thinking is partly explained by the fact that it was never intended to go beyond the small elite who were able to read Latin or afford a book. Not even the humanists believed that their discussions were suitable for the masses, and that included parish priests. In the days before seminaries, the ordinary cleric was nearly as uneducated as his flock, and the trickling down of theological discovery, when it occurred at all, was slow and uneven. Original sin remained the established dogma of the Catholic Church, and after a thousand years of cultural immersion it was much more widely understood than the latest newfangled notion emanating from the Sorbonne.

As we shall see, it was not the elite's intellectual insights but their greed which did most to undermine original sin's popular potency.

5

THE FORGIVENESS INDUSTRY

IN THE EARLY FIFTEENTH CENTURY, the castle church of the Elector of Saxony, Friedrich the Wise, housed a collection of more than nineteen thousand relics, including a sample of Mary's milk, the body of a holy innocent from Bethlehem, and straw from the famous manger – all of which were believed to confer eternal benefits on their owner. Friedrich employed eighty-three priests, whose principal duty was to say mass on his behalf – ten thousand were said in 1520 alone.[80] But how was this profitable industry reconciled with the doctrine of original sin, which emphasised the *futility* of human efforts to achieve salvation?

During the Middle Ages, the concept of a single, all-sufficient act of forgiveness was gradually put aside by the church. Infant baptism was still necessary, in order to be forgiven for inherited sin, but thereafter pardons were rationed, releasing the sinner only from the punishment owed for particular failings. The effect of this was that the Christian was now unable to trust in the grace of God alone.

The idea of purgatory, a distinctively Western dimension of the afterlife which was given formal sanction by the church at this time, came to the fore. How long a deceased person would spend in this place of temporary punishment depended on what they owed on their sins. God had been paid out in full by the sacrifice of Jesus, Mary and the saints, but the surplus they had earned was stored in a

35

treasury in heaven in the form of 'indulgences', which only the Catholic Church had the authority to distribute on earth.

Even Aquinas struggled to explain the system rationally – he resorted to the explanation that the church would not offer indulgences if they did not work – but purgatory proved to be an extremely profitable concept for Rome, which was seeking funds to finish its buildings (including those being adorned with Renaissance art), to finance its crusades and to pay for its ever-expanding bureaucracy.[81] While endowed masses – where priests or their religious orders were paid to say a mass to reduce a person's outstanding debt to God – were part of the system almost from the beginning, during the eleventh and twelfth centuries the prayers of ordinary Christians, pilgrimage and the giving of alms to the poor were equally central to drawing down the treasury of heaven. On the eve of the Black Death in 1343, which led to skyrocketing demand, the indulgences system was rationalised and codified in a papal bull by Clement VI. Securing indulgences by paying for church projects, prayers, a mass or relics became standard practice.[82] This was the system which the devout Friedrich the Wise utilised to ensure his passage to heaven.

A self-serving and pragmatic approach to salvation was also associated with the rise of the parish. By the eleventh and twelfth centuries a network of small parishes covered the western European countryside, and it was understandable that local priests would focus on how their tithe-paying parishioners could aid their own salvation in an uncertain and disease-ridden world. Doing penance for sins acknowledged in confession both rewarded the pious and enhanced priestly power.[83] Even though most people went to confession only infrequently (normal practice was once a year, during Lent, and on the point of death), the ritual became critical to the cycle of sin and absolution, a system in which ordinary people worked for their salvation under increasingly detailed clerical direction.

The new ideology of salvation meant that people were no longer confined to one of the two groups established by the doctrine of original sin: those outside the grace of God and condemned to eternal hell by the sin of the first Adam, and those made righteous by the sacrifice of Jesus, the second Adam. Instead, they could move in and out of salvation over the course of the year, or even over one day. The purpose of religious practice became to tilt the balance towards righteousness, but no Christian could ever be certain of the status of their heavenly balance sheet. This was in contrast to Augustine's pessimistic certainty about human endeavour and his unbridled confidence in the permanent power of God's forgiveness. Original sin might have been a harsh and terrible doctrine for the unsaved, but it was eternally generous for the saved: Christ's sacrifice was sufficient – nothing more was needed.

The micro-management of salvation particularly affected women, as they were seen as the chief hurdle to be overcome if men were to be saved. Not only were the sons of Adam irresistibly tempted to procreate with the daughters of Eve, but, in stark contrast to later religious stereotypes, women were assumed to lust right back, and because of their more physical and less rational nature, their desires were considered to be virtually insatiable.[84] Man's responsibility was to subjugate, control, remove and silence women, if temptation was to be resisted and redemption for both genders secured.

The emphasis on the seductress Eve in the creation story is well known, but it is not so often acknowledged that the doctrine of original sin actually reduced the focus on the fallen woman. While Augustine shared in the general prejudice against Eve, his concern to highlight the total corruption of human nature meant that he returned primary responsibility for original sin to Adam.[85] Precisely because he took the flawed character of women for granted, and assumed others did too, locating guilt and punishment primarily in the female compromised the extent of male depravity.

It was the scholastics who reconstructed a cleanly sexist creation story by appropriating the biology of Aristotle, who believed that women were defective humans who lacked the full capacity for rationality and moral self-control, in order to assert that Eve's behaviour in Eden reflected her innate biological character.[86] Echoes of their physiology remain to this day in the Catholic Church's insistence that it was not incidental that Christ was a male: he and his priests *had* to be so if they were to fully represent God on earth.[87]

The scholastics' understanding was popularised by medieval art, which often depicted a prostitute-like Eve enticing men away from piety and purity, represented by the Virgin Mary.[88] These images were targeted at the usually illiterate priests as much as at the laity, in an endeavour to prevent priests from forming long-term sexual relationships, initially with their wives, and then, after this was prohibited in the twelfth century, with their 'concubines'. The danger of Eve related not just to her body, but also to her words. It was Eve's conversation with the serpent that had got her into trouble, the church argued, and it stressed the risk posed by the chatter of women: such talk still let the Devil in.[89]

The paradox of the renewed emphasis on Eve was that Adam became a childlike figure, powerless in the face of a womanly command.[90] It has even been argued that Eve's role in the creation story – whereby *she* chooses knowledge, *she* directs the passive, baby-like man, and *she* is charged with bearing new life while the man tills the earth – empowers women to some degree. Marguerite of Navarre (1492–1549) dared to suggest that Eve was God's masterpiece and that man's subordination of women was a direct consequence of *his* transgression.[91]

Nor were all men blind to how self-serving it was to blame Eve for the Fall. In one of his *Canterbury Tales*, Geoffrey Chaucer has a female character observe that:

> By God, if women had written stories,
> as clerks have in their oratories,
> they would have written more of men's wickedness
> than all of the sex of Adam can redress.[92]

Chaucer's *Tales* stepped beyond the world of the celibate and cloistered male elite who wrote theology and ran the church. And it is
worth remembering that for the ordinary peasants of Europe, women
never ceased to be men's fellow workers in the struggle for existence,
with the marital bed affording one of the few comforts life afforded.
For the vast majority of the population, piety remained an inherently
earthy affair.

6

A PEASANT'S WORLD

As late as 1500, nine out of ten Europeans still lived in small hamlets or scattered farmsteads, with their lives shaped by the agricultural cycle. These people were deeply concerned with eternal salvation, but their focus was on the struggles of this life: how to preserve their health, crops, children, fertility and personal safety. Vulnerability to the natural world meant that they were always more likely to locate evil primarily in the environment around them, rather than deep within their own natures.[93] No doubt successive bubonic plagues, which wiped out as much as one-third of the population in the mid-fourteenth century and ensured the population continued to fall until the second half of the fifteenth century, also fostered the resilience of ancient belief systems.

The vibrant spirit world of the European countryside compromised original sin because it located evil *outside* the individual soul, and provided a means of placating it beyond church-mediated faith. In what Charles Taylor has termed the 'enchanted cosmos', ordinary folk could draw on a wide range of 'sacramentals', or 'locations of sacred power' located in the landscape, ritual, prayer, dance, song and the wisdom and spells of holy people, all of which offered people some hope of saving themselves.[94] Peasants believed in a complex array of demons, angels, fairies, goblins and ghosts, and these could often explain and moderate suffering better than the teachings formulated by an ecclesiastical elite which was quarantined from both the perils and the comforts of peasant existence.[95]

Although many of the spirits and rituals often had pre-Christian origins, popular piety should not be considered any less 'Christian' or 'Catholic' than papal bulls; every religious expression involves the enculturation of older customs and beliefs. Nor was the faith of the people distinct from that of their priests. Crumbling consecrated bread into an insect repellent to protect one's growing vegetables might not have been sanctioned by the church, but the efficacy of the mix came from the ecclesiastical claim that it contained Christ's body. No incantation to increase crop yields, control the weather or abate fires was as effective as the host. Joan of Arc helped the girls of her village prepare 'hats' of flowers, but they did this in the honour of the Virgin. And this illiterate peasant girl well knew the difference between an apparition of a saint and a fairy (which she insisted she had never seen).[96]

Moreover, even the church-sanctioned pilgrimage routes, holy sites, relics and intercessory-sensitive saints, which gave the medieval Christian a sense of being able to influence events in this life and facilitate his or her entry into the next, emerged as much from popular movements as from apostolic edicts.[97] Even official dogma sometimes only gave belated definition to customary belief. This included many of the teachings concerning the Virgin Mary, who by the late Middle Ages had almost supplanted Christ as the main object of devotion.[98] While the latter was increasingly confined to the cross, Mary could befriend and even appear to ordinary people, helping them in this life and advocating for them in the next.

Integral to this popular devotion was the belief that Mary had been conceived by her mother, St Anne, free from original sin. This idea, known as the Immaculate Conception, highlighted the compromise to the doctrine of original sin manifest in the focus on Mary in the first place. According to Augustine, Jesus alone was free from the common human inheritance of sin, which was why only his sacrificial death could save sinners. This partly explains why the Immaculate Conception did not become an official dogma of the Catholic Church until 1854, even though it had long enjoyed institutional support.[99]

Another standout example of the influence of popular piety was infant baptism, which continued to reflect its origins as a grassroots custom that the church had only retrospectively justified. Rome's belated appropriation of the rite was never absolute, since baptism's magical power derived from the water itself and the invocation which accompanied its decanting, rather than the ecclesiastical status of the person conducting the ceremony. As long as someone said 'I baptise you in the name of the Father, the Son, and the Holy Ghost' as the water was poured – and any water would do – directly onto human skin, the church accepted that ordinary women and men were empowered to send a dying soul to heaven.

Although it is not well publicised, this remains true to this day: if there is no alternative and it is done with the right intent, anyone can legitimately baptise anyone else[100] The pimp who was said, in a medieval London court case, to have baptised the child of a prostitute was upholding canon law. Even a non-Christian can perform a legitimate baptism.[101] This concession to popular piety reflected cultural history *and* the traditionally high infant mortality rate, which, especially during times of plague and other epidemics, could overwhelm the priestly capacity to respond. John Myrc's *Instructions for Parish Priests* (c. 1403) advised that midwives should baptise a baby when there was no time to call in a priest.[102] What was important was that a baptism occur, to ensure entry to paradise and membership of the church. Once achieved, the latter was considered as indelible as life beyond the heavenly gates, and unable to be revoked – even by later disbelief – without liability to the punishments ascribed to apostasy.[103]

Even when a baby was baptised by a priest in a church, the ritual reflected its popular origins. By tradition, a new mother absented herself from holy places for six weeks after birth, so it was usually the father who, generally on the birth day itself, assembled the god-parents. A godmother or midwife carried the baby to the church door, where they met the priest, who performed an exorcism by blessing the child and putting salt in its mouth (an ancient custom which Augustine unconvincingly claimed was evidence for the antiquity of belief in original sin). Only then did the party move to the baptismal font.[104]

So determined were the faithful to manage the danger posed by original sin that even dead babies were sometimes baptised, despite this being a theological impossibility. It was not uncommon to spray holy water on a protruding limb or into the womb using a 'baptis-mal sprinkler', so that a stillborn baby might nevertheless be said to have been saved; after all, no one could be certain when such a death had occurred.

People exploited other opportunities provided by the teaching that any water on any part of a living being, when accompanied by the right words, gave the guarantee of heaven. The custom at the statue of Mary at Oberbüren, near Berne, was to warm dead infants between glowing coals and burning candles, after which feathers were laid on their lips. As soon as the feathers moved, it was declared that the child was breathing, whereupon it could be baptised. The Bishop of Constance thought that what took place was 'in contempt of orthodox Christian faith and the sacraments of the church', but similar customs occurred in Catholic regions of Europe until the eighteenth century.

Even where the holy places were vandalised or destroyed (a fate that befell Oberbüren's chapel), the persistence of 'eaves children' – those 'baptised' with rain water from the church roof – bore witness to people's creativity in saving the newborn from the punishment ordained by the Bishop of Hippo.[105] Such flexibility reduced the danger of damnation even as it highlighted how seriously the threat of a baby's confinement to the fiery pit was taken. The creativity of custom was a testament to the doctrine's terrifying power. Managing a God who was so tempestuous that he could judge a baby unworthy of heaven because no water had touched its skin as the right invocation was said was as frightening as contending with the vagaries of the weather. It is no wonder that peasants also prayed their own spells.

The idea of limbo was another example of popular piety qualifying original sin. For over a thousand years, belief in the *limbus puerorum* (or 'suburb of children'), a concept that was first expressed in Pelagian thought and developed in the writings of John Scotus Eriugena, grew in popularity. Limbo was the place where unbaptised babies were sent by God as an alternative to the fires of hell. It was the scholastics who belatedly put this belief on a sure dogmatic footing by connecting it to their concept of privation. Aquinas claimed that babies in limbo were simply experiencing the absence of what was not rightfully theirs to receive, and consequently did not torment themselves 'any more than a peasant would because he is not the King'.[106]

Pope Innocent III gave formal sanction to limbo in the thirteenth century, but some theologians pointed out that it compromised original sin. A fourteenth-century general of the Order of Hermits of St Augustine, Gregory of Rimini, became known as *tortor infantium* ('torturer of infants') for upholding Augustinian teaching on the pains of hell experienced by unbaptised babies. Such conservatism meant that it was only at the turn of the twentieth century that limbo became part of the Catholic catechism; it was removed again in 1992.

The popular determination to moderate the consequences of original sin did not extend to children *after* they had been baptised. Once the saving rite had been performed, children faced the same challenges as adults, due to their corrupted human nature. Infants' crawling and feeding at the breast, both of which seemed to suggest an animal-like nature, were seen as direct products of the Fall. The custom of tightly swaddling infants so they could not crawl was not unique to the West, but it was carried further than in other cultures and was sometimes done until the child could walk. Similarly, wet nurses were employed by people a surprisingly long way down the social ladder. Much of the motive for both customs was practical – swaddled children could be taken to work and left safely on the ground or even hung on a hook, while wet nurses provided some relief for hard-working mothers – but the widespread belief in original sin probably encouraged both practices.[107]

It was only in the fifteenth century that a child began to be seen as a special class of human who required rigorous intervention to be redeemed. Philippe Ariès' *Centuries of Childhood* (1960) and Michel Foucault's *Surveiller et Punir* (or *Discipline and Punish*) (1975) revealed that in the late Middle Ages the child was more likely to become subject to humiliating systems of punishment at school and at home.[108] But the paradoxical fact is that the systematic attempt to banish inner depravity relied on the neo-Pelagian hope that the effects of original sin could be overcome by *human* intervention. The philosophy of the new schools was closer to the monastic hope of achieving redemption through strenuous effort than it was to Augustinian pessimism about the permanent incapacity of the human will. While beatings and rote learning were justified by original sin, they were fostered more by compromises to the doctrine than by its fervent proclamation.

It should be remembered, however, that we still know very little about the lives of the large majority of children who didn't go to school, spending their days and nights out in the fields and at home. The peasant perspective on children (let alone the child's own experience) is very difficult to glean from a historical record which concentrates almost exclusively on the elite. What solid research there is has, unsurprisingly, made it clear that although children might not have been idealised, they were generally loved and cherished, and their deaths mourned. In popular piety, children were perceived as neither little demons nor little angels, but, like everyone else, as limited and flawed human beings who, while expected to share in the labour and suffering of earthly existence, were also a gift from God. Although the elite had already begun to see their offspring as belonging to a special category of person who could be moulded into a better being, it was hundreds of years before ordinary farming folk had the time or the resources to share in this dubious dream.

How to survive this life and secure entry to the next remained the simple but anxious focus of popular piety as the plague randomly propelled its way through the towns and villages of Europe. Peasant religion should not be idealised; immersion in nature did not provide freedom from fear in this life or the next. The omnipotence of death largely defined life, a fact symbolised by the decaying bodies and skulls on wide display and the 'dance of death' that was commonplace in late medieval iconography.[109] In this fearful atmosphere, it is not surprising that a counter-spirituality emerged which focused on God's loving presence for all of humanity. Mystics preached that unity with the divine was not dependent on any ritual; it was *already* the reality.

7

ALL SHALL BE WELL

*For as body is clad in the cloth, and the flesh in the skin, and the
bones in the flesh, and the heart in the trunk, so are we, soul
and body, clad and enclosed in the goodness of God.*

—JULIAN OF NORWICH

IN THE LATE FOURTEENTH CENTURY, a holy woman living in a
small cell in central Norwich completed the first book written by a
woman in the English language. In *Revelations of Divine Love*, Julian
of Norwich (c. 1342–1420) proclaimed that God is 'the true Mother
of life and of all things' and 'to the property of motherhood belong
nature, love, wisdom and knowledge'.[110] Hers was a compassionate
confrontation of the patriarchal tenets of the Western tradition. The
metaphor of the divine as a 'kind, loving mother who knows and
sees the need of her child [and] guards it very tenderly' remains on
the fringe of permissible discourse in Western Christianity even
today. And Julian was but the latest in a distinguished line of medieval mystics who upheld the ancient tradition that God's loving
presence with human beings was never severed by an original sin,
and that every person, without exception, remained Her child.

For these mystics, a direct challenge to the authority of the institutional church was neither possible nor desired. Yet because they saw
God's loving presence in *all* of life, they undermined ecclesiastical
efforts to restrict and regulate salvation. Nevertheless, their writings

were largely tolerated because of their professed loyalty to the church, their educated and aristocratic backgrounds, and their comparatively small and influential audiences. Nor was the church hierarchy in any doubt about the limits of celibate contemplation as a mode of resistance. What serious threat could possibly arise from a scattering of pious and predominantly female virgins?

It is no coincidence that the mystic whose writings *were* condemned by the church was a comparatively well-known man who came close to open rejection of the doctrine of original sin. Meister Eckhart (c. 1260–1328) described the *ancilla animae*, or 'handmaid of the soul', within every human being as 'something like the original outbreak of all goodness, something like a brilliant light that glows incessantly and something like a burning fire which burns incessantly. This fire is nothing other than the Holy Spirit.'[111] Eckhart quoted approvingly the great Eastern theologian Origen, who 'tells us that God's image, the Son of God, is in the ground of the soul like a living fountain'. Redemption was not about the restoration of fallen human nature but the reclamation of its essential goodness; once the outer layer of darkness caused by sin had been stripped away, the true divinity within human beings and all of life could be revealed. When Eckhart wrote that 'the seed of Divine nature in us is never destroyed, although it may be covered up', he was well aware that he was challenging the orthodox understanding of the human condition, as formulated by the Bishop of Hippo.[112]

Meister Eckhart was fortunate that his writings were not condemned as heretical by Pope John XXII until 1329, shortly after his death. Perhaps more surprising is that his memory, especially within his own religious order, was kept alive; those copies of his work not given up for burning would become unlikely bestsellers in the spiritually hungry years of the late twentieth century.

Eckhart had drawn inspiration not just from the giants of the Eastern tradition, but also from an extraordinary fellow German who had died a century earlier. Hildegard (1098–1179), the founder and first abbess of the Benedictine community at Bingen, did not begin writing until her forty-third year, but thereafter compiled a massive trilogy which combined Christian doctrine and ethics with cosmology, an encyclopaedia of medicine and natural science, a body of music that included seventy liturgical songs, and the first known morality play. Hildegard (wrongly) believed herself to be the first woman writer in the world, so just to put quill to paper took courage enough. That she then embarked on a series of arduous preaching tours at the age of sixty, in which she confronted her largely male audience with the urgency of the need for clerical and monastic reform, was one of the braver acts of evangelism in Christian history, even considering her status as a well-connected aristocrat.[113]

Hildegard was politically savvy – she obtained papal sanction for her writings, with the help (ironically) of Bernard of Clairvaux, who recognised her as a holy woman – and cleverly exploited sexist stereotypes in her dealings with the church's male leadership, emphasising that she was but 'Adam's fragile rib graced with a mystical spirit'. Nevertheless, she urged her sisters to stand up for truth:

> Do not be like those who should have shown people the true way, but who perversely have remained silent about the justice they have come to know ... You, whom I have taught by mystical inspiration, even though you are trodden down by the masculine sex, speak openly and always of that fire you have seen and that burns within you.[114]

Hildegard's major spiritual work was *Scito Vias Domini* ('Know the Ways of the Lord' – generally known as *Scivias*), which documented a series of visions or revelations and vividly described the presence of God within human beings and all of creation. 'I saw a blazing fire,' she wrote, 'incomprehensible, inextinguishable, totally alive, Life itself.' But God also told Hildegard to inform her fellow humans that they would 'suffer much anguish when you conquer in yourselves what was sown in the lust of sin by the taste of the fruit' of Eden. Although Hildegard emphasised the capacity of human beings to achieve 'victory', the legacy of original sin ('the burning flame of lust ... anger, pride, wantonness and other vices of that sort') remained very real to her. Hers was a theology in which 'roses grow with thorns.'[115]

Perhaps the most important dimension of Hildegard's view of human nature was that it reclaimed the tradition, almost lost in the West, that God created men *and* women. While Hildegard accepted the truth of the third chapter of Genesis (in which Eve was created from Adam's rib to be man's helper), her interpretation of the creation story was in the spirit of the first chapter ('male and female he created them'): 'Man and woman are ... so involved with each other that one of them is the work of the other. Without woman, man could not be called man; without man, woman could not be named woman.'

Hildegard outwardly accepted the standard identification of man with reason and divinity, and woman with the body, but because she did not see the body to be the source of evil and temptation, her conclusions represented a radical departure from the misogynist orthodoxy. Hildegard argued that because God became human in Jesus (known as the incarnation), while man might be the 'indication of the Godhead ... woman is an indication of the humanity of God's son'. Where Aquinas had seen 'all men' in Adam, Hildegard dared to see all humanity in Eve: 'in her the whole human race was present in a latent way.'[116]

Moreover, in Hildegard's understanding of creation, Eve had not *chosen* to sin but had been poisoned by Satan with 'venomous vomit' because of his envy of her ability to bear children. The poison was passed on involuntarily, like a contagious disease, rather than by a deliberate act, so that, as Barbara Newman suggests, in Hildegard's thought, Eve 'is more sinned against than sinning'. Indeed, those who blame Eve for original sin are understood by Hildegard to be, in effect, taking the Devil's side.[117]

Another German woman pushed the boundaries of orthodoxy still further. Mechtild of Magdeburg (c. 1210–1285) was a Beguine, a fascinating movement primarily made up of ordinary women pursuing their calling in Christian communities outside the sanctioned religious orders.[118] Between 1250 and 1264 Mechtild recorded her visions and ideas in a book titled (on God's instruction), *Vliessende Lieht miner Gotheit in allu die Herzen die da lebent ane Valscheit* ('Light of My Divinity, Flowing into All Hearts that Live Without Guile'), which was published after her death. Mechtild condemned the sins of the clergy, vividly portrayed hell and purgatory, and directly confronted the doctrine of original sin:

> Some learned people say that it is human to sin. In all temptations of my sinful body, all feelings of my heart, all understanding of my senses and all nobility of my soul, I could find none other but that it is *devilish* that man sins ... More than that, wickedness acquired of our own free will is always more harmful to us than all the rest of our weaknesses such as hunger, thirst, heat, frost, pain, sorrow, longing, sleep, weariness. These are all things which Christ too suffered who became true man for and with us. Moreover, if sins were only human then He too had sinned, for He was true man in the flesh.[119]

The Christian revelation, for Mechtild, was not that Adam's sin changed human nature, but that with Christ 'the *divine* nature now has bone, flesh, body and soul'.[120]

It was more than two hundred years after the death of Hildegard, and over a century after the passing of Mechtild, that England's most celebrated female mystic wrote down her understanding of the Christian faith for posterity. In May 1373 Julian received her series of sixteen 'shewings' during a severe illness and became an anchoress, confined to a cell attached to St Julian's Church. (It is probable that she took her name from the church, which was already about

51

four hundred years old.) For twenty years Julian meditated on her visions, finally recording them in *Revelations of Divine Love*. It is surely appropriate that in the territorial stronghold of Pelagianism, and in the first book written by a woman in English, one of these shewings was a compassionate reinterpretation of creation:

> I understood that the lord who sat in stately rest and peace was God. The servant ... was Adam; thus one man was shown as falling at a particular time, to make it clear how God regards all men and their falling. For in the sight of God all men stand for one man, for one Man stands for all men. This man was hurt in the day of his strength and made very weak ... But his will was kept constant in God's sight; for I saw the lord commend and approve his will, but, he, himself, was hindered and blinded from knowing his own will; and this causes him great sorrow and grief; for neither does he see clearly his loving lord ... nor does he see truly what he is in himself in the sight of his gracious lord. And I know well that when these two things are wisely and truly seen, we shall have rest and peace in part in this life, and by his bounteous grace, the fullness of joy in heaven ...[121]

Julian's conclusion that human 'pain alone blames and punishes, and that our courteous Lord comforts and succours ... loving and longing to bring us to his own blessedness' represented a profound rejection of original sin.[122] She maintained that God 'is the ground ... the substance ... the very essence of nature', and that 'he is the true Father and the true Mother of nature', because 'we are all bound to God by nature'. Far from a desire to sin having taken over human beings, 'it belongs to our nature to hate sin ... for nature is all good and fair in itself ... nature has been tried in the fire of tribulation and ... no lack of defect is found in it. So are nature and grace of one accord; for grace is God, as uncreated nature is God.' The reason sin is 'more vile and painful than hell' is precisely because it is 'in *opposition* to our fair nature'.[123]

Julian was no isolated hermit; people flocked to her window for counsel, and she railed against the desolation she saw there: 'It is our enemy who wants to retard us with his false suggestions of fear about our wretchedness ... For it is his purpose to make us so depressed and so sad in this matter that we should forget the blessed contemplation of our everlasting friend.'

She set no bounds on God's love for humanity – *every* bodily function was sacred because it reflected His presence. Her God did not even disdain the privacy of the privy:

> A man walks upright, and the food in his body is shut in as if in a well-made purse. When the time of his necessity comes, the purse is opened and then shut again, in most seemly fashion. And it is God who does this, as it is shown when he says that he comes down to us in our humblest needs. For he does not despise what he has made, nor does he disdain to serve us in the simplest natural functions of our body, for love of the soul which he created in his own likeness. For as body is clad in the cloth, and the flesh in the skin, and the bones in the flesh, and the heart in the trunk, so are we, soul and body, clad and enclosed in the goodness of God.[124]

Julian was the mystic's mystic, her wisdom transcending time, culture and even Christianity itself. No other Western writer had so simply or eloquently presented an alternative to the received theology based on original sin:

> From the time that it was shown I desired often to know what was our Lord's meaning. And fifteen years after and more, I was answered in inward understanding, saying, 'Would you know your Lord's meaning in this? Learn it well. Love was his

meaning. Who showed it to you? Love. What did he show you?
Love. Why did he show you? For love. Hold fast to this, and you
shall learn and know more about love, but you will never need
to know or understand about anything else for ever and ever ...
And so I saw ... surely that before ever God made us, he loved
us. And this love was never quenched nor ever shall be. And in
this love he has done all his works, and in this love he has made
all things profitable to us ... In our making we had beginning,
but the love in which he made us in him from without beginning, in which love we have our beginning.[125]

Julian believed that there was too much emphasis on guilt, and her
most famous saying confronted the widespread despair concerning
sin and judgement: 'All will be well, and you will see it yourself, that
every kind of thing will be well.'[126]

These were much more than maternal words of comfort to a
plague-ravaged generation. In daring to document her radical vision
of God's embrace of all humanity, this pioneer woman writer of the
vernacular tongue presented an enduring alternative to the central
tenet of the muscular Roman church. But it was a testament to the
power of the patriarchal institution and the centrality of its defining
doctrine that it was more than five hundred years before her caring
words would be widely heard beyond the small opening in her East
Anglian city cell. Reform of the church would not be achieved by
women who quietly undermined original sin, proclaiming God's
loving presence with every person, but by fervent men who loudly
restored the doctrine to an ancient and uncompromised purity.

8

THE MEANING OF
MARRYING A NUN

ON 13 JUNE 1525 A ONE-TIME AUGUSTINIAN MONK, Martin
Luther, married a former nun, Katharina von Bura, in the German
town of Wittenberg. More than any religious teaching, this act gave
expression to the revolutionary understanding of original sin that
underpinned the Protestant Reformation. In Luther's marriage bed,
the thousand-year association between Adam's sin and sexual temptation was broken. His nuptials revealed what Christianity's carnal
obsessions had come to obscure: that the consequences of the Fall
concerned not bodily desires alone, but every dimension of human
existence.

The Reformation, which tumultuously transformed Europe
during the sixteenth century, was grounded in original sin.[127] The
reformers' essential belief was not that the Catholic Church was corrupt or moribund (there was nothing new in either sentiment), nor
that society was immoral and semi-pagan (even if this was also
widely believed), but that the *only* way in which anyone, however
righteous or powerful, could escape damnation was through the
unearned forgiveness of God – his 'grace'. This could be accessed by
faith in Christ alone. The reasoning behind this radical concept of
salvation, a belief which could cost people their jobs, families and
even their lives, relied on the depravity of human nature. People
could do nothing to save themselves, however godly, generous or

chaste, because people did not simply sin, they were *sinners*, innately and unavoidably subject to the just punishment of God. Because sin defined the human condition, the whole medieval salvation package, from pilgrimage to purgatory, was a Satanic detour from the only road to heaven.

The intellectual resources for this renewed focus on original sin were provided by the scholastic and humanist scholars who made new translations of Augustine and the Bible, and provided the techniques to study them. The first printed scholarly editions of Augustine's works were published over sixteen years from 1490, with the new printing presses ensuring they were widely disseminated across the monasteries, universities and towns of Europe. One of the many young monks who read these texts, and who was sufficiently trained in the humanist and scholastic techniques needed to unpack them, was Martin Luther (1483–1546), who in 1511 had moved from his cloister in Erfurt to teach the Bible at the University of Wittenberg.[128] Luther was to spend the rest of his life in this small town on the banks of the Elbe, and would never leave his post at the university founded by his early patron and protector, the ever-pietistic Friedrich the Wise.

Like Augustine before him, Luther's spiritual journey began with an overwhelming sense of his own sinfulness, from which he found no escape through confession, pious practice or theological study. Here is Luther's testimony of the dramatic impact that Paul's 'Letter to the Romans' had on him:

> My situation was that, although an impeccable monk, I stood before God as a sinner troubled in conscience, and I had no confidence that my merit would assuage him. Therefore I did not love a just and angry God, but rather hated and murmured against him. Yet I clung to the dear Paul and had a great yearning to know what he meant. Night and day I pondered until I saw the connection between the justice of God and the statement that 'the just shall live by his faith'. Then I grasped that the justice

of God is that righteousness by which through grace and sheer mercy God justifies us through faith. Thereupon I felt myself to be reborn and to have gone through open doors into paradise. The whole of Scripture took on a new meaning, and whereas before the 'justice of God' had filled me with hate, now it became to me inexpressibly sweet in greater love. This passage of Paul became to me a gate to heaven …[129]

Making almost as much use of Augustine (especially his anti-Pelagian writings) as of Paul, in September 1517 Luther prepared ninety-seven 'theses' or arguments (he never abandoned scholastic techniques) against the scholastic understanding of salvation, in which he asserted that human beings are a 'corrupt tree', and can neither 'will nor do anything but evil'.[130] In 1518 he went further, with ninety-five theses and a sermon on indulgence and grace, written in what became his trademark polemical style. Luther's assertion that no human being could of their own free will do anything but evil now led him to embrace predestination, on the grounds that even the decision to choose salvation must be the initiative of God. These ideas found a wide audience, and from this time on, Luther faced the wrath of the church.[131]

Luther's attack on the system of indulgences no doubt aided his popular appeal and stiffened the resolve of his self-interested opponents. But his views on this subject were a direct expression of his understanding of sin and salvation, rather than an attack on church corruption per se. By promoting the purchase of indulgences, he said, the church was doing the work of Satan – not because it was making money but because it was misleading sinners about how they could be saved. Luther shared the patriotic resentment that hard-working Germans were propping up a corrupt and overblown Curia in Rome, but his ultimate concern was that the church's teaching that an innately sinful people might do something to save themselves was sending people to hell.

Luther's trial for heresy opened in 1518 and he was excommunicated in 1520, provoking an unprecedented pamphlet war across Germany and much of Europe.[132] Reform-minded humanists, most notably Desiderius Erasmus (c. 1467–1536), sought a middle way, but as Luther's attacks on the pope and the church grew more vitriolic, the pressure on Erasmus to declare his position grew. When in 1524 he finally did so, with *A Discourse on the Freedom of the Will*, Erasmus differed with Luther not on indulgences, church authority, the vernacular mass or the myriad issues associated with the Reformation, which by then was well underway, but on the central question of how original sin affected human nature. Luther acknowledged that his foe 'alone saw what was the grand hinge upon which the whole [dispute with Rome] turned'.[133]

In his bestselling satirical book *In Praise of Folly* (1510), Erasmus had mocked the way theologians preoccupied themselves with the question of 'how original sin is transmitted down through the generations'. Who could 'understand all of this', he asked, 'unless he has frittered away thirty-six whole years over the physics and metaphysics of Aristotle and Scotus'? But despite his sympathy for the simplicity of Luther's teaching, Erasmus was adamant that people could make right choices, because humanity's God-given capacity to reason had not been fully corrupted by original sin, but only damaged by it. In *Freedom of the Will*, Erasmus pointed out that it would be unjust of God to create human beings who were incapable of fulfilling the conditions of salvation, and to save or damn people for something for which they cannot be responsible. The Christian's task was to become a genuine disciple through holy living, as 'true religion' meant doing good deeds for those in need. Finally, even if it did turn out that the will was not free, the church must still act as if it were; otherwise, 'what a window to impiety would the public avowal of such an opinion [denial of free will] open to countless mortals'.[134]

The importance which Luther placed on this critique is revealed by the fact that, during the frantic year of 1525, in which he remained the head of a movement already violently fracturing, he found time to respond to his scholarly foe. Late in life, Luther came to hope that most of his writings would be forgotten, but he was 'certain' that *On the Bondage of the Will* contained 'the unchangeable truth of God'.[135]

Luther's landmark text is not, as one might expect from the father of the Reformation, full of scripture. As his biographer Michael Mullett has observed, Luther relied on 'dialectic methods of argument from premise to conclusion'. And the first premise for Luther's scholastic-style discourse, the foundation on which his whole argument rested, was that 'Original sin itself ... will not allow of any other power in Free-will, but that of sinning and going on unto damnation'. Luther was certain that 'original sin has so destroyed us, that ... nothing [is] left in a man ... which can turn itself towards good'. He maintained that to qualify the impact of original sin on human nature would be to qualify the redemption achieved by Christ: 'If we believe that Christ redeemed men by his blood, we are compelled to confess, that the whole man was lost: otherwise we shall make Christ superfluous, or a Redeemer of the grossest part of man only – which is blasphemy and sacrilege!'[136] For Christ alone to save us, original sin must first have destroyed us completely, meaning that, for Luther, justification by faith alone and the destruction of human nature wrought by original sin were more than related ideas – they were one.

In 1526–27 Erasmus published *The Shield Carrier*, which broadened his critique of Luther and his movement, although he was still looking for olive branches. Luther made no reply, and ever after would speak of Erasmus only with scorn. But although the debate did not replicate the ongoing tit-for-tat of Augustine and Julian, both men continued to put original sin's implications for salvation at the heart of the Reformation divide.

Luther devoted ten years of labour, from 1525 to 1535, to the compilation of a series of published lectures on Genesis in which he reviewed in detail the creation and the Fall. Erasmus, meanwhile, laboured throughout the 1520s on new scholarly editions of the works of the Church Fathers. As an old man, despairing of the religious divisions and conflicts that had engulfed Europe, Erasmus seems to have opted out of the debate altogether. When he died in July 1536, he was writing again on Origen, the giant of Eastern Christianity distrusted by Catholics and Protestants alike. Did Erasmus sense that that if the Reformation's divisions were ever to be overcome, it was necessary to reconnect with a Christian tradition in which God was present with *everyone*, regardless of what they believed?[137]

Luther's ideas on sin and salvation might have been central to his break with the Catholic Church, but why did so many people rush to embrace a teaching that celebrated human incapacity? For the first generation of reformers, this was heretical and therefore a dangerous choice, so why make it at all?[138]

In emphasising the universal consequences of original sin, and in shifting the emphasis from sin to sinner, Luther preached a radical spiritual equality. No one, be they priest, monk or pope, was perceived to be more righteous or further ahead in the race for salvation. *All* people were innately and unavoidably sinners, and, through the grace of God alone, *all* could become saints (thus being *simul iustus et peccator* – 'at the same time saved and lost' – according to Luther's famous formula). Once the power to mediate salvation, in this life and the next, was moved away from the church, with its complex rules and rites, authority was effectively returned to the believer. Luther asserted 'the lofty dignity of the Christian' by offering every human being the keys to paradise.[139]

In abolishing all spiritual distinction between 'religious' and 'lay' ways of life, and in bridging the ancient divide between high reason and low physical instincts, Luther sanctified ordinary human existence. The millions of words he wrote in pamphlets, books, letters and hymns, reproduced by the increasingly busy printing presses in German and Latin, radically redefined the holy life. It is difficult for the modern mind (and it wasn't easy for the late medieval one) to see how Luther's emphasis on the depravity of human beings under-pinned his extension of the sacred. It was precisely because original sin affected the whole person, and could never be quarantined to a particular dimension of human existence, that Luther's God no longer blessed a distinctively 'religious' life. God's redemption was not focused on good people but on sinners, meaning the pope had no more power to command celibacy than 'he has to forbid eating, drinking, the natural movement of the bowels, or growing fat'.[140] 'What do you mean,' Luther asked in his *Large Catechism*, 'by the words "I believe in God, the Father, the Almighty, the Creator ..."? Answer: "What I mean and believe is that I am God's creature, that means that he has given me and continuously maintains body, soul and life, limbs small and large, all the senses, intellect and reason."'[141]

Now that heterosexual marriage and the 'family' have become synonymous with evangelical Christianity, it is easy to overlook how Luther's teaching that sexually active people were as worthy in God's eyes as celibates and virgins restored spiritual dignity to the majority of believers. For Luther, sexual desire was part of God's creation, and marriage a 'divinely noble business'. 'Whoever is ashamed of marriage,' he wrote, 'is also ashamed of being called human and tries to improve on what God has made.'[142]

Luther's sanctification of the body and its desires forced him to address the novel problem of what to do with runaway nuns. From 1520, the Reformation was characterised by thousands of women walking away or being expelled from their religious houses.[143] These women had, on entering their order, usually at a young age, renounced all claims on their family, and by leaving it they were foregoing their only means of economic survival and the sole socially permissible identity available to them as a single person. It was understandable that Luther felt a responsibility for these vulnerable converts to the Reformation's cause; he personally sheltered many of them. In fact, in the midst of the chaotic political upheaval sweeping across Germany, Luther's home became something of a dating agency, as he linked eligible men (including one-time monks) to former nuns. It was in this context that he, too, decided to marry.

To understand the revolutionary significance of Luther's wedding to Katharina von Bura, one must remember his station in life. It was not such a large step to imagine that priests might again be permitted to marry – as they had been until 1139, when the custom was declared invalid and lawful wedded wives were often replaced by priestly concubines – but for a monk, whose whole life was dedicated to pursuing holiness, to marry a nun was to break a taboo and court disaster. Every venerated church leader since St Peter (whose apparently abandoned wife was forgotten by scripture and tradition) had been an ascetic celibate.[144] Even today, it would be difficult for the Catholic Church to imagine that a truly holy man might tell another human being, as Luther did, 'I would like to be your lover now.'[145]

Even the Lutheran Church, although it would come to idealise its founder's 'model' family, never came to terms with his enjoyment of sex. The decision to censor the published version of the letter Luther wrote in December 1525 to explain why he could not attend the wedding of a friend deprived generations of sexually anxious Protestants of one of Luther's most tender reflections: 'When you sleep with your Katharina and embrace her, you should think: "This child of man, this wonderful creature of God has been given to me by my Christ. May he be praised and glorified." On the evening of the day on which ... you will receive this, I shall make love to my Katharina while you make love to yours, and thus we will be united in love.'[146]

The image of Luther in bed with his nun-wife, much publicised in counter-Reformation propaganda for centuries, was disturbing not only to the conservative Curia.[147] Luther's colleague Philipp Melanchthon saw his marriage as an unnecessary impediment to the possibility of reaching a compromise with Rome; other Reformation leaders, still loyal to canon law, also opposed it. Even Luther's closest friend, Justus Jonas, wrote on the day after the fateful act:

'Yesterday I was present and saw the bridegroom on the bridal bed – I could not suppress my tears at the sight ...' But on this matter Luther mocked both friends and foe: 'Getting married has brought me so much contempt that I may hope that the angels are laughing and all the devils weeping.'[148]

The virtue of monastic virginity found popular expression in the superstition that a union between a monk and a nun would produce a two-headed monster, and so it was with understandable relief that, after Katharina gave birth to a boy on 7 June 1526, the proud father wrote to family and friends that the baby had been born without any defects. (One wonders what would have happened to the Reformation if the child had been disabled.)

The many historians who casually link original sin with harsh child-rearing practices would do well to consider Luther's family life. The physical punishment of children so characteristic of the late medieval period had been experienced by Luther himself as a school-boy.[149] Cruel discipline was a daily part of rote learning, but Luther would later condemn teachers who did not distinguish in their assaults between laziness and a lack of ability. In the schools he established, and in his own home life, he sought a more moderate path.[150] He saw children as 'God's little fools', who needed firm guidance but were also close to the divine. He was devastated when two of his daughters died young, and, despite his fervent belief in judgement and the afterlife, he was ever reluctant to consign babies to hell.

Compared with Christian teachers before him – and with most of those who followed, for that matter – Luther was an earthy leader, who enjoyed women, children, wine and music.[151] It is ironic that the Reformation, which would do so much to banish the sacred from the natural world, had a founding father who enjoyed and sanctified ordinary human existence. Luther's beliefs that 'God provided the body with limbs, arteries, ejaculation, and everything that goes along with them', and that 'if someone wants to stop this and not permit what nature wants and must do', he is 'preventing nature from being nature, fire from burning, water from being wet, and man from either drinking, eating, or sleeping', are not easily reconciled with the image of sixteenth-century Protestantism as a severe, life-denying creed.[152]

The fact that every person and every dimension of ordinary life were blessed by God and equally sacred in His eyes did not mean that people were *social* equals. Luther's understanding of the status of women highlights this. This was a man who could claim that 'when a father goes ahead and washes diapers … and someone ridicules him as an effeminate fool', 'God, with all his angels and creatures, is smiling'; he was making a theological point about the sanctity of all forms of labour, not doing the washing.[153] Luther's argument was 'only' that a wife's lower station (like all other earthly stations) did not affect her status before God. Yet for ordinary women whose lives were made up of endless chores demeaned by scripture and tradition, their elevation to full spiritual equality with priests and monks was nevertheless a potentially transformative teaching. Luther's disapproval of the traditional practice of wife-beating was of equal import.

Luther emphasised that Adam, not Eve, was responsible for original sin. In part this was because every teacher who gave priority to original sin still had no choice but to maintain Augustine's masculine emphasis, since a womanly sin lacked sufficient spiritual status (how could a *woman's* sin be transmitted to every *man*?), but Luther also emphasised Adam's fall in order to sever the association of original sin with female sexual desire.

The practical consequences of the Reformation's focus on original sin went far beyond the convent and the family home, or what Luther could have intended or foreseen. With poverty no longer to be sought as a holy calling, with salvation not aided by giving alms, and with the major institutional source of relief, the Catholic Church, undermined or expelled, the Reformation came at some cost to the poor. Luther did preach that faith should be expressed through charity, but with believers' entry to heaven guaranteed, the incentive to follow this injunction was weakened. In Wittenberg he established a community chest for those deemed deserving of aid. And, like most Catholic theologians, he condemned the charging of interest on loans, asserting that 'after the devil there is no greater human enemy on earth than a miser and usurer'. But in wanting usury to be condemned as vigorously as stealing and murder, Luther was, as in so many other areas of his social and political thought, a medieval conservative whose world was passing into history.[154]

Another instance of this was his traditional belief that everyone belonged, by infant baptism, to the one church. It is unsurprising that others saw his teachings on sin and salvation as leading to a different conclusion.[155] The best known of these dissident groups, the Anabaptists, pointed out that a person could not be justified by faith alone while still a baby, and sought to rebaptise believers who then made up their true church. To Luther, their exclusive theology was replicating the mistake of monks and nuns.[156]

Luther's vigorous defence of universal infant baptism occurred at a new stage of the Reformation, in which rulers of political and administrative units became Protestant, bringing all their subjects with them as a matter of course. From the mid-1520s, whole states (remembering that in Germany alone there were scores of self-governing towns and other political entities within and beyond the Holy Roman Empire) became Protestant. In Lutheran regions, this ensured there was as much continuity as change, with only those religious practices abandoned which Luther saw as distracting the believer from facing up to their innate incapacity to do anything to save themselves.[157]

The most significant of these was the practice of confession, on the basis that this sacrament implied that sin primarily comprised discrete acts which could be dealt with, one by one, by the church. A Lutheran confession, best done in private before God alone, required the believer not to focus on this sin or that, but to face the guilt that came with their whole being and very existence. Only then would one know the totality of God's love and forgiveness.[158]

The most controversial consequence of Luther's emphasis on original sin was the justification it gave to the use of force to maintain order. This issue came to the fore during the Peasants' War of 1525, a rural uprising in which perhaps 100,000 people died.[159] The catalyst for the rebellion was increased taxes and new laws that removed traditional rights of access to forests, waterways and meadows. Luther expressed some early sympathy for the farmers' cause, but as the insurrection spread and violence increased, he published a pamphlet that sanctioned violent reprisals by the state. His perceived betrayal was bitterly felt and reduced Lutheran support in the rural south of Germany.

Luther's actions warrant criticism, but they were not, as is sometimes suggested, a 'sell-out' of his principles to achieve political support. Not only was Luther a medieval man in his understanding of the social order, but his belief in original sin also led him to believe that 'it is the function and honor of worldly government ... to prevent men from becoming wild beasts'.[160] Ultimately, Luther's defence of coercion in the service of order was not intended to justify war, but to prevent it. He was consistently horrified when the cause behind the Reformation was used to justify violence, describing war as 'one of the greatest plagues that can afflict humanity; it destroys religion, it destroys states, it destroys families. Any scourge, in fact, is preferable to it.'[161]

During the 1520s, the Reformation spread but also fragmented, and in Zurich arose a more militaristic leader, Ulrich Zwingli, whose philosophical differences with Luther centred on original sin. Zwingli preferred to talk of *Erbprest* ('original weakness'), rather than *Erbsünd* (the usual term for 'original sin').[162] He did not believe that Adam's disobedience transmitted an actual sin or guilt to every human being, but only an inclination to sin.

Because Zwingli placed comparatively less emphasis on the whole person and more on actual wrongdoing, he believed that sin could and should be actively confronted through preaching, education, law and, when necessary, force. Zwingli shifted the emphasis back to the moral teachings of the Bible, including Old Testament law, arguing that through these passages God had given man 'a sure knowledge of his will'.[163] He maintained that such 'commandments of God are not advice, as the papists maintain, but are the direct orders of God which he requires us to obey, and we cannot come to him unless we are as guiltless, pure and devout, as he wishes us to be'. Faith in Christ 'made obedience to God's commands possible for us', and the danger for believers was to remain 'evil and corrupt rather than reaching out towards everlasting righteousness'.[164] The contrast with Luther's forlorn view of human capacity – which not even conversion could overcome – was profound.

It was because they had such different understandings of the consequences of original sin for human nature that these two Reformation leaders had opposing positions both on the *need* to uphold all of scriptural law, and on people's *capacity* to do so. While Lutheran towns carried on dancing, drinking and singing, in Zurich the idols were smashed and many customary pleasures outlawed. Such theology also underpinned Zwingli's decision to use force against both the independent-minded Anabaptists and the resolutely Catholic Swiss cantons.[165]

Zwingli was killed on the battlefield on 11 October 1531, and a report soon spread that when his friends came to find his body three days after his death, his heart lay whole and undamaged among the ashes. As this myth suggests, not even Zwingli had been able to banish ancient superstitions concerning the redemptive power of relics and saints.[166]

Despite Zwingli's violent death, it was the non-Lutheran branches of the Reformation (which, confusingly, came to be called the Reformed Churches) that had the greatest long-term influence. The future spread of Lutheranism was limited: with the notable exception of Scandinavia, it never expanded much beyond its early strongholds in Germany. By contrast, the Reformed Churches would convey the Reformation across much of Europe and, ultimately, to the New World.

The theology of the worldwide Reformed Churches would differ from Zwingli's in one crucial respect. As early as the 1530s, they shifted closer to Luther's understanding of the meaning and consequences of original sin. The person most responsible for this was John Calvin, the celebrated author of the Western world's most influential doctrinal manual, *The Institutes of the Christian Religion.*

9

JOHN CALVIN'S *INSTITUTES* OF THE CHRISTIAN RELIGION

I am aware of the superior plausibility of that opinion, which invites us rather to a consideration of our goodness, than to a view of our miserable poverty and ignominy, which ought to overwhelm us with shame. For there is nothing more desired by the human mind than soothing flatteries; and ... to hear its excellences magnified.

—JOHN CALVIN[167]

ONE SUNDAY MORNING IN OCTOBER 1534, Parisians on their way to church found themselves confronted with placards attacking the mass and ridiculing priests. The response from the authorities to this provocation was fierce, and many reformers fled to Protestant territory as some of their brethren were burnt at the stake. One of the refugees was a young law graduate from the University of Orléans, John Calvin (1509–1564), who arrived in Basel in January 1535. Calvin spent his exile in the Swiss city writing, and by March 1536 the first edition was published of the book that would define the central teachings of Reformed religion and determine the brand of Protestantism that would do so much to mould the modern West.

The full title of Calvin's tome expressed its ambition and ultimate achievement: *The Institutes of the Christian Religion, Containing almost the Whole Sum of Piety and Whatever It Is Necessary to Know in the Doctrine of Salvation.*[168] This book set out doctrine and provided a guide to the interpretation of ancient, inconsistent and often inaccessible Biblical texts. Like the Catholic Church (and unlike some of his future followers), Calvin took it for granted that the Bible had to be interpreted.[169] He understood that if Protestantism was to triumph over its established foe, it must not only reject the thousand years of dogmatic development in the Catholic Church, but also provide a comprehensive replacement for it, and to achieve this became his life's work.

In 1539 Calvin released the first expanded edition of his book, a process of revision which did not end until the sixth and final version of 1559. Protestant polemicists have always proclaimed that 'the Word' of the Bible defines their faith, but the *Institutes* was the equally significant scripture of their religion.

Calvin believed that papist dogma had distorted the central message of the Gospels. Even the early Church Fathers ('except Augustine', he emphasised) had explained salvation by faith alone, 'with less perspicuity than it required'. Calvin presented himself as a modern-day Bishop of Hippo, seeking to defeat 'the Pelagians of the present age'.[170] In dedicating his book to the King of France (who he hoped would protect Protestants), Calvin explained that the sole reason some reformers 'are bound in chains, others are lashed with scourges, others are carried about as laughingstocks, others are outlawed, others are cruelly tortured, [and] others escape by flight' was their zeal for the doctrine of salvation. The only point of this suffering and persecution was that 'our doctrine must stand, exalted above all the glory, and invincible by all the power of the world; because it is not ours, but the doctrine of the living God'.[171]

This 'exalted doctrine' began with original sin. Despite their many theological differences, Calvin respected Martin Luther and his legacy, because both men placed the West's creation story at the centre of Christianity. Calvin was as certain as the Wittenberg professor that to lay claim to even a residual goodness within human beings proffered the false hope that people could do something to save themselves, and that this was the well-trodden road to hell.

Although the two leaders began as one on this question, the greater emphasis in the Reformed churches on naming and confronting specific sins was grounded in Calvin's determination to clearly define what original sin meant in human life. For Luther, a Christian's understanding of original sin came from self-knowledge rather than from a theological treatise, but Calvin's determination 'to remove all uncertainty and misunderstanding' led him to define it explicitly: original sin was 'an hereditary depravity and corruption of our nature, diffused through all the parts of the soul, rendering us obnoxious to the Divine'.[172] Calvin also employed his training as a lawyer to clarify and modernise Anselm's legal metaphor through the notion of substitution: Christ secured salvation by suffering on the cross in the sinner's place.

Affirming hereditary depravity meant rejecting every carefully crafted theological compromise of the past. This project extended to the ever-sensitive issue of the eternal fate of dead babies, which Luther had largely avoided confronting, even though it remained the doctrine's most contentious front. Calvin stressed that 'the impurity of the parents is so transmitted to the children, that all, without a single exception, are polluted as soon as they exist', and that because all people at their birth had received the 'pollution to which the punishment is justly due', there could be no respite in limbo or purgatory for babies or anyone else who had not been saved by faith in Christ. Babies were not innocent: their 'whole nature is as it were a seed of sin, and therefore cannot but be odious and abominable to God'. Even in the womb, 'before we behold the light of life … we are in the sight of God defiled and polluted'.[173]

Nevertheless, there is a sign in the *Institutes* that even Calvin found it difficult to send babies to hell. Buried in his lengthy tome is the concession that because God's grace knew no limits, he might give justifying faith to infants. This seems akin to the medieval softening of original sin which Calvin was so concerned to repudiate, and is perhaps a testament to how hard it has been for any pastor of sensitivity to squash a grieving parent's hope that his or her deceased child was in heaven.

Calvin also allowed that the human mind, 'even by natural instinct, possesses some sense of a Deity'. He saw in the 'diversity' of human wisdom 'some remaining marks of the divine image', a *sensus divinitatis*, the residue of a religious sense which distinguished 'the human race in general from all other creatures'.[174] But that most Calvinists would overlook Calvin's sensitive side is not surprising, given that he made no attempt in the *Institutes* to integrate these beliefs with the book's central teaching. Moreover, even at his mystical best, Calvin stressed that the 'natural' gifts that remained after the Fall 'have ceased to be pure to polluted man'. The 'first and universal curse' remains what is 'denounced on human nature'.[175] Just as it had with Augustine, Calvin's attempt to distinguish between created human nature and its fallen reality was a conceptual devise that made little practical difference. Calvin claimed that man's 'natural depravity' did not 'originate from nature' because he was concerned to protect the character of the creator, not his creation.[176]

In another critical respect, however, later Calvinists did distort the teaching of their founder. Calvin has come to be closely associated with the doctrine of predestination, including the notion of an 'elect' chosen by God to be saved before the beginning of history. As with Luther and Augustine, Calvin's belief in predestination was a logical consequence of his determination to uphold unqualified original sin: every human being had become 'so enslaved by sin, as to be of his own nature incapable of an effort, or even an aspiration, towards that which is good', so that even seeking God 'is attributed solely to Divine Grace'. Because human beings were totally ruled by sinful desires, 'the cause of election must not be sought in men' but 'proceeds from the same decree by which we were elected before the creation of the world'. Yet there is only a relatively short discussion of the 'sublime mystery' of predestination in the *Institutes*; Calvin did not believe it should be the basis on which to build a Christian society.[177] The fact that predestination is now associated with Calvinism is because the churches of Augustine and Luther did not accept their teachers' instruction on the subject, whereas many of Calvin's followers became so fixated on identifying the elect that it came to define their community.

Calvin's reputation as the promoter of godly government is better deserved. He believed original sin brought down God's judgement on all of human society, so that salvation required action by individuals and institutions. His first attempt to implement his vision in the reformed Geneva was rebuffed, but after returning to the city in 1541, he spent the rest of his life translating the theory of the *Institutes* into a program of practical ecclesiastical and political reform.

The Scottish reformer John Knox declared that under the rule of Calvin, Geneva became 'the most perfect school of Christ that ever was in the earth since the days of the apostles'.[178] Calvin's social agenda was ambitious, ranging from outlawing most traditional forms of pleasure to a prohibition on giving non-Biblical names to children – which therefore eliminated most saints' names as well as many traditional local names.[179] Reportedly asserting that 'we must have rough halters for rough donkeys', Calvin imposed orthodoxy through an institution called the Consistory, a church court that either excommunicated or handed over to secular authorities as criminal defendants those who held dissenting beliefs. House-by-house tests of knowledge of religious doctrine were carried out annually in the 1550s, with education in Calvin's detailed doctrine requiring a level of rote learning beyond anything previously required of ordinary people. His second Catechism comprised three hundred and seventy-three questions and answers.[180]

Calvin's political activism might seem to be in tension with the doctrine of salvation by faith alone – until it we recognise that he believed original sin meant that not just the individual but the entire community was subject to the wrath of God; thus, receiving His saving grace required personal conversion and corporate repentance. The capacity to achieve social change was based on the *Institutes'* distinction between inner and outer human realities. While the Fall had led to the complete corruption of man's inner nature, God in his mercy had moderated the consequences for his outer nature, which was what allowed the construction of a godly society. This was a conceptual delineation foreign to Martin Luther, for whom facing reality involved accepting that there was only one truth about yourself; everything else was ultimately masks and mirrors.[181]

The *Institutes* rejected the idea that the state was a mere concession to human sin, 'a polluted thing' which must be tolerated but 'which has nothing to do with Christian men'. Civil government was a 'benevolent provision' of God that was not merely the unavoidable consequence of the Fall, but 'equally necessary to mankind as bread and water, light and air, and far more excellent'. Like Zwingli before him, Calvin believed the role of church and state was to glorify God by creating a holy community that was brought into harmony – by coercion, if necessary – with the divine will.

Calvin gave both a positive and a negative justification for the imposition of the godly state. He believed it was every Christian's responsibility to channel divine grace to implement God's will in the world, but original sin also meant that an inherently sinful people needed an authoritarian government. Calvin warned that 'the transition is easy from monarchy to despotism; it is not much more difficult from aristocracy to oligarchy ... but it is most easy of all from democracy to sedition'.[182] However, the increasing persecution of Protestants in France, and Calvin's loss of faith in the monarchy, meant that the final edition of the *Institutes* (1559) emphasised the fact that even the most exalted human ruler was a sinner:

... it does not often happen ... That kings so control themselves that their will never wanders from what is just and right. In addition, it is truly rare that they have sufficient prudence and cleverness that each of them can see what is good and useful. It follows that the vice or defects of men is the reason that the most acceptable and surest form of superiority is that in which several govern helping one another of their duty. If one raises himself too high, the others act as censors and teachers.[183]

Calvin never supported sharing political power beyond a select elite, but the long-term implication of his admission that original sin corrupted even the rule of kings was profound. The citizens of rigidly reformed Geneva already knew that no member of the elect, including Calvin himself, was immune from the corruption of the Fall, but as Europe descended into religious turmoil, original sin's perversion of political power was most readily seen in the persecuting old regimes. During the seventeenth century Calvinists came to see their church as a godly community that stood apart from the world and its sinful rulers. The project to construct a universal Christian society continued, but increasingly the focus was on building a new world rather than pursuing reformation of the old.

10

SPREADING THE WORD

By the mid-seventeenth century, the grand vision of the first generation of reformers, a Protestant Europe, seemed unachievable. A century of religious flux had produced many voluntary assemblies of Reformed Christians – especially in France – but only three large Reformed kingdoms: England, Scotland and the Netherlands. Moreover, of this trinity only Scotland had achieved a Calvinist consensus.

While the ideas of John Knox were still being successfully resisted in the Scottish highlands (this would change in the centuries to come), by the 1650s such was the strictness of the laws designed to counter the human inclination to sin that children in the lowlands were being punished for playing on Sundays, and more witches were being burnt in Scotland than in any other Reformed region of Europe. By contrast, in the comparatively tolerant and diverse new nation of the Netherlands, Catholics remained the majority of the population.[184] England, either because of its Pelagian undercurrents or due to its unusual level of intellectual and cultural freedom, remained a very different place from its northern neighbour even at the height of its enthusiasm for Reformation religion.

It is even sometimes denied that the Church of England ever was a Calvinist church. While there was a vibrant diversity of beliefs in English Christianity (which is evident in Shakespeare's *Hamlet* and Milton's *Paradise Lost* as much as in theological debate), before the mid-seventeenth century the English church's essential harmony with other Reformed churches was rarely questioned.[185] This was reflected both in the strong resistance to Arminianism, which asserted no more than that all people could choose to be saved, and in the poetic prose of *The Book of Common Prayer*, composed largely by Archbishop Thomas Cranmer in the middle of the sixteenth century.[186]

Fragments of Cranmer's poetic prose persist in the popular imagination around marriage and death: 'for richer, for poorer, in sickness and in health … till death us do part' and 'earth to earth, ashes to ashes, dust to dust' are fragments of this inheritance.[187] By contrast, the words of the christening service now seem grating:

> Dearly beloved, forasmuch as all men are conceived and born in sin, (and that which is born of the flesh is flesh), and they that are in the flesh cannot please God, but live in sin … I beseech you to call upon God the Father, through our Lord Jesus Christ, that of his bounteous mercy he will grant to this Child that thing which by nature he cannot have.

The contrast is suggestive of the ambivalent place of original sin in English Christianity.

The climax of Calvinist influence came with the Westminster Confession of Faith of 1647, which asserted: 'Mankind is wholly defiled in all parts and faculties of soul and body … utterly indisposed, disabled, and made opposite to all good, and wholly inclined to all evil.'[188] But the execution of King Charles in 1649 and the imposition of a 'godly commonwealth' widened the distrust of Puritan extremism; following the Restoration in 1660, the influence of Calvinism in the Church of England significantly declined.[189] The newly formulated Articles of the Church of England on 'Original or Birth-sin' expressed this change with the comparatively moderate assertion that human beings were 'very far gone from original righteousness' and '*inclined* to evil'.[190]

A confidence in the capacity of human beings to choose the good
and the godly can be seen in the most famous Protestant text of its
age, John Bunyan's *The Pilgrim's Progress*, first published in London
between 1678 and 1684. The cave in the Valley of the Shadow of
Death is guarded by Pope and Pagan, but although they make the
heroes suffer, they don't make them fail. As Linda Colley points out,
'The Pilgrim's Progress is celebration of the importance of willed
activity, a paean to individual commitment and indomitable struggle, and an assurance that they will indeed win through.'[191]

The relative diversity and tolerance of English religion and culture meant that Reformed purists were increasingly marginalised,
and this encouraged some of the more zealous among them to construct a more godly society across the Atlantic. When the Puritans
set sail from Plymouth in 1620 on the *Mayflower*, and when John
Winthrop followed them a decade later to found Massachusetts,
they carried with them the baggage of uncompromised Calvinist
thought about sin and salvation.

During the seventeenth and eighteenth centuries, many other
Calvinists arrived in the North American colonies. The Dutch settled New Amsterdam, which the British renamed New York. French
Protestants, known as Huguenots, emigrated to North America in
considerable numbers. And by the end of the seventeenth century,
Scottish Presbyterians, already present in New England, had also
firmly established themselves in the middle colonies and were well
on their way to becoming as influential in American life as the Congregationalists (as the New England Puritans came to be called).
Religious wars in France, the Netherlands and Germany – which
culminated in the Thirty Years' War from 1618, the conflict which
largely cemented the religious divide of Europe through to the present time – displaced hundreds of thousands of people and promoted further Protestant migration across the Atlantic.[192]

All forms of Calvinism in North America were underpinned by
a rigid belief in the doctrine of original sin, but there were subtle

shifts in how the story of Adam and Eve was interpreted. Calvin's notion that God had formed a 'covenant' with humankind was applied to the telling of the creation story. Adam, as the 'federal' head of humanity, had broken the contract with the divine, and all people now bore the debt that resulted from this. The corresponding certainty that Calvinist believers were a chosen people whom God had set aside to be saved faced a degree of questioning in the cultural melting pot which the American colonies were already becoming. This constraint was sadly absent from the Dutch and Scottish communities established by Calvinist emigration to southern Africa and Ulster, respectively; in these lands the notion of an elect people became a political ideology that underpinned centuries of rigid separatism.

Such was the decisive long-term importance of the Calvinist push into the New World that it is easy to forget that most Calvinist missionary effort was aimed at achieving spiritual conformity within Europe. A particular focus was taking the Reformation message out from the Protestant strongholds of the towns.

The Calvinist assault on the countryside represented the first serious attempt to confront those popular beliefs that contradicted the doctrine of original sin. Whereas the Catholic hierarchy had largely been content to tolerate peasant beliefs and practices so long as people accepted the sacraments and authority of the church, the reformers set out to destroy all sources of salvation – every demon, holy site and spell – other than the Christ they proclaimed. It is true that Reformation religion heightened the concern with Satan (partly because all his rivals in the dominion of evil had been rendered redundant), but even Satanic work aimed to tempt individuals to deny their own sinfulness and find ways of saving themselves. Using the power of the pulpit (which was very real, in an age of few alternative sources of information), pastors sought to replicate in villages across Europe what Calvin had achieved in Geneva: a godly society built on a dogma of human depravity.[193]

Depending on the level of missionary vigour and the resistance that could be mounted, the change in rural lifestyles could be dramatic. When the Church of Scotland (known as the Kirk) sent its missionaries into the stubbornly Celtic Western Isles, it was not only the traditional dances, prayers and songs that were vigorously attacked. Even such seemingly secular matters as clothing and communal systems of farming and local decision-making could be targeted. The missionaries often worked in partnership with the secular authorities, who were equally concerned to bring the rebellious Gaels into line, and even the speaking of the local language, which had rightly been identified as the carrier of the alternative spiritual and political tradition, was banned in schools. Churches were established to convert and civilise what was seen as a superstitious and savage people.

Historians dispute the overall impact of this process. At one time it was standard to see the Calvinist assault on the countryside as producing 'modern people', but the emphasis has now shifted to recognising the similarities between pre- and post-Reformation culture. Alexandra Walsham argues that the Reformation played a more marginal role in the 'disenchantment' of the universe than Max Weber and other scholars have argued. She sees a 'battleground', where even as the reformers 'eradicated one set of legends, contemporaries were busy creating others to fill their place'. For example, while there were widespread attacks on and ordinances against traditional holy sites, such as holy wells, wayside crosses and monasteries, there was also an increased focus on the sacredness of the parish church.[194] Euan Cameron suggests that there has been an overreaction: people did resist, were far removed in their outlook from modern Europeans and did not conform to the reformers' expectations, but the cultural change was nevertheless significant.[195] As when Christianity was imposed on the cultures of foreign lands, the response seems to have been resistance *and* accommodation. Missionaries were not solely responsible for the decline of traditional beliefs and practices, but they did have a considerable long-term impact.[196]

The impact of the Calvinist mission also varied across the different regions and even localities of Western Europe. While the speed of change in Geneva is well documented, even in the neighbouring region of Vaud the Reformed experience was quite different. Between 1630 and 1670, a century after the Reformation, there were still numerous complaints about people venerating a sacred tree trunk which was supposed to cure gout, visiting a fountain which cured evil spirits, observing traditional holy days like St Bridle's Day, when no horses were meant to work, and bedded-down newlyweds being made to drink a 'furry soup' in order to receive unnameable blessings.[197]

It is also important to remember that in an age when religion was still enmeshed with every other dimension of human life, the interests of Calvinism went beyond personal piety and cultural practice. As new forms of work and trade supplanted the fixed medieval order, anxiety over salvation remained much more than a spiritual concern. Fears of undue suffering in this life and the next were not removed by the Reformation, and, as Max Weber would famously document, the Calvinist response to people's unending worries seems to have been surprisingly well suited to the times. As capitalism slowly came into being, no creed would do a better job of sanctifying the old-fashioned sin of greed.

THE PURITAN FOUNDATION
OF MODERN LIFE

Poor soul, the centre of my sinful earth.

—William Shakespeare, Sonnet 146

The Reformation has been described as 'the first great
expression of the search for certainty in modern times', the age in
which magic and mystery were banished from the cosmos.[198] But
while this was true of the West's relationship with nature as a whole,
it was certainly not true of human nature. The confrontation of the
sinful self, the foundation of Western Christianity since Augustine's
Confessions, became a radically more uncertain undertaking once it
was no longer regulated by ecclesiastical authority or closely associated with sexual desire. The Reformation meant that the mind was
no longer quarantined from the corrupting influence of original sin;
now believers were expected to find evidence of its corrosive power
in every dimension of their thought and being. With the correlation
between sin and the body undermined, the Western creation story
could penetrate the once secure citadel of the inner soul.

It is more than a hundred years since Max Weber highlighted
the broader consequences of Reformation angst. In *The Protestant
Ethic and the Spirit of Capitalism* Weber argued that an 'unprecedented inner loneliness' was critical to the ethical revolution which
underpinned the emergence of capitalist society.[199] Weber noted that

because Calvinism taught that human beings could do nothing to save themselves, all the initiative and power lay with God alone. The believer had 'no agent to intercede with God on his behalf – no priest, no sacraments, no Church'. Even a committed and active faith was no guarantee of salvation. Who could know whom God had predestined for heaven?

Calvinist ministers were forced to confront the problem which had undermined the preaching of extreme versions of original sin since the age of Augustine: if believers could do nothing to save themselves, what could the church offer in the way of solace or moral direction? Unable to question predestination itself, ministers sought to give believers certainty in their 'state of grace'.[200] Calvin himself wrote that perseverance in faith was a sign of the elect, and pastors advised their flocks that all doubts about their own salvation came from Satan. Weber argued that the 'Protestant ethic' emerged from the requirement that the Christian continually believe in his or her own election, and ensure that all dimensions of life provided evidence for it. Believers were required to live out their sainthood not in the other-worldly sense of monasticism, but while immersed in family, church, work and commerce.

The negative aspect of the Protestant ethic, Weber argued, was the denial of pleasure and the rigorous self-control it demanded, but the positive aspect was equally significant: the confident pursuit of one's calling in the world. Weber believed that both these dimensions made up the 'the spirit of capitalism': 'The positive sanction entailed a moral premium in support of closely managed and continuous profit making, and the negative sanction entailed an unconditional prohibition against the consumption of these profits or their diversion from the enterprise that the believer, as God's faithful steward, treated as his calling.'[201]

Weber's thesis has been disputed on many grounds. John Wesley pointed out that Methodists succeeded because they drank less and saved more, and a link between a disciplined lifestyle and material prosperity is not hard to establish. But the Reformation was associated with a profound cultural shift towards the sanctification of what had previously been regarded as 'sin', particularly the pursuit of profit through commerce and usury (the charging of interest on loans). And while this was not confined to Calvinist countries, it was particularly pronounced in them. Whether it was a cause or effect (or cause *and* effect) of capitalism, it was predominantly in Reformed regions that diligent participation in profit-making became a godly duty, rather than sinful compromise.[202] The most dramatic ethical convulsion of the Reformation was undoubtedly the blessing conferred on trade, which, in the growing towns of England, Scotland and Holland, must have encouraged the emerging capitalist economy.

Weber's ideas also help to explain the strange self-doubt which became characteristic of the wealthy West. The threads are difficult to untangle, but the anxiety induced by a religion that emphasised the dire consequences of original sin while simultaneously removing the power of the Catholic sacraments to secure salvation (especially baptism, confession and the mass) is likely to have promoted a restless, accumulative and questioning spirit. Any large disruption to a people's established sense of spiritual security makes for anxiety, and this must be amplified still further when the new teaching ridicules all traditional sources of redemption.

The consequences of salvation insecurity were perhaps most evident in people's heightened concerns about child-rearing. Although the education of children was a focus of the Reformation generally, it was Calvinistic Puritans who pioneered and dominated the new genre of parenting manuals. During the sixteenth and seventeenth centuries, on both sides of the Atlantic, the Puritans wrote twice as many advice books on rearing children as did all other groups combined.

It was in these books that the modern assumption that early childhood is a critical formative stage in human development was first expressed. The reason parents were 'especially bound to instruct the children, pray for them and train them up in fear of God', as Sir Simonds D'Ewes explained in one typical book entry, was 'because they drew original corruption from their loins'.[203] Cotton Mather, a leading minister in early New England, noted that children 'go astray as soon as they are born. They no sooner *step* than they *stray*, they no sooner *lisp* than they *ly*.'[204] Mather knew from personal experience how quickly death (and thus judgement) could come to little sinners, as eight of his fifteen children died before the age of two. Although the Puritans eventually accepted that there might be an eternal benefit in baptism, consistent clarity on this matter was never reached, meaning the fate of dead infants remained terrifyingly uncertain. The best hope for children was rigorous training, and the Puritans discovered that their infants could be taught to repent from a remarkably young age.

Because babyhood, with its irrepressible self-centred demands, remained mired in original sin, parents were encouraged to teach their children to walk upright as soon as humanly possible. Crawling, seen as a disturbingly animal-like behaviour, continued to be discouraged, but the traditional European means of doing this – swaddling a child so that his or her movements were restricted – was also criticised. Infants were instead dressed in long robes or petticoats and placed in wooden go-carts, complete with neck-stays to keep their heads upright.[205] Mather and others also condemned the still widespread practice of wet nursing, claiming it exposed infants to outside influences.

Catechisms and scripture were taught so early that children readily recited what they could not hope to understand, but the capacity to read and write for themselves was a more important aid to salvation. The *New England Primer*, first published around 1690 and in print for nearly 200 years, shaped the education of millions of children in North America. Its most famous feature was its alphabet pages, used to teach letters. The first of these, and the only one that never changed throughout the *Primer*'s many editions, was on original sin: 'In Adam's Fall / We Sinned all.'[206] Its enduring influence is shown by the fact that as late as the early 1930s, at Doomadgee, in a remote region of northern Australia, when the missionaries taught Aboriginal children to read and write, '"A" still stood for "Adam" and "All have sinned".'[207]

Once they could read and write, children were encouraged to keep journals to record their spiritual state. Samuel Mather, aged twelve, was fearful that he might 'belong not unto the election of grace'. John Clap had a 'thorow conviction of his misery by reason of sin both original and actual' by the time he turned eleven. At the same age, Priscilla Thornton declared that 'she knew she was made up of all manners of sin'. And at age thirteen, Nathanael Mather wrote: 'I confess, O Lord, I have fallen from thee by my iniquity, and am by nature a son of hell.'[208]

During the seventeenth century, it was primarily a patriarchal responsibility to promote a child's salvation. The father was the family pastor and had the responsibility to lead daily prayer and Bible reading for the household, as well as to teach the Catechism, so it was not surprising that early child-rearing manuals were specifically addressed to him.[209] It was only at the end of the seventeenth century that parenting manuals began to be aimed at women. This reflected the feminisation of the faith that was characteristic of most voluntary Christian assemblies. By the early eighteenth century, seventy per cent of Puritan worshippers were women, which meant that many mothers now had primary responsibility for dealing with the consequences of original sin in their children.[210] Not only was motherhood taken more seriously, but instructions on how to raise children into godly adults became increasingly intense, as anxiety mounted about the departure of young men from their parents' faith.

A question which has long absorbed historians is why, given their belief in predestination, the Puritans were so focused on the question of how to save themselves and their children. If the elect had already been chosen, why was virtuous living so critical? The point was that every person had to prepare for the offer of salvation, and to ensure that he or she was ready whenever the opportunity arose. Conversion happened through the grace of God alone, but it was also a developmental stage which required that believers progress to the point where they could respond to the call. It was because of the necessity of being *ready* that parents needed to make young children cognisant of their sinful nature, the ever-present possibility of death and the urgency of repentance.[211]

A focus on child-rearing also gave Puritan parents and pastors something positive to say and do, which was surely both a psychological and an institutional necessity. Nevertheless, the Puritan parent's apprehension can readily be imagined when it is recalled that failure in one's duty meant not just a misspent life on earth, but also an eternity of suffering for their child in the fires of hell. The great comfort that baptism afforded the Catholic and Lutheran parent was not available to the Puritan; they could never be certain of their children's eternal fate, and whether there was more they might do to secure it. The distinguished historian of childhood Stephen Mintz believes that the intense parental anxiety which this uncertainty induced has been a Puritan legacy to the American nation.[212]

12

RECLAIMING AUGUSTINE

WHILE CALVIN LABOURED IN GENEVA, the Catholic Church was also undergoing radical reform. During the mid-sixteenth century, the church comprehensively overhauled its teachings, a change that largely defined its dogma and direction for the next five hundred years.[213] The compromises of the Middle Ages were rejected as the church sought to define what it stood for and to ensure conformity with its every ukase.

While the members of the Catholic hierarchy were particularly determined to mark every point of difference with the Protestant heretics, the irony of their project was that it, too, centred on a return to the creed of Augustine and a rejection of those teachings and customs which contradicted it. As a religious wall was constructed through early modern Europe, with each group colourfully describing the damnation awaiting those on the other side, few recognised that the bitter conflict involved a shared commitment to restoring the purity of the doctrine of original sin, which ensured that it became the improbable foundation of *modern* man's quest for meaning.

Much of the work of reforming the Catholic Church was undertaken by the influential Council of Trent, which met from 1545 to 1563.[214] The council put original sin at the top of its agenda, asserting: 'If anyone says that recently born babies ... incur no trace of the original sin of Adam needing to be cleansed by the water of rebirth for them to inherit eternal life ... let him be anathema.' Because of original sin, salvation could not be achieved 'by the powers of human nature or by any other remedy than by the merits of the one mediator, our Lord Jesus Christ'.[215]

The Council of Trent attempted to distinguish Catholic teaching from Protestant by affirming the potential for a Christian to overcome, with God's help, the consequences of original sin. It stated that the inherent inclination to sin (termed 'concupiscence') 'cannot harm those who do not give consent but, by the grace of God, offer strong resistance'.[216] Affirming the capacity to resist sin distinguished the Catholic position from that of Martin Luther (about whom the council seemed to know much), but it was also broadly consistent with what the Reformed churches were preaching. The view that humans could, by God's grace, lead holy lives underpinned both the renewal of Catholic religious orders through to 1700 (with a new emphasis on engaging with the outside world) *and* godly living in Calvinist communities. Zealous Catholics and Protestants alike sought to stand out from the sinful crowd.

This unintentional consistency was even evident in Trent's codification of canon law, which meant that sin was more clearly defined. Luther's focus on the all-encompassing impact of original sin meant that measured distinctions between different sins had been effectively abolished. The council's demand that sins be confessed according to their kind, the number of times they had been committed and the circumstances in question thus seemed to differentiate the Catholic Christian from lax Protestants. Yet the enhanced theological interest in detailed behaviours and rules concerning what was permissible bore an obvious similarity to the rigid moral laws and detailed regulations characteristic of many Calvinist communities. For example, the contemporary Roman Catholic and evangelical Protestant obsession with criminalising the ancient practice of abortion dates from this period. In the wake of Trent, the old tradition that a male foetus could be aborted for forty days after conception, and a female foetus for eighty days (which in practice meant that abortion was exempt from punishment for eighty days, since there was no way of determining gender) was suspended.[217]

Ultimately, it was only the Catholic denial of predestination that made for an obvious denominational difference, but even this diminished over time as first the Lutherans, then most Anglicans and finally even many Calvinists, changed their minds about the incapacity of human beings freely to choose faith in Christ.

During the sixteenth century, the Catholic Church also became as committed as the Calvinists to living out faith in the world. The Protestant caricature of the celibate monk fighting his sexual fantasies in a cloistered cell retained an element of truth, but the renewal of old orders and the establishment of new ones meant that professed religious were now at the vanguard of activism. These men and women were generally better trained and resourced than ordinary clergy, and they were often the ones taking reformed Catholicism into the European countryside and out to the vast Catholic empires of Spain and Portugal.

That this activism had its own form of inspirational leadership is best seen in the life of Ignatius of Loyola. This one-time soldier and courtier from the Basque region underwent a Luther-style confrontation with self, then, as a mature-age student at the University of Paris, gathered around him a small group of soldiers for Christ. Members of the Society of Jesus, sanctioned by the Pope in 1540 (after Ignatius had endured multiple interrogations by the Inquisition), did not live in monasteries at all, but sought to lead transformative Christian lives in the world. The Jesuits, as they came to be called, brought a level of professional focus to the ordering of a human life that sometimes made even Puritan discipline look amateurish.[218] But underpinning Ignatius' renowned *Spiritual Exercises* (which every Jesuit had to undertake) was a surprisingly optimistic assumption about humanity's deepest desires.

Ignatius believed that the 'the human spirit seeks goodness and truth rather than the opposite and tries to reassert those values in people who neglect them'. The temptations which took people away from Christ – riches, honour and pride – were the 'enemy of human nature', not a reflection of it. Yet Ignatius' comparative confidence in human nature coexisted with an emphasis on the dire consequences of original sin. Right at the start of the *Exercises*, novices were required to reflect on 'the sin of Adam and Eve' and their own 'bodily corruption and foulness'; they were to recognise themselves as 'as a sore and ulcer, for which have sprung so many sins and so many iniquities and so very vile poison'.[219] Nevertheless, the point of difference in Ignatian spirituality was significant. It might be hard work to dig down through the layers of sin to find the true self, but if, at the ultimate centre, was created goodness rather than vile lust, then God's will could be discerned *through* the body's emotions and desires.

It is not surprising that this departure from orthodoxy produced a counter-reaction. In his posthumously published book *Augustinus*, the Bishop of Ypres, Cornelius Jansen (1585–1638), sought to confront 'the very splendid advocates of lust' who had compromised the teachings of Augustine on the absolute depravity of human nature.[220] Jansen followed Augustine's teaching all the way to accepting the Protestant heresy of predestination, which was why he was reluctant to publish *Augustinus* in his own lifetime, and ensured that it was condemned by the pope in 1641.[221] Nevertheless, Jansenism prospered, especially in France, for one hundred and fifty years, and the movement's political influence was such that it even secured the suppression of the Jesuits by Pope Clement XIV in 1773, which forced the order to go underground to survive.

Other religious orders and lay movements – both male and female, and both newly reformed and altogether new – were also energetically expanding, and became central to the vibrant diversity of Catholicism, which coexisted with its increasingly rigid dogma.[222] The success of such activism meant that the Catholic Church had, by the late seventeenth century, seemingly emerged victorious – on points, if not by knockout – in the territorial fight with its Protestant foe.[223] Moreover, the ecclesiastical elite were now much better equipped to assert control over their vast domain. Parish priests, trained for orthodoxy in newly established seminaries, were bound more closely to diocesan discipline. One arm of Roman power was the infamous Inquisition, which ensured an unprecedented level of conformity with official dogma.[224] Rome became almost as virulent as Geneva in its determination to stamp out the superstitions of its flock.

One manifestation of this was the practice of witch-hunting, which, at least in part, represented an attack on those who sustained hope in popular piety's diverse sources of salvation. Tens of thousands of newly discovered witches and heretics were burnt at the stake, usually after undergoing torture to elicit a confession; the craze predated the Reformation but was intensified by it. It was even possible to be killed simply for denying the truth of original sin. In 1600 a miller from an obscure Alpine village, Domenico Scandella, was found guilty of communicating a number of heretical beliefs, including that man is not a sinner until 'he begins to feed on his mother's milk when he comes out of her belly'. Given Scandella's old age and limited influence, even the inquisitors recommended clemency, but the level of official fear concerning the attractiveness of heretical ideas became clear when Pope Clement VIII personally intervened to ensure Scandella's execution.[225]

It was not only the people of Europe who experienced the reformed power of Catholicism. Its focus was on Central and South America, but Catholic missions also penetrated the Philippines, India, Japan and China. Missionaries were both integral to conquest and sometimes lonely defenders of native peoples. In parts of Asia, the Jesuits ensured that Christianity was adapted to local cultures in ways which would be considered bold even today. Even where the mission was most tragically played out, in the wake of the Spanish sweep through South America, it showed itself more culturally sensitive than many of the Christians who would follow.

Nevertheless, the work of even the most compassionate mission-aries was rendered cruel by original sin. As the first Catechism devel-oped for the Indians put it: God had made heaven and hell, and in heaven are all who convert to Christ and in hell are 'all your dead, all your ancestors, your fathers, mothers, grandparents, relatives, and who have existed and departed this life. And you shall go there as well, unless you become friends of God, and are baptized and become Christians, for all who are not Christians are God's enemies.'[226] Because of their unquestioned belief in the doctrine of original sin, missionaries took for granted that Indians who did not convert to Catholicism were destined to be punished by God for eternity, and this in turn justified their conversion at almost any cost.

So central has original sin been to Western Christianity that it is now difficult to imagine how the religion could have been preached *without* a belief in the doctrine. If every non-believer was not by their very birth destined for hell, and if God was understood to be already present with the Indians, might the missionary effort in South America have been more akin to the peaceful Celtic missions to northern Europe a millennium before? Was it only a thousand-year immersion in original sin which led the Spanish to assume that baptism offered the only hope of escape from the wrath of God? There is no possibility that an alternative theology would have ensured a peaceful conquest or a tolerant cross-cultural encounter, but might it have made the religion of the conquistadors a less sub-servient partner to their force of arms?

Ultimately, a version of Western Christianity devoid of original sin is now so hard to imagine that these questions cannot be consid-ered in any informed way. It is near impossible to demarcate the influence of original sin because it was enmeshed in both the reli-gious and the cultural dimensions of European expansion. All that is certain is the troubling truth that the creation story of the Western world proved particularly well suited to conquest.

PART II

ORIGINAL SIN IN
THE MODERN WORLD

PREFACE

It is evident, that all the sciences have a relation, greater or less,
to human nature; and that, however any of them may seem to
run from it, they still return back by one passage or another.
                                        —DAVID HUME[227]

IT IS A PECULIAR PARADOX THAT THE West's thousand-year-old
creation story helped to shape the emergence of the modern world.
The sixteenth and seventeenth centuries saw the demise of the medieval age, yet this was also the time when original sin reached the
zenith of its influence. The apparent divisions of the Reformation
only distilled and unified the core teaching, and strengthened the
institutions charged with imposing it. Far from original sin being a
medieval idea, early modern Europe took it to heart.

The reason this truth has been obscured is that shortly after the
consensus was achieved, a profound shift began to occur in the world
view of Western Europe's educated elite: achieving eternal salvation
ceased to be the orienting principle of their lives. The historic shift
towards *this life* became ever more noticeable through the eighteenth century. In what has come to be called the Age of Enlightenment, the doctrine of original sin was not so much defeated as
bypassed; it slowly faded away, as the answers it provided ceased to
be relevant to the questions being asked. Or that, at least, is what
most educated people believed, then as now.

What is forgotten in this view of history is that original sin was not only a religious dogma; it also supplied a framework in which to understand what it meant to be human. As my nineteenth-century namesake James Petigru Boyce pointed out, the doctrine concerned not what people did, but 'what they are'.[228] The widespread assumption that the principal tenet of Western Christianity is the Judeo-Christian moral code is based on a fundamental misunderstanding of the West's religious tradition. Salvation did not come from being 'good' or worthy. Rather, the religion was grounded in a deeply personal emphasis on the broken self, and a corresponding reliance on an external divinity to provide salvation.

Original sin did not just see humans as limited creatures who made mistakes. It was because people were inherently corrupt in a way no other creature could be – inclined to evil by their very being – that *judgement was central to the Western perspective on human nature. There is no doubt that the divine dimension to this spirituality was banished from the modern mind – eventually not even most Christians believed in a sin inherited by all humans since the Fall. But the issue being considered is more basic: was the essence of the story passed on, and a new language found for an old tale? Did the secular story still begin with a broken self and end with a search for salvation?*

The Enlightenment was an era of new insights and discoveries, and it is understandable that its thinkers emphasised their break with the dogmatic past. There is no doubt that they believed their theories were based on empirical observation alone. It is equally certain that this conviction was naïve. Modern rationalists were not secret or unconscious followers of Augustine, but they were Western people who carried within them aspects of their ancestral inheritance. Leading thinkers in philosophy, economics, psychology and evolutionary science were often agnostics or atheists, but their consideration of the human condition was nonetheless shaped by a shared spiritual tradition. For this reason, the question of what happened when a suddenly old-fashioned religious dogma was replaced by secular thought requires more scrutiny than rational people have wanted to believe.

13

A CHRISTIAN ENLIGHTENMENT

FEW HISTORIANS NOW VIEW THE Enlightenment as the 'anti-Christian' movement it was once taken to be. The much-publicised and sometimes ferocious anti-clericalism of the eighteenth-century French philosophers was the exception, not the rule. Francis Bacon, the seventeenth-century English natural philosopher, set the scene for the English Enlightenment with his conviction that the pursuit of knowledge was a sacred task, one that brought human beings closer to 'the character of the Deity'. The very reason that Bacon considered 'atheism ... in all respects hateful' was because it 'depriveth human nature of the means to exalt itself above human frailty'. Without knowledge of God, 'man is a busy, mischievous, wretched thing; no better than a kind of vermin'.[229]

The gulf between Bacon and the anti-clerical French philosophers illustrates that rather than a single Enlightenment perspective, there were many, and they varied by chronology, country (French, English, Scottish, American) and belief (radical or otherwise). When Edward Gibbon visited Paris in 1763, he was disturbed by the 'intolerant zeal' of the *philosophes*, who 'preached the tenets of atheism with the bigotry of dogmatists, and damned all believers with ridicule and contempt'.[230] Nevertheless, the leading thinkers of the Enlightenment shared a faith in their capacity to obtain sure knowledge of the world around them. It was this common belief that came closest to defining an Enlightenment that crossed geographical, chronological and ideological borders. And it was this approach to knowledge, not hostility to Christianity, that most effectively undermined faith in the idea of original sin.[231] The religious doctrine that had so recently inspired the Reformation proved to be redundant for Enlightenment radicals and conservatives, the moderate Christian gentlemen of Britain *and* the anti-clerical revolutionaries of France. Why? Because it mocked *human* knowledge and *human* effort.

Almost every Enlightenment thinker recognised the unreasonableness of the doctrine of original sin, at least as it pertained to guilt. What rational person could believe that the guilt of one man had been passed on to everyone else? The *Dictionary of Philosophy* compiled by François-Marie Arouet (1694–1778) – usually known by his pen name, Voltaire – quoted extensively from scripture, from the early Fathers and from alternative Christian beliefs to challenge original sin. He concluded: 'We admit that St. Augustine was the first who brought this strange notion into credit; a notion worthy of the warm and romantic brain of an African debauchee – who passed his life in perpetual self-contradiction.'[232]

Even in seventeenth-century England, Christian philosophers and theologians such as Jeremy Taylor, Richard Baxter and John Locke had exposed the doctrine's logical limitations and sought to reinterpret the meaning of the Fall. In *The Reasonableness of Christianity*, Locke accepted that the 'doctrine of redemption, and consequently of the Gospel, is founded upon the supposition of Adam's fall', and that Christ came to 'reform the corrupt state of degenerate man', but sought to separate Christian insights about the human condition, including the universality of sin and the need for repentance, from notions of inherited guilt and divine punishment.[233]

The Enlightenment, especially in Northern Europe, generally did not confront Christianity but largely operated within its increasingly diverse borders, and this was highly significant for the history of original sin. If the direct confrontation with the doctrine seen in pre-revolutionary France had been more widespread, original sin might have been flushed out of cultural discourse. But where clerical power was not aggressively repudiated, the doctrine seemed just to disappear from educated conversation (thus sparking an evangelical reaction that will be considered later). Yet was this an indication that original sin's perspective on human nature had been rejected or absorbed?

Underpinning the intellectual innovation of the era was a taken-for-granted anthropology. The widespread view that the philosophers of this period saw human nature as a 'blank slate' is a crude misrepresentation of their thought.[234] Entire books have been premised on the mistaken assumption that the Enlightenment effectively banished the concept of an innate human nature, and thereby laid the foundation for the modern social-scientific orthodoxy that a person's environment largely determines what he or she will become.[235]

The blank slate metaphor is attributed to Locke, on the basis of his reflection that 'It has been only an empty assertion and no one has proved it ... that the souls of men when they are born are something more than empty tablets capable of receiving all sorts of imprints but having none stamped on them by nature'.[236] However, neither Locke nor, for at least a century, his readers understood the blank slate to mean a denial of human nature or an innate tendency to sin. His argument pertained only to 'moral principles', which he believed must be established by 'reasoning and discourse' because they do not 'lie open as natural characters engraven on the mind'. Locke accepted that God gave human beings a 'definite constitution', was ready to acknowledge 'the narrow measure of our capacities' and admitted that the voice of reason was often drowned out by contrary 'appetites and prevailing passions'.[237]

Locke's orthodox view of human nature was most accessibly expressed in his influential book *Some Thoughts Concerning Education* (1693). As befitted the work of a bachelor son of a captain in the parliamentary army, this fell into the genre of the Puritan parenting manual. While there is no questioning its centuries of progressive influence on dutiful middle-class parents and serious educational-ists, or the significance of its framing notion of natural rights, the Calvinist tenor of *Some Thoughts* is obvious.[238] Locke asserted that what children love most is 'dominion', and that this:

> ... is the first original of most vicious habits, that are ordinary and natural. Their love of power and dominion shows itself very early, and that in these two things ... We see children (as soon almost as they are born ...) cry, grow peevish, sullen, and out of humour, for nothing but to have their wills ... Another thing, wherein they show their love of dominion, is their desire to have things to be theirs; they would have property and possession, pleasing themselves with the power which that seems to give, and the right they thereby have to dispose of them as they please. He that has not observed these two humours working very betimes in children has taken little notice of their actions: and he who thinks that those two roots of almost all the injustice and contention that so disturb human life, are not early to be weeded out, and contrary habits introduced, neglects the proper season to lay the foundations of a good and worthy man.[239]

The objective of parenting was to ensure that children 'learn the art of stifling their desires, as soon as they rise up in them', in order to bring 'their unruly and disorderly appetites' under control. Teaching self-discipline was essential to making a virtuous person: 'the great principle and foundation of all virtue and worth is ... that a man be able to deny himself his own desires, cross his own inclinations, and purely follow what reason directs as best, though the appetite lean the other way'.[240] The intensity with which Locke approached the duty of parenthood sprang from his certainty about the destructive resilience of human nature. Here, the child was no blank slate.

Most other English philosophers also accepted the existence of an innate human propensity to sin, even if they were less interested in children. The Earl of Shaftesbury stressed the 'hateful passions' that beset mankind, and even William Godwin (a rare English atheist and a true radical) wrote that 'It is comparatively easy for the philosopher in his closet ... to show how mankind, if they were without passions and without prejudices, might best be united in the form of a political community', but unfortunately, 'men in all ages are the creatures of passion'.[241]

Then there was Thomas Hobbes (1588–1679), whose belief in the innate evil of human beings rivalled that of Martin Luther. After the horrors of the English Civil War, Hobbes concluded that human society, left to govern itself, leaves:

> ... no place for industry ... no culture ... no navigation, nor use of the commodities ... no commodious building ... no knowledge of the face of the earth; no account of time; no arts; no letters; no society; and which is worst of all, continual fear, and danger of violent death; and the life of man [becomes] solitary, poor, nasty, brutish, and short.[242]

The major difference between Hobbes and the leaders of the Reformation is that Hobbes *accepted* the selfishness, self-absorption and aggressive pursuit of individual self-interest that he depicts. What was important for Hobbes was to face up to the reality of human nature and make the necessary political and social arrangements. He believed rational self-interest demanded that people support autocratic authority in order to restrain other humans from expressing their natural inclinations.[243]

While most Enlightenment thinkers were more optimistic than Hobbes, they shared his commitment to accept human nature *as it was*. The profound schism between the spiritual and intellectual sentiment of the Reformation and that of the Enlightenment arose because the link between human nature and divine judgement had been severed. From the mid-seventeenth century, it is not that descriptions of the human condition change markedly, but that this condition is no longer linked to a transcendent story of salvation. The Enlightenment approach to human nature is reflected in Alexander Pope's famous couplet in *An Essay on Man* (1733): 'Know then thyself, presume not God to scan / The proper study of mankind is man.'

The commitment to describe human beings dispassionately reached its British culmination in the work of the Scottish philosopher David Hume (1711–1776). In his major work, *A Treatise on Human Nature*, Hume maintained that 'the science of man is the only solid foundation for the other sciences' and that the 'only solid foundation we can give to this science … must be laid on experience and observation'.[244] But this was not inconsistent with Augustinian theology, which also began with observations of the human condition. Hume's view – that reason was the mere 'slave of our passions' because it can only show us how to achieve what we already want – also upheld the Western Christian tradition. It was because human preferences, desires and 'instincts' are unable to be influenced by reason, or even by social pressure, that Hume believed 'men must endeavour to palliate what they cannot cure'. It is precisely because people 'cannot change their natures' that human passions must be channelled in proper directions, and government authority be accepted.[245] However, governments too are made up of human beings, and the people may have to withdraw consent when those in authority become consumed by their *own* self-interested passions. Customs and conventions deserve respect because they had developed over time to deal with the reality of human nature as it is, not as some might wish it to be.

Despite the improbability of the still solidly Calvinist Kirk conferring a blessing on a man it considered eternally lost, Hume sounded remarkably like one of the church's own in the conclusion to his treatise: 'There is some benevolence, however small, infused into our bosom; some spark of friendship for human kind; some particle of dove kneaded into our frame, along with the elements of the wolf and the serpent.'[246] Hume was no less sure that every human being was born with a tendency to be selfish and cruel than John Calvin; the difference was that the gentle Scot would not condemn anyone to hell because of it.

When Hume died, his friend Adam Smith paid tribute to him in terms that well expressed the spirit of the Scottish Enlightenment, which both men embodied: 'Upon the whole, I have always considered him, both in his lifetime and since his death, as approaching as nearly to the idea of a perfectly wise and virtuous man, as perhaps the nature of human frailty will permit.'[247]

The idea that it was important to take human beings as they were rather than as one would like them to be was developed by Edmund Burke, who vigorously defended the 'latent wisdom' in habit and custom, which had developed over time to deal with the sorry reality of the human condition.[248] In *Reflections on the Revolution in France* (1790), Burke condemned the way that religious beliefs 'which the heart owns and the understanding ratifies as necessary to cover the defects of our naked shivering nature and to raise it to dignity in our own estimation' were now 'exploded as a ridiculous, absurd, and antiquated fashion'.[249]

Nor was the gap between the French philosophers and their colleagues in Northern Europe regarding human nature (even before the brutality of the Terror undermined Gallic optimism) as great as is sometimes imagined. Helvétius could claim that any shepherd boy of the Cévennes could be turned into an Isaac Newton by suitable education – and who would deny that *some* could have? – but many French philosophers were less sanguine about human nature, at least as it was found in the mass of humanity, than their British counterparts.[250]

The great work of the French Enlightenment was the *Encyclopédie*, which appeared in thirty-five volumes comprising some twenty million words, and was issued over nearly three decades from 1751. Its principal editor, Denis Diderot, described its purpose as being 'to collect all the knowledge that now lies scattered over the face of the earth, to make known its general structure to the men among whom we live, and to transmit it to those who will come after us', thus making men, of this time and all time, not only wiser but also 'more virtuous and more happy'. However, in the *Encycopédie* Diderot made it clear that the common people would not be included in this worthy mission, because 'the general mass of men are not so made that they can either promote or understand this forward march of the human spirit'. In another entry Diderot expressed his 'distrust [of] the judgement of the multitude in matters of reasoning and philosophy; its voice is that of wickedness, stupidity, inhumanity, unreason, and prejudice'. The esteemed editor informed Voltaire that the poor were 'too idiotic – bestial – too miserable, and too busy' to enlighten themselves and would not change.

Voltaire himself argued that religion was necessary to keep the poor in check: without it, they would be nothing but 'a horde of brigands' and would pass 'their miserable lives in taverns with fallen women', each day beginning anew an 'abominable circle of brutalities'. Voltaire's view moderated over time, but he never ceased to associate the mass of humanity with passion, and the educated classes with reason.[251]

Other philosophers echoed the theme. In 'Discourse on Happiness', Julian Offray de Lamettrie (1709–1751), best known as the author of *L'Homme Machine* (1748), wrote: 'Man in general seems a deceitful, tricky, dangerous, perfidious animal; he seems to follow the heat of his blood and passions rather than the ideas which were given to him in childhood and which are the basis of natural law and remorse.'[252]

Even Jean-Jacques Rousseau (1712–1778), who famously rejected original sin (the Archbishop of Paris condemned his influential tract *Émile* specifically because of this), believed in both an original innocence *and* a historical fall, which he linked to the introduction of private property. Indeed, the opening lines of *Émile* might have been written by the otherwise critical Archbishop:

God makes all things good; man meddles with them and they become evil. He forces one soil to yield the products of another, one tree to bear another's fruit. He confuses and confounds time, place, and natural conditions. He mutilates his dog, his horse, and his slave. He destroys and defaces all things; he loves all that is deformed and monstrous; he will have nothing as nature made it, not even man himself, who must learn his paces like a saddle-horse, and be shaped to his master's taste like the trees in his garden. Yet things would be worse without this education, and mankind cannot be made by halves. Under existing conditions a man left to himself from birth would be more of a monster than the rest. Prejudice, authority, necessity, example, all the social conditions into which we are plunged, would stifle nature in him and put nothing in her place. She would be like a sapling chance sown in the midst of the highway, bent hither and thither and soon crushed by the passers-by.[253]

Rousseau summarised *Émile* as 'a treatise on the natural goodness of man, intended to show how vice and error are foreign to his constitution, invade from outside, *and imperceptibly alter it*'. Rousseau's logic resembled Augustine's insistence that even though God created people good, Adam's sin had made everyone bad.[254] Just like the doctrine he sought to supplant, Rousseau maintained that human beings were born with a nature that had been corrupted from its true self. Nor does the fact that Rousseau socialised sin, transferring the burden of guilt from individuals to human beings collectively, weaken the comparison.[255] Ever since Ambrosiaster had explained that 'in Adam all sinned as in a lump', original sin theorists from Aquinas to Calvin had made use of this conceptual device.[256]

Rousseau's affirmation of a childhood innocence, too, was not the straightforward rejection of original sin that it is commonly taken to be. In his autobiography, *Confessions*, Rousseau recounts his own fall from this blessed state, which came after he had been punished unjustly for breaking the tooth of a comb:

> This affair was thought serious; the mischief, the lie, the obstinacy, were considered equally deserving of punishment ... This occurrence terminated my infantine serenity; from that moment I ceased to enjoy a pure unadulterated happiness, and on a retrospection of the pleasures of my childhood, I yet feel they ended here. We continued at Bossey [where Rousseau was boarding in the Swiss countryside] some months after this event, but were like our first parents in the Garden of Eden after they had lost their innocence; in appearance our situation was the same, in effect it was totally different. Affection, respect, intimacy, confidence, no longer attached the pupils to their guides; we beheld them no longer as divinities, who could read the secrets of our hearts; we were less ashamed of committing faults, more afraid of being accused of them: we learned to dissemble, to rebel, to lie: all the vices common to our years began to corrupt our happy innocence, mingle with our sports, and embitter our amusements. The country itself, losing those sweet and simple charms which captivate the heart, appeared a gloomy desert, or covered with a veil that concealed its beauties. We cultivated our little gardens no more: our flowers were neglected ...²⁵⁷

Far from positing a radical alternative to the West's ancient creation story, Rousseau helped to reconnect it to the contemporary world by again making it a personal story. The author of this *Confessions* proclaimed: 'The man I shall portray will be myself. Simply myself.' This was not true of other French philosophers, who sought to communicate objective knowledge, and one of Rousseau's purposes was to highlight how spiritually barren he considered their project to be.

In July 1749 Rousseau recalled that, while walking to visit Diderot, who was in prison outside of Paris, he experienced a form of conversion, after which he believed that the civilising process only threw 'garlands of flowers over the chains which weigh us down' and that people were becoming so alienated that eventually they would beg God to give them back their 'ignorance, innocence, and poverty'. What separated Rousseau from Diderot and Voltaire, and connected him to Western spirituality, was, in the words of Tim Blanning, his 'insistence on doing everything from the inside ... And what he found inside himself was a witches' brew of emotions, neuroses and paranoia.'[258]

Rousseau's self-exploration placed him on the margins of the French Enlightenment, which generally remained confident that human nature could be redeemed rationally. But from the perspective of German philosophers, he was an optimist. Immanuel Kant's (1724–1804) *Religion within the Limits of Reason Alone* (1793) argued that 'the propensity to evil in mankind is universal, or, what here comes to the same thing, that it is woven into human nature'. Kant sought to demonstrate that a human being 'is evil by nature', arguing that even when people lived in a 'state of nature', there was abundant evidence of 'unprovoked cruelty' and the 'vices of barbarity'. In the tradition of Augustine and Luther, Kant also sought to challenge his readers to face up to the truth of their own selves, including the 'secret falsity even in the closest friendship', the 'propensity to hate him to whom one is indebted' and the fact that even 'in the misfortunes of our best friends there is something which is not altogether displeasing to us' (not to mention the 'many other vices still concealed under the appearance of virtue'). His philosophy drew explicitly on a metaphorical Fall. God created humans as good but also free, and in their freedom they went wilfully against their true nature.[259]

Like other major Enlightenment thinkers, Kant parted with Reformation Christianity and the doctrine of original sin in his view not of human nature but of redemption. Kant had a Pelagian confidence in the freedom of human beings to restore 'original goodness' through sustained efforts at 'virtue ... won *little by little*'. But his view of what was required to achieve this would not have been out of place in a Puritan tract. It was only through 'continuous labor and growth' that a person could become 'a good man', but 'this change must be regarded as nothing but… a gradual reformation of the propensity to evil, the perverted cast of mind'. In other words, the fight was not 'against vices one by one' but against the core of character, the 'common root' of self-love, towards the ultimate goal of 'ascendancy … over … sensuous nature'.[260]

While Kant stretched the boundaries of Enlightenment thought, Goethe rejected its rationalist borders altogether. In the 'Walpurgis Night' episode of *Faust*, on the night before May Day, Faust and Mephistopheles make their way up to the highest point of the Harz mountains to attend the Witches' Sabbath. Here the doyen of the Berlin Enlightenment, Friedrich Nicolai, is parodied as Proktophantasmist (translated by David Luke as 'Mr Arsey-Phantarsey'). Enraged that his world has been invaded, he cries out:

> Damned spirit-rabble! Stop this insolence!
> Hasn't it been quite clearly proved to you
> You don't exist as proper people do …
> This is outrageous! Why are you still here?
> The world has been enlightened! You must disappear! …
> All my life I've tried to sweep away
> This superstitious junk. It's an outrage I say![261]

As a remarkable century closed, Goethe gave voice to the contradictions involved in trying to impose Enlightenment order on the Western soul. But his was a prophetic voice out of kilter with the rationalist tenor of his age. In the century that followed, even evangelical Christians would come to celebrate the capacity of human beings to direct their own desires. The groundwork for this revolution in Christian thought, on both sides of the Atlantic, was laid by an extraordinarily energetic Church of England cleric, the Reverend John Wesley.

14

THE PERFECT EVANGELICAL

JOHN WESLEY IS THE FOUNDER OF WHAT is now understood as evangelical Christianity. Whereas Calvin and Luther remained, in significant respects, medieval men, Wesley is the prototype of the self-confident preacher who confronts a rapidly changing and increasingly secular society with an upbeat message of salvation. Born in 1703, he reflected *and* reacted to the Age of Enlightenment in which he lived, rebutting 'reasonable' Christianity from *within* empiricism and merging the era's intellectual insights with an intensely personal call to conversion that proved perfectly suited to its times. No radical did more to democratise the Enlightenment, but no one was so adamant in holding on to the Reformation emphasis on original sin and proclaiming that salvation was attainable by grace alone. Yet it was also this towering evangelical, not the doubting deists, who ensured that Augustine's doctrine would ultimately be made subservient to the celebration of individual freedom.

John Wesley was born and brought up in Lincolnshire's Isle of Axholme – so called because, before serious drainage works commenced in the mid-seventeenth century, its farms and villages were surrounded by wild marshland, whose rich natural resources were exploited by an unruly people. Wesley's homeland changed dramatically during his lifetime, as neat fields and an industrious peasantry were imposed on it. The change became a metaphor for his life as he confronted the chaos caused by Britain's economic and social transformation. It is still sometimes said that John Wesley single-handedly prevented an English revolution. However improbable the claim, such was the significance of his labour that it is not surprising that it continues to be made.

Wesley was always a pious and conscientious Christian, but it was not until 1738 that he was reborn. One Sunday evening he attended evensong at St Paul's Cathedral in London and then proceeded to a Moravian prayer meeting, where he heard a reading from Martin Luther's restatement of Paul's message to the Romans on justification by faith alone. Wesley recalled that his 'heart was strangely warmed', an experience he thereafter sought to share, as the leader of the movement which became known as Methodism, with what he perceived to be the near-heathen population living in the backblocks and urban wastelands of Britain and Ireland.[262]

In keeping with the spirit of his conversion, Wesley's understanding of salvation outwardly conformed to Reformation orthodoxy: because of Adam's sin, every human being was under God's judgement and must rely on Christ alone to be saved. Wesley was as convinced as Luther that people could not understand the need for salvation by Christ alone until they acknowledged the truth of their forlorn nature: 'If we are not diseased, we do not want a cure. If we are not sick, why should we seek a medicine to heal our sickness?' He preached and wrote on original sin extensively before putting his ideas into a tome of over four hundred pages entitled *The Doctrine of Original Sin According to Scripture, Reason and Experience, Answer to Dr Taylor* (1756). In this book Wesley asserted that Taylor and others who denied that man is 'by nature filled with all manner of evil' were not even Christian: 'Is [man] void of all good? Is he wholly fallen? Is his soul totally corrupted? ... Allow this, and you are so far a Christian. Deny it, and you are but a Heathen still.'[263]

Wesley's argument for the truth of original sin was based firmly on observation. He saw 'the flood of miseries, which covers the face of the earth, which overwhelms, not only single persons, but whole families, towns, cities, kingdoms', as the 'demonstrative proof of the overflowing of ungodliness, in every nation under heaven'. He believed that the conclusion from any 'just survey of this world' was clear: the earth was 'a grand and magnificent structure in ruins: wherein lie millions of rebels against their Creator, under condemnation to misery and death: who are at the same time sick of a moral distemper, and disordered in their minds even to distraction'.264 In other writings and sermons he pointed to the extent of sin even within his beloved England, including 'thefts, cheating, fraud, extortion ... injustice, violence, oppression ... robberies, sodomies, and murders'. Wesley pointed to both 'the sloth, laziness, luxury, and effeminacy of the English gentry', and to the 'drunkenness, and stupid, senseless cursing and swearing which are daily seen and heard in our streets'.265

Nevertheless, the Englishman parted from Luther and Calvin in one highly significant respect: he rejected the teaching that the impact of the Fall was so profound that human beings were incapable of making real choices – first to be saved, and second to be sanctified. Wesley declared that 'free grace is free in all and free for all' and drew heavily on the teachings of the sixteenth-century renegade Dutch reformed minister Jacobus Arminius, wearing the once-derided label 'Arminian' with pride.266

Wesley's unbridled confidence in the capacity of human nature *post*-conversion was foreign to Western Christianity, which had always relegated complete healing to heaven. 'Know your disease! Know your cure!' he wrote. 'You were born in sin: Therefore, "ye must be born again", born of God. By nature you are wholly corrupted. *By grace ye shall be wholly renewed.*'267 It was because he rejected all limits on human capacity that Wesley unintentionally undermined the doctrine he so passionately supported. The purpose of original sin was to direct believers to rely on God alone. Wesley did acknowledge that few Christians (including himself) ever became wholly free of sin, but every believer could stride with confidence towards that end, since 'this great gift of God, the salvation of our souls, is not other than the image of God fresh stamped on our hearts'.[268]

Although all varieties of Western Christianity had found a way to ascribe value to human effort, Wesley did this more boldly than any scholastic, Puritan or Arminian before him. Nor was he embarrassed when this teaching was described as Pelagian, asserting that Pelagius was wrongly called a heretic for claiming that Christians may 'go onto perfection' and fulfil the law of Christ.[269]

Wesley was similarly Pelagian in his concern, as he put it to his brother and collaborator Charles in 1772, to 'join faith and works in all our preaching'. He warned against 'what is usually called gospel preaching' but was actually 'useless' 'mischievous' and 'dull' harangues 'on the sufferings of Christ or salvation by faith, without strongly inculcating holiness'. He came to believe 'more and more, that this [preaching] naturally tends to drive holiness out of the world'.[270] While Wesley warned that it must always be remembered 'that God, not man, is the Physician of Souls', and 'that it is he and none else, who giveth medicine to heal our natural sickness', he maintained that it was 'generally his pleasure to work by his creatures: to help man by man'. Thus, for Wesley, God 'honours men, to be ... workers together with him'.[271]

In other respects, too, John Wesley was a man who embraced the celebration of human endeavour associated with the Enlightenment. Wesley believed that reading and study were integral to the Christian faith. In his address to the annual Methodist Conference in 1766 he called on preachers to 'spend all the morning, or at least five hours in twenty four in reading the most useful books and that regularly and constantly', and specifically denounced the belief that it was sufficient to 'read only the Bible'. Frustrated with the excuse that his lowly paid preachers could not afford books, he promised to 'give each of you as fast as you can read them books to the value of £5; and [to ensure] ... that all large societies provide the Christian library for the use of preachers'.[272]

Many Methodists no doubt felt that keeping up with Wesley's personal literary output of two hundred and thirty-three books was challenge enough. His projects included a 'Christian Library' of some eighty volumes, in which he tried to 'condense all that is most valuable in the English tongue'. This included a four-volume history of England; a complete English dictionary; a host of tracts on medicine, electricity and natural history; abridged versions of Shakespeare, Milton, Spenser, Locke and other classics; translations and editions of theological works (not just of the evangelical variety); and a three-volume natural philosophy, which paid tribute to Francis Bacon. One of his most widely distributed tracts was *Primitive Physick* (published in twenty-three editions by 1828), which provided remedies for some two hundred and eighty-eight specific ailments; it was much used by his itinerant preachers, who often doubled as medical practitioners to the poor. All Wesley's books were produced in inexpensive editions, and while it is easy to mock the quality of Wesley's medical knowledge or his understanding of Shakespeare, no one did as much to take Enlightenment knowledge to the ordinary people of England, or to create a mass reading public.[273] In this respect, he humbled both the French philosophers and home-grown intellectuals alike.

Wesley's merging of Enlightenment and neo-Augustinian values also found expression in his establishment of Kingswood School. His concern with the existing 'great schools' was that they were deficient not simply 'with regard to instruction in religion', but also 'with regard to learning', including in 'arithmetic', 'writing', 'geography', 'chronology' and languages. There was certainly time enough to teach a broader curriculum at Kingswood, where, Wesley boasted, students 'rose at four in the morning [and] have no play-days, the school being taught every day in the year but Sundays'. Before a child entered the school, his parents had to agree that they would not take him 'from school, not, not for a day, till they take him for good and all'.[274]

Kingswood was the template for all the nineteenth-century evangelical institutions that sought to remove children's innate tendency towards sloth and sin, whether it be the boarding schools of the English elite or the dormitories of the mission schools established for native peoples in the increasingly far-flung empire. Children across the globe would suffer the consequence of Wesley's conviction that 'evil passions or irregular appetites continually prevail in them', and that 'from their first capacity of acting as moral creatures' they were led 'to practice falsehood and injury to their play-fellows; perhaps with cruelty or revenge'.[275] But it was less his dire diagnosis of human nature, and more his confident belief that children could be cured of this, which created the hungry, sleepy, play-deprived and overly disciplined children who populated Wesleyan schools and homes. Always ready to detail 'the general diseases of human nature', Wesley asked: 'Is it not the grand end of education to cure them?'[276]

Despite having no children himself, Wesley felt no qualms about drawing on personal experience to tell parents what to do. He had been brought up in a Church of England vicarage, but both his parents had dissenting family backgrounds. This non-conformist Calvinist heritage infused his impassioned pleas for parents to 'break their [child's] will, the first moment it appears'.[277]

Much of Wesley's message was taken verbatim from his mother, Susanna, whose advice, written down at her son's request in 1732, reflected her Presbyterian upbringing:

In order to form the minds of children, the first thing to be done is to conquer their will and bring them to an obedient temper. To inform the understanding is a work of time … but the subjecting of the will is a thing that must be done at once … I insist on the conquering of the will of children betimes, because this is the only strong and rational foundation of a religious education … As self-will is the root of all sin and misery, so whatever cherishes this in children insures their after wretchedness and irreligion:

whatever checks and mortifies it, promotes their future happiness and piety. This is still more evident if we further consider that religion is nothing else than doing the will of God and not our own: that the one grand impediment to our temporal and eternal happiness being this self-will ... Heaven or hell depends on this alone; so that the parent who studies to subdue it in his child works together with God in the renewing and saving a soul. The parent who indulges it does the Devil's work; makes religion impracticable, salvation unattainable, and does all that in him lies to damn his child body and soul forever.[278]

Wesley's promotion of Susanna's account helped create the legend of a perfect home, in which 'not one' of the ten children 'was ever heard to cry aloud, after it was a year old', and where all understood that they were 'fallen spirits ... more ignorant, more foolish, and more wicked, than they can possibly conceive'.[279] But the sad lives of Wesley's seven sisters challenged this mythology.[280] All were given a good education at home, but this afforded them no respite from oppressive regulation. Mehetabal (known as Hetty) suffered especially because her will seems never to have been broken by Susanna. Hetty eventually eloped with her lover but he did not follow through with the promise of marriage, leaving her pregnant and dependent on her parents, who rejected her. Married off to the local plumber, Hetty had, like most of her sibilings, a deeply unhappy marriage characterised by domestic violence, and all her children died in infancy.[281] In 1733, only a year after Susanna's triumphal parenting testimony was compiled, Hetty wrote a poem to her own baby, 'Infant Expiring on the Second Day of its Birth', which began:

Tender softness, infant mild,
Perfect, purest, brightest child;
Transient lustre, beauteous clay,
Smiling wonder of the day.[282]

Clearly, Susanna Wesley's perspective on the character of children was not the only one in the vicarage.

If Wesley's approach to child-rearing remained broadly within the Calvinist tradition, in other respects his activism went far beyond it. Wesley exaggerated in asserting that Methodists 'do not insist on your holding this or that opinion ... they think and let think', but his boast that 'one condition, and one only, is required [for Methodist membership] – a real desire to save their soul' contained a significant measure of truth.[283] Notably, for example, there was no Methodist confession of faith. A straightforward focus on salvation, combined with a passionate zeal to take the message to the expanding working class of an increasingly industrialised and urbanised economy, was to give Methodism its competitive advantage in the religious market-place of not just the United Kingdom, but eventually much of the New World as well.

Wesley's radical reinterpretation of original sin means that his fervent defence of the doctrine tells only part of the story. Wesley's ultimate achievement was to comport with Reformation zeal while creating a Protestant religion that celebrated the unlimited potential of human beings.

The influence of Wesley's activist religion on British society and politics was profound. Methodism became not only the dominant religion of the working class in many industrial and mining regions, but also the seedbed for their cultural and political development. The role played by Methodism in the emergence of the union move-ment, the Labour Party and mass democracy in England and Wales has been much debated, but there is little doubt that the creed had latent political implications, or that its mode of organising provided an ideal forum in which to practise activism.

Original sin had always been a spiritual leveller, and in the vac-uum created by the turmoil of the Industrial Revolution, it became in its activist Wesleyan expression a social and political one as well. In a letter to the Countess of Huntingdon, the aristocratic patron of the evangelical revival, the Duchess of Buckingham warned that Methodist teachings were:

> ... most repulsive and strongly tinctured with impertinence and disrespect towards their Superiors, in perpetually endeavouring to level all ranks and to do away with all distinctions. It is monstrous to be told you have a heart as sinful as the common wretches that crawl on the earth. This is highly offensive and insulting; and I cannot but wonder that your ladyship should relish a sentiment so much at variance with high rank and good breeding.

A woman who was rumoured to be the illegitimate daughter of King James II was perhaps more sensitive than most on the subject of good breeding, but once the doctrine of original sin was freed from the strictures of traditional church control and the rigid social hierarchy of Reformation Europe, it clearly did undermine the very aristocratic determination to separate 'us' from 'them'.[284]

Nor was Wesley's successful adaptation of evangelical religion to the modern world confined to the various Methodist societies which emerged in the century after his death. From the late eighteenth century, a Wesleyan-style revival was also witnessed in the established church and other Protestant groups, and this movement collectively transformed British Christianity. By 1830, it has been estimated, perhaps sixty per cent of British Protestants were involved in some variety of evangelical practice. Furthermore, through various missionary societies, this was the primary form of Protestantism that was exported into the ever-growing British Empire.[285]

But before moving on to the heyday of imperialism, we should first return to the *old* empire and consider how Wesley's celebration of free choice was seen in Calvinist America.

15

CELEBRATING CHRISTIAN CHOICE

THE KEY FIGURE IN THE EXPORT OF the evangelical revival across the Atlantic was George Whitefield, an early collaborator of John Wesley and the pioneer of open-air preaching. Whitefield parted company with Wesley on the subject of predestination and lacked the latter's organisational skills, but his oratory was unmatched by any of his evangelical colleagues.

Whitefield's mission to the North American colonies between 1739 and 1741 enjoyed unparalleled popular support, and he became the model for the many celebrity preachers who followed him: an on-message entertainer who held the crowd spellbound before inviting them to repent. He challenged his audience 'to see and feel that in your flesh dwelleth no good thing; that you are conceived and born in sin; that you are by nature children of wrath; that God would be just if he damned you, though you never committed an actual sin in your lives'. Whitefield relied on his listeners' ingrained sense of guilt to justify the call to repentance: 'If you have never felt the weight of original sin, do not call yourselves Christians.'[286]

Whitefield's sermons were printed in America by a young Benjamin Franklin, who became a lifelong friend and recalled 'the extraordinary influence of [Whitefield's] oratory on his hearers, and how much they admir'd and respected him, notwithstanding his common abuse of them, by assuring them that they were naturally half beasts and half devils'.[287]

While Whitefield provided the template for the mass marketing of revival-style religion, it was the home-grown American intellectual Jonathan Edwards (1703–1758), a Congregationalist cleric, who shared in Wesley's achievement of reconciling the Enlightenment with Reformation Christianity.

Edwards was a precocious teenager who immersed himself in the writings of British philosophers. When he read Locke's *Essay on Human Understanding* in 1717, he described himself as like a miser who had discovered gold.[288] Locke's writings helped Edwards navigate a formative intellectual and spiritual crisis, and he emerged as a young man committed to demonstrating how his New England Calvinist heritage held the answer to the questions posed by the Enlightenment thinkers of his day. As a minister in Northampton, Edwards became an influential sponsor of the revivals known as the 'Great Awakening' of 1734–35 and 1740–42, but of greater long-term impact was his literary output, which ensured that Calvinism was impregnated with an intellectual vigour that helped it make the transition into the modern world.[289]

Original sin was one of Edward's principal concerns. In his highly influential book *Freedom of the Will*, he took on the philosophical critics of the doctrine, and in *The Great Christian Doctrine of Original Sin Defended*, he targeted John Taylor's ideas.[290] Edwards believed that Christianity depended on the acceptance of original sin, as 'the salvation by Christ stands in direct relation to this ruin, as the remedy to the disease; and the whole Gospel, or doctrine of salvation … and all real belief, or true notion of that Gospel, must be built upon it'.[291] Edwards employed new metaphors to explain ancestral guilt and responsibility, and sometimes tortured metaphysical argument to maintain a collective identity for the human race 'in Adam', which was consistent with the theology of his New England forefathers.[292]

Original Sin Defended was written mostly in the mission village of Stockbridge, after the congregation of Northampton had voted to expel Edwards in 1750 in the wake of the turmoil engendered by the Great Awakening. In an open letter to his former congregation, he challenged the continued admission of people to the church simply on the basis that they were seen as virtuous Christian citizens; he warned that the congregation was forgetting the true state of all human beings. Such thinking also moulded Edwards' approach to Native Americans: while he was highly critical of indigenous culture, he also told his new flock: 'We are no better than you in no respect.' The principal problem was not that they were *Indian* (as most European Americans assumed), but that they were *human*; Edwards wrote that 'the poor savage Americans are mere babes and fools (if I may so speak) as to proficiency in wickedness, in comparison with of multitudes that the Christian world throngs with'.[293]

Despite his intellectual depth and literary output, Edwards had less success in adapting evangelical religion to modernity than John Wesley because he continued to deny the existence of free will. The American never wavered from the Puritan orthodoxy that *no* good was left in humanity as a result of original sin – not even the capacity to freely choose God. Edwards refused to compromise even on the depressing fate awaiting the non-elect newborn: 'As innocent as children seem to be to us, if they are out of Christ, they are not so in God's sight, but are young vipers, and infinitely more hateful than vipers.'[294] Because Edwards' defence of New England Calvinism extended to a belief in predestination (as it did for Whitefield and most other preachers in the Great Awakening), it would be another generation before Wesley's reconciliation of original sin with the responsibility to choose to be saved and sanctified became embedded in American Protestantism.[295]

It was left to Nathaniel Taylor (1786–1858), a professor of theology at Yale, and other so-called New Haven theologians to break the Calvinist nexus and ensure that American Protestantism was compatible with the notion of free choice that was becoming the ideology of the nation. Taylor was an early and articulate advocate of the necessity of individuals to decide to be 'born again'. In his best-known sermon, *Concio ad Clerum* (1828), he did not deny an inherent tendency to sin, but maintained that every sin was nonetheless 'a free and voluntary act', as 'God does not compel [a human being] to sin by the nature he gives him'. Taylor admitted that all people 'are born destitute of holiness', and thus 'are by nature totally depraved', but sought to 'throw all the guilt of sin with its desert of wrath, upon the sinner's single self. Let us make him see and feel that he can go to hell only as a self-destroyer.'

Taylor's theology created a storm that nearly split the Connecticut Congregationalists. In series of letters published in 1832, Joseph Harvey wrote that 'the friends of sound doctrine in the State, will soon seek other seminaries for their children, and Yale will become, in Connecticut, what Harvard [already] is in Massachusetts'. There was a similar conflict among Presbyterians concerning the implications for free will of original sin.[296]

What can be confusing in this controversy is that it was the 'liberals' who were the most concerned to secure converts through evangelical outreach. It was precisely because they wanted individuals to take responsibility for their sins and the judgement which would follow them that they attacked the traditional Puritan understanding that people were so lost in inherited sin that they could never choose God for themselves.

Nathaniel Taylor was far from alone in recognising the difficulty of selling predestination in America's increasingly free religious marketplace. During the Second Great Awakening, which began at the turn of the nineteenth century, the key forum was the frontier camp meeting, the first of which was held in 1800 at Creedence Clearwater Church in Kentucky, and these were premised on people *choosing* to be saved. During the revivals that continued up to the Civil War, the rejection of predestination gathered momentum. Famous preachers such as Charles Grandison Finney (1792–1875) were even more pro-choice than Wesley. Wesley had suggested God must first prepare the sinful heart, but for Finney no divine act could inhibit divinely sanctioned individual liberty.[297]

The new confidence Christian activists showed in human action was also reflected in their campaign to build a godly nation. Evangelicals on both sides of the Atlantic became focused on the possibilities afforded by the new communication technologies and by democratic politics. While some of their programs, such as temperance and Sabbath-protection, now seem reactionary, they involved confronting not just working-class custom but profitable vested interests in a way that evangelicals of the twenty-first century conspicuously avoid. There was little room for humility about human capacity in this vision of the Christian life: believers were to foster change on a personal, national and imperial scale through an energetic commitment to mission that, ultimately, was intended to transform life everywhere on earth.

Evangelical activism extended into the home and provided a powerful stimulus for the nineteenth-century exaltation of motherhood. The Puritan stress on the maternal responsibility to save the sinner and create a Christian became mainstream in the Anglo-American middle class, and strenuous efforts were made to extend this to the lower orders too. In *The Mother at Home* (1833), John S. C. Abbott warned that 'mothers have as powerful an influence over the welfare of future generations, as all other earthly causes combined'.[298] In *Christian Nurture* (1867), the Congregationalist minister Horace Bushnell argued against the still widespread belief that a child could not be expected to live a 'right life, until *God* gives him a new heart'. On the contrary, asserted Bushnell, there was nothing in 'any scheme of depravity ... to forbid the possibility that a child should be led, in his first moral act, to cleave unto what is good and right'.[299]

This confidence in parental intervention greatly boosted children's literature. By 1857 Samuel Goodrich, who wrote and edited one hundred and fifty-seven books for children, could observe that 'it is difficult now ... to conceive of the poverty of books suited to children' during his youth, 'except for the New England primer ... and some rhymes, embellished with hideous [wood]cuts of Adam's fall, in which "we sinned all"'.[300] The youngsters who suffered most from the conviction that the effects of original sin could be overcome were the Aboriginal, Native American and other indigenous children, who were removed from their communities and taken to schools or families far from home in order to be moulded into new beings.

The beliefs that every Christian had the potential to become holy or even perfect, that heathens could be converted *and* civilised (there was a long-running debate on which should come first), and that social evils could be overcome all meant that, by the late nineteenth century, Protestants put far less emphasis on original sin than Jonathan Edwards or even John Wesley had. But despite the dramatic shift, it was as difficult as ever for pastors to justify the *universal* need for salvation without making some reference to original sin. The doctrine still provided the simplest answer to an age-old question: why did good people require salvation through the death of Christ? But while evangelical churches might hesitantly affirm the traditional meaning of Adam's fall, this was never allowed to complicate the triumphant proclamation of free choice that was forging 'Christian America' and giving certainty to Britain's providential empire. Moreover, the resurgent evangelicals added to the growing cultural isolation of Christianity. No amount of activism could change the fact that a private faith adopted through individual choice could be more easily quarantined to a 'religious' sphere of life. This meant that evangelical fervour did not interfere, except on the margins of human misery, with the dynamics of industrialisation, the most important force shaping the emergence of the modern West.

Evangelical Christianity also had little influence on the many specialised fields of secular study which emerged in the nineteenth and twentieth centuries – psychology, sociology, anthropology and so on. The irony was that many of these schools of thought remained closer to the old religious orthodoxy in their understanding of human nature than the increasingly cheery evangelicals. It is appropriate that the first case study exploring this paradox should focus on the ideas of Adam Smith, founder of the most influential new discipline of all: free-market economics.

16

ADAM SMITH AND MARKET SALVATION

THE EXTRAORDINARY, EXPLOITATIVE ENERGY of nascent capitalism could be seen in some regions of England and Scotland by the end of the eighteenth century. Capitalism did not begin with the Industrial Revolution, nor did the older economic order end with it, but contemporaries watched with growing fear and awe the forces driving the swift transformation of the age-old agricultural economy and the mercantile order of the towns. The rampant pursuit of self-interest on show was consistent with the view of human nature propounded by Augustine, Luther, Calvin, Wesley and Edwards. The question was how this behaviour would be judged. Would greed still be condemned in this life or the next? Would it even stay a sin? Adam Smith, a leading figure of the Scottish Enlightenment and a resident of Glasgow, a city which was being rapidly altered by the forces of industrialisation, would do more than any other thinker to answer these questions for the Western world.

Adam Smith is regarded as the founder of *laissez faire* economic theory and remains the best-known advocate of the free market. It might therefore come as a surprise to learn that he was professor of moral philosophy at the University of Glasgow, and that his concept of the 'invisible hand', in which the pursuit of individual economic self-interest acts for the betterment of all, was first described not in *The Wealth of Nations* (1776) but in a preceding book equally

influential in his lifetime, *The Theory of Moral Sentiments* (1759).[301]
The two were not independent projects and should be considered as
parts of a whole: *The Wealth of Nations* took the theory of human
nature developed in *Moral Sentiments* and applied its insights to the
economic sphere.

Smith's observations on human nature were the foundation of
his economic theory. He did not believe that the market determined
behaviour; human nature did. His famous theory was built on an
understanding of innate human 'passions' far removed from the
Enlightenment optimism that one might anticipate from this hero
of liberal thought.

Smith believed that the 'original passions of human nature' are
independent of culture and time. Like his friend David Hume, he
accepted that 'mankind are so much the same in all times and places
that history informs us of nothing new or strange in this particular'.
Moral Sentiments explored the successful working of human society, given that human nature was always and everywhere fundamentally selfish. Smith was critical of his former teacher Francis
Hutcheson for failing to give weight to the fact that 'every man ... is
much more deeply interested in whatever immediately concerns
himself, than in what concerns every other man'.[302]

Even love and compassion were distorted and restricted by baser
passions: 'As to love our neighbour as we love ourselves is the great
law of Christianity, so it is the great precept of nature to love ourselves only as we love our neighbour, or what comes to the same
thing, as our neighbour is capable of loving us.' These cruder passions were, in part, physical, and Smith had an almost Augustinian
view of the human body, asserting that it was a fact of human nature
that 'such is our aversion for all the appetites which take their origin
from the body [and] all strong expressions of them are loathsome
and disagreeable'. Of sexual desire – 'the passion by which nature
unites the two sexes' – Smith wrote that 'though naturally the most
furious of all the passions, all strong expression of it are upon every

occasion indecent, even between persons in whom its most complete indulgence is acknowledged by all laws, both human and divine, to be perfectly innocent'. Even within marriage, Smith believed that it was a fixed fact that sex was innately indecent.[303]

It was only when humans rose above their natural passions that their behaviour could be considered virtuous: 'to feel much for others, and little for ourselves, that to restrain our selfish, and to indulge our benevolent affections, constitutes the perfection of human nature'. Virtue depended on the potential of human beings to transcend their own nature, but while the potential of self-command 'astonishes by its amazing superiority over the most ungovernable passions of human nature', few would ever exercise sufficient discipline or restraint to realise this.[304]

The individual and communal behaviour of almost all people, rich and poor alike, was governed by innate passions, all of which (including love and compassion) were connected to self-interest, since the 'feeble spark of benevolence which nature has lighted up in the human heart' was incapable of 'counteracting the strongest impulse of self-love'. Furthermore, innate compassion did not extend much beyond a person's immediate circle. Smith gave the example of a man's response to news of a great earthquake in China: he will profess compassion and concern before going to sleep, to 'snore with the most profound security over the ruin of a hundred million of his brethren'.[305]

Not only were people self-centred and selfish, most were also unaware of the fact and lost in self-delusion, unable and unwilling to face the truth. Smith saw 'this self-deceit, this fatal weakness of mankind', as the 'source of half the disorders of human life', and maintained that 'if we saw ourselves in the light in which others see us, or in which they would see us if they knew all, a reformation would generally be unavoidable. We could not otherwise endure the sight.' But to face one's true self took considerable moral courage:

He is a bold surgeon, they say, whose hand does not tremble when he performs an operation upon his own person; and he is often equally bold who does not hesitate to pull off the mysterious veil of self-delusion which covers from his view the deformities of his own conduct.[306]

Smith did not deny the existence of God, but assumed that God was too distant and too dimly glimpsed to influence human behaviour directly, except to the limited degree that fear of punishment after death might restrain bad behaviour. The fundamental question was, therefore, how society held together, given that so few people were virtuous and 'every man is, no doubt, by nature, first and principally recommended to his own care'.

Smith found the answer not in divine agency or the practice of virtue, but in the pursuit of self-interest itself. It is people's self-centred concern for what others think that ensures the continuance of human society: 'When we first come into the world, from the natural desire to please, we accustom ourselves to consider what behaviour is likely to be agreeable to every person we converse with.' It is primarily because of this sensitivity that 'the coarse clay of which the bulk of mankind are formed' is 'impressed with a regard to general rules, as to act upon almost every occasion with tolerable decency'. The internalised moral code finds social expression in the system of justice, 'the pillar that upholds the whole edifice. If it is removed, the great, the immense fabric of human society ... must in a moment crumble into atoms.' Without justice, men 'would like wild beasts ... at all times ready to fly upon [offenders], and man would enter an assembly of men as he enters a den of lions'.[307]

For Adam Smith, social order emerges *because of* self-centred human nature, not in spite of it. The operation of the free market is Smith's principal – and most misunderstood – example of this. The market is driven by people pursuing their own material interests, but this is not the result of an abstract economic 'law', but rather a manifestation of vanity:

> To what purpose is all the toil and bustle of this world? What is the end of avarice and ambition, or the pursuit of wealth, of power, and pre-eminence? Is it to supply the necessities of nature? The wages of the meanest labourer can supply them ... Do they imagine that their stomach is better, or their sleep sounder, in a palace than a cottage? The contrary has been so often observed, and, indeed, is so very obvious ... that there is nobody ignorant of it. From whence, then, arises that emulation which runs through all the different ranks of men, and what are the advantages which we propose by that great purpose of human life which we call bettering our condition? To be observed, to be attended to, to be taken notice of with sympathy, complacency and approbation, are all the advantages which we can propose to derive from it. It is the vanity, not the ease, or the pleasure, which interests us.[308]

Smith's understanding of the operation of the free market could not be further removed from the faith of twenty-first-century neoliberals or 'economic rationalists'. He wanted to explain why people behaved *irrationally*, given that it was rational to obtain the material necessities and then to cease striving and working for more. He believed that people pursue their self-interest far beyond any personal benefit because innate human nature is *not* subject to reason. It is only in the 'imagination' that the supposed 'pleasures of wealth and greatness' become 'grand and beautiful and noble', and their attainment 'well worth all the toil and anxiety which we are so apt to bestow upon it'.

Smith saw the pointless striving for riches and honour as a sign of how few people attain virtue. Nevertheless, delusory behaviour does, by the benevolence of the 'author of nature', promote the common good because 'it is this deception which rouses and keeps in continual motion the industry of mankind.' An example of this is the 'proud and unfeeling landlord' who has not 'a thought for the wants of his brethren'. Even this greedy, selfish man, despite the 'immensity of his desires', can actually consume 'no more [of the harvest] than that of the meanest peasant', meaning that he will spend his surplus on 'luxury and caprice', and thus will ultimately ensure that the poor receive a 'share of the necessaries of life, which they would in vain have expected from his humanity or his justice'.[309]

This is the context for Smith's famous invisible hand. The common good is promoted not despite the selfishness and greed of human nature, but because of it:

> In spite of their natural selfishness and rapacity, though they mean only their own conveniency, though the sole end which they propose from the labour of all the thousands whom they employ, be the gratification of their own vain and insatiable desires, [the wealthy] divide with the poor the produce of all their improvements. They are led by an invisible hand to make nearly the same distribution of the necessaries of life, which would have been made, had the earth been divided into equal portions among all its inhabitants, and thus without intending it, without knowing it, advance the interests of society and afford means to the multiplication of the species.[310]

In a famous passage from *The Wealth of Nations*, Smith made the point that that this logic applied not only to the surplus of the rich, but to all trade and human labour:

> [M]an has almost constant occasion for the help of his brethren, and it is in vain for him to expect it from their benevolence only. He will be more likely to prevail if he can interest their self-love in his favour, and show them that it is for their own advantage

to do for him what he requires of them. Whoever offers to another a bargain of any kind, proposes to do this ... It is not from the benevolence of the butcher, the brewer, or the baker, that we expect our dinner, but from their regard to their own self-interest. We address ourselves, not to their humanity but to their self-love, and never talk to them of our own necessities but of their advantages.[311]

Smith's explanation for and justification of the free market was thus firmly grounded in an Augustinian perspective on human nature. His work ensured that the innate selfishness of humanity was given a powerful secular endorsement. Smith's primary point of difference with the Western Christian tradition was that, consistent with the spirit of the Enlightenment, he did not believe in divine redemption from the human condition. John Wesley might have had Smith in mind when, in a sermon on original sin, he deplored the fact that 'this fatal disease ... which is so deeply rooted in our nature ... the desire of praise, of the honour that cometh of men' was now seen as 'strictly natural; as natural as the sight, or hearing, or any other of the external senses'.[312]

Nevertheless, there was a redemptive bent to Adam Smith's thought. Smith never equated the invisible hand with salvation, but presented it as an external force that saved people from the fate that would otherwise be theirs. Hence, as society became more openly secular, 'the Market' increasingly took on a role that had formerly belonged to God alone. Christopher Lasch is wrong to claim that in Smith's work 'private vices' became 'public virtues' through stimulating industry and invention.[313] Smith, like Bernard Mandeville before him, whose *Fable of the Bees* (1714) was subtitled *Private Vices, Publick Benefits*, identified the common wealth which arose from the pursuit of self-interest, but if he no longer labelled this behaviour as 'vice', it was certainly not virtue. However, although Smith was adamant that the free market was not of itself 'good', nor greed virtuous, the increasing intensity with which he asserted this late in his life reflected the fact that others were already drawing a different conclusion from his thought.

Smith spent the last year of his life revising *Moral Sentiments*, and the biggest alteration he made was to add a new chapter with a title that says much about how he regarded those who devoted their life to pursuing riches and status: 'Of the Corruption of our Moral Sentiments, Which is Occasioned by This Disposition to Admire the Rich and the Great, and to Despise or Neglect Persons of Poor and Mean Condition'.[314]

Sounding more like a more like a Church of Scotland minister than a hero of the Enlightenment, Smith challenged people to see themselves from the perspective of their 'infinite Creator' rather than accept the illusory image conveyed by their 'fellow-creatures'. A person facing up to the truth of who they are:

> ... can easily conceive, how the numberless violations of duty, of which he has been guilty, should render him the proper object of aversion and punishment; neither can he feel any reason why the divine indignation should not let loose without any restraint, upon so vile an insect, as he is sensible that he himself must appear to be ... Some other intercession, some other sacrifice, some other atonement, he imagines must be made for him, beyond what he himself is capable of making, before the purity of the divine justice can be reconciled to his manifold offences. The doctrines of revelation coincide, in every respect, with those original anticipations of nature; and, as they teach us how little we can depend upon the imperfection of our own virtue, so they show us, at the same time, that the powerful intercession has been made, and that the most dreadful atonement has been paid of our manifold transgressions and iniquities.

Those who applied and developed Smith's theory were not fellow moral philosophers. Smith had advocated that the government ought to largely stay out of the market because politicians and bureaucrats were also self-centred human beings, and while individuals had to suffer the consequences of their actions (especially bankruptcy, a form of public shaming), governments generally did not. But for those who saw the market as a force for good – and often benefited financially from doing so – all attempts to regulate it were a restriction on its redemptive power.

The free market is not the only pillar of modern Western liberalism to rest on an anthropological foundation of original sin. In the same year that *The Wealth of Nations* was published, the nation in which Smith's philosophy would find its most energetic expression declared independence from Britain. Augustine's legacy would contribute in no small measure to the meshing of the free market with a new vision of political liberty. The paradox of government – that it was a consequence of sin, yet necessary because of it – would be foremost in the thought of the Founding Fathers. The constitution of the United States of America would be their attempt to rationally manage the conundrum of sin.

17

IMPERFECT DEMOCRACY:
THE FOUNDING FATHERS

It may be a reflection on human nature that ... devices should be necessary to control the abuses of government. But what is government itself, but the greatest of all reflections on human nature?

—James Madison[315]

THE YEAR 1789 WAS A MOMENTOUS ONE. It saw both the outbreak of revolution in France and the inauguration of the federal constitution of the United States of America. Despite the close connections between these seminal upheavals of modern history, they were shaped by two radically different views of human nature. The philosophy of the French Revolution was premised on the potential to perfect humanity, while the American system of government was grounded in an acceptance of its innate imperfection. The anti-clerical revolutionaries of France criticised Christianity generally and the doctrine of original sin in particular, while their New World cousins were immersed in Protestantism and the Fall. And while France would descend into terror and dictatorship before the century's end, the American constitution became the single most influential political document in history, inspiring and directing democratic reform across the globe through to the present day.

The doctrine of original sin had always had political implications. For most of Western history it was used to justify autocratic authority as a necessary constraint on sinful subjects. But since the sixteenth century, it had also become commonplace to use the doctrine to challenge autocracy: if kings and bishops were fallen men too, why should their authority go unquestioned? Original sin was part of the political battleground; it was employed by conservatives to defend established elites, and by reformers to challenge them. But it was in the United States, after two centuries of debate, that both sides of the argument were in large part reconciled in the constitution of the new nation.

The founding fathers of America believed that government could be constituted to promote liberty rather than tyranny, but their confidence was grounded in the nation's Calvinist heritage. While they did not follow their thinking through to a final conclusion – universal adult suffrage was still more than a century away, and the equality of slave owners and slaves was restricted to the purely spiritual realm – their understanding of equality was grounded in a belief in universal sin as much as universal rights. An ingrained scepticism about human nature guided what could be expected of individuals as rulers and citizens. Liberty meant protecting people from the state *and* from each other. What was wanted was a strong central government *and* a balancing determination to limit and disperse its power.

The need to acknowledge in the constitution the truth about human nature was a major theme of the Federalist Papers, a series of newspaper articles written by Alexander Hamilton, James Madison and John Jay in 1788. The constitutional task, as Madison described it, was to strike a balance between the dangers posed by the power of sinful rulers and the rights of sinful citizens. There would be no problem 'if men were angels' or 'if angels were to govern men', but the reality was that it was necessary to frame 'a government which is to be administered by men over men'. Madison concluded: 'It is a melancholy reflection that liberty should be equally exposed to danger whether the Government have too much or too little power, and that the line which divides these extremes should be so inaccurately defined by experience.' The best that could be done to manage this dilemma was to disperse the power held by the legislative, executive and judicial branches of the new state: 'Where the power, as with us, is in the many, not the few, the danger cannot be great that the few will be thus favoured. It is much more to be dreaded that the few will be unnecessarily sacrificed to the many.'[316] Madison was particularly concerned to reduce the danger of armed conflict, recognising that the 'strongest passions and the most dangerous weakness of the human breast – ambition, avarice, vanity, the honourable or venial love of fame – are all in conspiracy against the desire and duty of peace', and ensured that the constitution gave Congress, not the president, the power to declare war.[317]

Ultimately, though, a perfect system of government was neither expected nor sought, and the Founding Fathers, in stark contrast to the French revolutionary leaders, sought to downplay expectations of what could be achieved by any manmade political system. In the final of the Federalist Papers, Hamilton warned his countrymen against expecting 'to see a perfect work from imperfect man'.[318] Hence the determination to ensure a permanent capacity to amend and improve the constitution.

There were, of course, some radical deists such as Elihu Palmer, who believed man was perfectible and that 'this great truth ... had been hidden from mankind by the sinister alliance of priests and kings, whose chief reliance had always been the absurd doctrine of original sin'.[319] But during the early years of the American republic, this was a marginal view. As John Witherspoon, president of Princeton and a signatory of the Declaration of Independence, put it: 'Others may, if they please, treat the corruption of our nature as a chimera: for my part I see it everywhere, and I feel it every day.'[320]

To affirm the importance of the Western religious tradition for those who formulated the American system of government is not to claim that the United States was founded as a Christian nation, as many contemporary evangelicals and conservative culture warriors seem determined to assert. There was no contest for supremacy between the values of the Enlightenment and those of Christianity in the nascent republic. The mundane truth is that, unlike in modern times or in revolutionary France, no contradiction was generally perceived between Enlightenment liberalism and Christianity. America was not the evangelical society in the late eighteenth century that it would become, but Protestant Christianity, especially its views of human nature derived from original sin, saturated the culture and permeated the world views of most progressive thinkers of the time.[321]

Benjamin Franklin's rationalist religious faith is often contrasted with that of Jonathan Edwards; yet Franklin's understanding of human beings did not diverge much from that of his Calvinist forebears. Franklin believed there were 'two passions which have a powerful influence on the affairs of men. These are ambition and avarice; the love of power and the love of money.' He informed his fellow scientist, moral philosopher and reformer Joseph Priestly that he found men to be 'beings very badly constructed. They are generally more easily provoked than reconciled, more disposed to do mischief to each other than to make reparation and much more easily deceived than under deceived.'[322] In his autobiography, Franklin reflected how hard it was to change human behaviour, as:

> ... there is, perhaps, not one of our natural passions so hard to subdue as pride. Disguise it, struggle with it, beat it down, stifle it, mortify it as much as one pleases, it is still alive, and will every now and then peep out and show itself; you will see it, perhaps, often in this history; for, even if I could conceive that I had completely overcome it, I should probably be proud of my humility.[323]

Pride was the traditional cause of Adam's disobedience, so it is not surprising that Max Weber used Franklin as an example of how Calvinist ideas could persist in a non-doctrinal modern form.

John Adams was another who explicitly rejected the doctrine of original sin, but it would be hard to deduce this from his perspective on human nature:

> Those who have written on civil government lay it down as a first principle ... that whoever found a state, and make proper laws for the government of it, must presume that all men are bad by nature; [and] that they will not fail to show that natural depravity of heart whenever they have fair opportunity.[324]

Adams was in no doubt that the 'heart is deceitful above all things and desperately wicked ... [for] it must be remembered, that although reason ought always to govern individuals, it certainly never did since the Fall, and never will till the Millennium'.[325]

Adams maintained that it was human 'weakness' which 'renders men unfit to be trusted with unlimited power', and he issued an early warning to victorious revolutionaries on both sides of the Atlantic, 'amid all their exultations', to remember that:

> ... the perfectibility of man is only human and terrestrial perfectibility. Cold will still freeze, and fire will never cease to burn; disease and vice will continue to disorder, and death to terrify mankind. Emulation next to self-preservation will forever be the great spring of human actions, and the balance of well-ordered government will alone be able to prevent that emulation from degenerating into dangerous ambition, irregular rivalries, destructive factions, wasting seditions, and bloody civil wars.[326]

Like Adam Smith (and we should note that the Scottish Enlightenment was an influential source of ideas for many of the Founding

Fathers), John Adams saw that the 'desire for the esteem of others is as real a want of nature as hunger. It is the principal end of government to regulate this passion.' Alexander Hamilton agreed: 'The love of fame [is] the ruling passion of the noblest minds.'[327]

The celebrated political radical Thomas Paine also accepted that revolutionaries needed to take account of human nature. He believed government was made necessary 'by our wickedness', its primary purpose being to restrain 'our vices'.[328] Paine was adamant in *Common Sense* (1776) that while 'society in every state is a blessing ... government even in its best state is but a necessary evil', a 'badge of lost innocence'.[329] Even Thomas Jefferson, who despised Calvinism and was optimistic about human potential, believed that 'the human character ... requires in general constant and immediate control, to prevent its being biased from right by the seductions of self-love'.[330] Jefferson's idealism was grounded in an acknowledgement that the 'seeds of moral decay were in all people', and that a man's 'self-love often seduced him from the start'. He was particularly adamant that it was important to guard against 'human weakness, competition and wickedness' in government.[331]

The anthropology of the Founding Fathers meant that they were cautious about the potential of democracy to change human society. But over time the constitution took on a quasi-scriptural status, and this work of 'imperfect man' was increasingly seen to be redemptive in its own right. The great strength of those who developed the American system of government, their consciousness of human frailty, was largely forgotten, as they and their words assumed a quasi-Biblical status, announcing how Americans could fulfil the potential of their promised land through the exercise of unfettered personal freedom.

It was no coincidence that the deification of the Founding Fathers coincided with a growing certainty in the capacity of human beings to create a godly nation if individuals were freed from regulatory and legal constraints. The dangers posed by the state were given ever greater emphasis as unfettered economic, political and religious choice was transformed into a national ideology. God was integrated surprisingly easily into what was essentially a secular belief system, but this was only possible because evangelical Christianity had rejected the doctrine of original sin's limits on free will. The paradox at the centre of the confusion concerning America's Christian heritage is that the political theory of eighteenth-century sceptics such as Franklin, Washington and Jefferson was more consistent with the Western Christian tradition than was that of the evangelicals who would increasingly define American politics and culture in the century to come.

18

ORIGINAL SIN IN
AN AGE OF PROGRESS

THE NINETEENTH CENTURY was a triumphant epoch of exploration in which ancient mysteries became the subject of science and subservient to the human will. In this age of progress, every unknown came to be defined as a question, and every question was assumed to have an answer. Even sin could be understood and dealt with. Rather than blaming primal parents or unalterable human nature for individual and social failings, people were expected to embrace the effort and labour needed to improve themselves and to build a godly nation.

The power of human beings to progress was seen to depend on personal freedom, which alone could unleash the spirit of enterprise. Liberal free-market and political theory increasingly moved away from its more cautious origins in the anthropology of original sin and towards an unprecedented confidence in human nature, although all but the most progressive thinkers still qualified this with various assumptions about race, gender and class.

During this century, the United Kingdom reached the height of its economic, military and imperial power. At a time when the United States was focused on fulfilling its manifest destiny within its own continental borders, Britain imposed its brand of Protestantism on some of the most isolated people on the planet. Nevertheless, the human ties within the Anglo world were strong, and the Atlantic was no barrier to the sharing of ideas.

The most influential liberal thinker of the age was John Stuart Mill (1806–1873). Mill was educated at home by his father, James Mill, with the assistance of the utilitarian philosopher Jeremy Bentham, and his tutors set out to prove what a 'blank slate' exposed to the right influences could achieve. Such was the 'appalling success' (to quote Isaiah Berlin) of the famous experiment that belief in the *tabula rasa* has rarely been straightforward since. A child who could read Plato in Greek by the age of seven and be debating Aristotle's works of logic at eleven was clearly both well educated *and* of high natural intelligence.[332]

Mill himself regretted the loneliness of his childhood, and abandoned Bentham's philosophy of maximising happiness for one focused on individual freedom, but he ever upheld the liberal tenet that 'the prevailing tendency to regard all the marked distinctions of human character as innate, and in the main indelible', rather than as the product of 'differences in circumstances', was 'one of the greatest stumbling blocks to human improvement'.[333] Mill was not naive: he believed not in humanity's present goodness but in its potential for change, and he was in no doubt about the discipline and sacrifice necessary for intellectual and moral development. Nor did Mill deny the existence of human nature; it was just that his priority was to promote conditions in which people could undertake the work of improving it. He wrote that 'the duty of man is the same in respect of his own nature as in respect to the nature of all other things, namely not to follow but to amend it'.[334] In this sense, Mill and other morally serious liberals of a similarly diligent bent might even be understood as the latest manifestation of a Pelagian tradition that had survived in Britain in various guises since the fifth century.

The paradox of the nineteenth century, however, is that at the apex of the trans-Atlantic optimism, just when it seemed that both progressive thinkers (such as Mill) and evangelical Christians (such as Taylor and Finney) had ensured modern people could free themselves of the burden of self-doubt, a *secular* creed emerged which did much to revive the ancient Western pessimism about human nature.

In *The Origin of Species* (1859), Charles Darwin developed the theories of evolution and natural selection which brought to a definitive end the dominance of Christianity in Western thought.[335] While Darwin still referred to a 'Creator' or an 'author of life' who had set evolution in motion, and although he placed his book in the tradition of Francis Bacon's revelations of the work of God, it became impossible after the publication of *Origin* for a thinking person to take the Biblical account of creation literally.[336] It seemed to most thoughtful people at the time – as it does today – that the creation story presented in Genesis had been rendered ridiculous.[337]

Darwin had studied to be a Church of England clergyman. Even during the epic five-year journey of scientific discovery on the *Beagle* which followed his degree at Cambridge, it was Milton's *Paradise Lost* which was his 'chief favourite' book.[338] However, the straightforward account Darwin gave late in his life of how 'disbelief crept over me at a very slow rate, but was at last complete', makes the ongoing debate over his religious convictions superfluous. There is no reason to doubt the man's own testimony, or his heartfelt conviction that:

> I can indeed hardly see how anyone ought to wish Christianity to be true; for if so, the plain language of the text seems to show that the men who do not believe, and this would include my Father, Brother and almost all my best friends, will be everlastingly punished. And this is a damnable doctrine.[339]

The unresolved question concerning Darwin and Christianity concern neither his personal beliefs nor the truth of evolution. What is open to debate is not Darwin's status as an agnostic or as a scientist, but what he took for granted in developing his influential theories of human behaviour, and what these assumptions owe to his culture's religious tradition.

The Origin of Species did not deal specifically with human beings, except to the extent that its celebration of evolution related to the emergence of the 'higher animals', which were 'the most exalted object which we are capable of conceiving'.[340] Darwin was aware that humans were a uniquely complex form of life whose diverse behaviours and cultural practices were not easily explained by evolutionary biology. To delve seriously into the human condition required a tome of its own.

In *The Descent of Man* (1871) Darwin made explicit what was implied in *The Origin of Species*: that self-interested competition is integral to human nature. That this was less a scientific argument than a culturally derived assumption can be seen by considering the book's central arguments. In the introduction, Darwin set out the three objects of his study: 'firstly, whether man, like every other species, is descended from some pre-existing form; secondly, the manner of his development; and thirdly, the value of the differences between the so-called races of man'.[341]

The first question was settled and remains so in every Western country apart from the United States, where modern Biblical literalism has a peculiar history all of its own. *Descent* was not a controversial book in England and was favourably reviewed even by the Christian press. Only eleven years after its publication Darwin would be given the highest posthumous honour that can be conferred on an Englishman by both church and state: burial in Westminster Abbey. It is Darwin's second question – the extent to which evolutionary biology can explain human development and behaviour – which was the subject of serious debate, and has remained so to the present day. The third, racial question, while mainstream until the 1930s, has been banished from civilised discourse since then because its suspect science and abhorrent assumptions underpinned racist policies.

In considering human development, *The Descent of Man* drew heavily on the work of others, including Thomas Malthus, Herbert

Spencer, Alfred Russel Wallace, William Greg and Walter Bage-hot.[342] Whereas *Origin* had been a highly original work based on a lifetime's research, Darwin admitted that *Descent* 'contains hardly any original facts in regard to man'.[343] In it, he largely reproduced the perspective of the upper-class Victorian gentleman living in a nation at the height of its imperial and industrial power. This can be clearly seen in *Descent*'s conclusions concerning women and indig-enous people. Darwin believed that his biological strength had given man a competitive advantage, which in turn meant he had evolved to be 'more courageous, pugnacious, and energetic than woman, and has a more inventive genius'. He thought it 'fortunate that the law of the equal transmission of characters to both sexes has com-monly prevailed … otherwise it is probable that man would have become as superior in mental endowment to woman, as the peacock is in ornamental plumage to the peahen'.[344]

There were similar assumptions in *Descent*'s treatment of 'sav-ages'. Darwin was greatly affected by his encounter with the indige-nous inhabitants of Tierra del Fuego during the voyage of the *Beagle*. The man who rightly prided himself on his ability 'in noticing things which easily escape attention, and in observing them carefully' was so mesmerised by the notion of savagery that he observed almost nothing of the complex cultures he encountered. The Yaghan (one of four Fuego peoples) needed a language with over thirty-five thousand words, sixteen vowels and fifty-four sounds to express their vibrant social and religious life. But all Darwin saw was a primitiveness so profound that he hoped it would provide comfort to those who were worried about being descended from monkeys:

> The main conclusion arrived at in this work, namely, that man is descended from some lowly-organized form, will, I regret to think, be highly distasteful to many persons. But there can hardly be a doubt that we are descended from barbarians. The astonishment which I felt on first seeing a party of Fuegians on

a wild and broken shore will never be forgotten by me, for the reflection at once rushed into my mind – such were our ancestors. These men were absolutely naked and bedaubed with paint, their long hair was tangled, their mouths frothed with excitement, and their expression was wild, startled, and distrustful. They possessed hardly any arts, and, like wild animals, lived on what they could catch; they had no government, and were merciless to everyone not of their own small tribe. He who has seen a savage in his native land will not feel much shame, if forced to acknowledge that the blood of more humble creature flows in his veins. For my own part, I would as soon be descended from that heroic little monkey ... or from that old baboon ... as from a savage ...[345]

The decade after *Descent* was published saw the death of most of the Fuego people, a consequence of the discovery of gold in the region in 1878.[346] Even during the voyage of the *Beagle*, Darwin had believed that the 'varieties of man seem to act on each other in the same way as different species of animals – the stronger always extirpating the weaker', and had maintained that the British inhabitants of Van Diemen's Land (now called Tasmania), where the Aborigines were almost all dead or living in forced exile by the time of his visit in 1836, enjoyed 'the great advantage of being free from a native population'.[347] To his credit, Darwin never lost sight of the tragedy attendant on the march of civilisation, but, like most privileged and educated Westerners, he believed the passing away of indigenous people was a necessary and ultimately beneficial process. His contribution to the cultural discussion was to 'prove' scientifically that this was underpinned by evolutionary law.[348]

Darwin's anthropology remains a sensitive subject, though, largely because of the tragic consequences of social Darwinist thought, especially as applied by eugenic movements in the West generally and Nazi Germany in particular. Like his cousin Francis

Galton (who coined the term 'eugenics'), Darwin was profoundly troubled by the uncontrolled rapid breeding of the lower orders, which was putting social progress at risk. To his credit, however, Darwin consistently rejected the eugenicists' proposals on this issue – such as withdrawing charity for the poor – on moral grounds.[349]

Nevertheless, he was convinced that if civilised man 'is to advance still higher he must remain subject to a severe struggle'.[350] Like Adam Smith, Darwin took it for granted that human beings were innately self-centred, and argued that this served the greater good: 'There should be open competition for all men; and the most able should not be prevented by laws or customs from succeeding best and rearing the largest number of offspring.'[351] He readily acknowledged a moral dimension to human life, but struggled to locate the source of ethical behaviour. He resorted to describing moral sentiment as an evolutionary product of sensitivity to the opinions of others, but, as Smith had recognised, this placed morality closer to the traditional understanding of sin than virtue.[352]

Darwin's understanding of human development was applied to a vast range of social questions, not least child-rearing.[353] A highly influential theory known as 'recapitulation' claimed to have proven that children began life as savages with fearsome appetites who had to be trained to be civilised. James Sully, the founder of the first child study laboratory, noted in his *Studies of Childhood* (1895): 'As we all know, the lowest races of mankind stand in close proximity to the animal world. The same is true of infants of civilised races.' Children, he noted, are 'in general accomplished little liars, to the manner born and equally adept with the mendacious savage'. The resemblance was empirically established by their mutual love of vanity and gaudy clothes, and by the similarities in their drawing and painting.[354]

These ideas about children soon spread beyond intellectual circles. The rigorous routine and disciplined regime required to mould children into socially acceptable human beings, and to avoid 'spoiling' them, was set out for middle-class parents by the paediatrician

L. Emmett Holt, whose *Care and Feeding of Children: A Catechism for the Use of Mothers and Children's Nurses* (1894), served as a parenting manual for Dr Benjamin Spock's own mother.[355]

Darwin was a scientist of the highest integrity, whose work on the origin of species arguably represents the greatest intellectual achievement of all time. But his attempt to apply evolutionary science to human nature was distorted by a failure to understand that, in this field, his research was not independent of the culture in which he was immersed. What *The Descent of Man* highlights is that biological science cannot be applied to human society without a rigorous examination of underlying cultural assumptions.

Darwin could not know that one explanation for the speed with which his ideas were applied, and the principal explanation for their popular resonance, was that they were in large measure a reflection of the Western Christian understanding of human beings which both he and his readership had absorbed as part of their cultural inheritance. Original sin had always seen human beings as innately self-centred creatures whose nature was to pursue their own interests at the expense of others'. Darwin provided a language in which this old religious idea could be renewed and given social scientific credence.

It was partly because Darwin's theory was so much closer to the anthropology associated with original sin than to the ideals being propounded by contemporary liberals and evangelicals that his scientific retort to their theorising was so successful. The fact that his ideas also provided a solution to the reality of human nature further resonated with Western peoples. The salvation he proffered was that evolution resulted in continual progress, first to the higher animals, then to man, then to civilised man, and then, if natural law was allowed to do its work, to higher planes still.

But there is no scientific reason why evolution should lead to any form of progress at all.[356] This was also just taken for granted. One reason this assumption was rarely challenged was that Western discussion of the mortal body and its selfish desires had always been intimately associated with the need for salvation.

Despite celebrating the redeeming power of progress, Darwin was distinguished from his optimistic age by his view that although civilised man had progressed to a higher plane, his competitive, self-interested and savage character remained firmly in place. When Darwin explained how 'the savage' still lived within every person, he sounded like a gentlemanly version of Augustine:

> Man may be excused for feeling some pride at having risen ... to the very summit of the organic scale ... [but] we must acknowledge ... that man with all his noble qualities, with sympathy which he feels for the most debased, with benevolence which extends not only to other men but to the humblest living creature, with his godlike intellect which has penetrated into the movements and constitution of the solar system – with all these exalted powers – Man still bears in his bodily frame the indelible stamp of his lowly origin.[357]

Darwin's acceptance of a savage core within civilised beings also had parallels with the anthropology of the artists, thinkers and poets known as the Romantics, whose commitment to 'absolute inwardness' had led them beyond the bounds of civilisation. While their distrust of rationalism put the Romantics on the other side of the methodological fence from Darwin, they also confronted liberal complacency concerning essential human nature.[358]

The eighty etchings of Goya's *Caprichos* (1799) comprise a grotesque menagerie of humanity engaged in monstrous acts. Goya wrote that they were all products of his dreams, and that 'as soon as day breaks, they fly each one his own way, the witches, the hobgoblins, the visions and the phantoms ... no one has ever been able to find out where they hide and lock themselves up in the daytime'. But whereas Goya and many of the Romantic artists who followed him during the nineteenth century assumed, like Augustine and Luther, that the true self was ultimately a mysterious creature of the night, Darwinists believed that all dimensions of human nature could ultimately be illuminated by science.

The challenge to expose the primitive darkness of the mind to the light of scientific inquiry would be taken up by a young Viennese researcher in the final decade of the nineteenth century. While progressive reformers assumed there were solutions to human depravity, for Sigmund Freud the hidden impulses lying beneath the veneer of civilisation could be controlled but never banished. Almost exactly fifteen hundred years after St Augustine had first formulated the doctrine of original sin, this secular scientist would again seek to confront people with the sorry truth of their inner selves.

19

FREUD AND THE
SCIENCE OF SELF

BY THE EARLY TWENTIETH CENTURY it was commonplace for
intellectuals to mock Christianity and its mythical stories. Since the
publication of *The Origin of Species* half a century before, Adam and
Eve had been the subject of more jokes than scholarship. More recent
was a new level of ignorance about the Genesis story; even highly
educated people might know little more than the caricatures penned
by satirists or proclaimed by fundamentalist preachers. Indeed, the
progress of secularism meant that for the first time since the collapse
of the Roman Empire, it was possible for leading thinkers in the
Western world not even to know that there was a distinctively Western interpretation of the Fall.

When this ignorance was combined with a naive faith in the scientific method to deliver culture-free knowledge, it led many scholars in the expanding social sciences to assume that their research
into human nature was revealing something altogether new.
Whereas most Enlightenment philosophers knew where they stood
in relation to their religious tradition – even when they were rejecting it – over a century later many writers assumed that their conclusions had no antecedents, that they were original insights that had
emerged from pure empirical observation. Thus, the paradox of the
secularisation of the West – at this stage still more evident in the
universities than the streets – was that an *old* and *Christian* idea

such as original sin could live on as a *new* and *scientific* theory. The standout example of this was the work of the most influential exponent of the science of the mind, Sigmund Freud (1856–1939).[359]

Because he has become a figure of caricature in modern popular culture, it is easy to forget just how influential Freud's ideas have been. While he is now little read and relatively few psychologists describe themselves as 'Freudian', concepts as basic as the ego and the libido were first set out in his writings. And his central conclusion – that human beings are driven by inaccessible instinctual drives, especially sexuality and aggression, which exist in tension with morality and conscious thought – have been so internalised that they are now often taken to be common sense.

Freud believed it to be a scientific fact that 'the deepest essence of human nature consists of instinctual impulses which are of an elementary nature, which are similar in all men and which aim at the satisfaction of certain primal needs'. While he did not pass moral judgement on these drives ('these impulses in themselves are neither good nor bad'), he admitted that 'it must be granted that all the impulses which society condemns as evil – let us take as representative the selfish and cruel ones – are of this primitive kind'.[360]

Freud maintained that although the 'sublimation' of instincts generated neurotic behaviour, the abolition of civilisation and a return to a state of nature would be far worse. He maintained that, left to itself, nature 'destroys us – coldly, cruelly, relentlessly, as it seems to us, and possibly through the very things that occasioned our satisfaction', and that 'the principal task of civilization, its actual *raison d'être*, is to defend us against nature.'[361] And nature, in this instance, includes *human* nature.

The 'element of truth behind all this, which people are so ready to disavow', Freud concluded, was 'that men are not gentle creatures who want to be loved, and who at the most can defend themselves if they are attacked'. Rather:

... their neighbour is for them not only a potential helper or sexual object, but also someone who tempts them to satisfy their aggressiveness on him, to exploit his capacity for work without compensation, to use him sexually without his consent, to seize his possessions, to humiliate him, to cause him pain, to torture and to kill him.[362]

Freud believed that most people were like 'little children' who 'do not like it' when 'there is talk of inborn human inclination to "badness", to aggressiveness and destructiveness, and so to cruelty as well'.[363] He wanted to confront Western people with a harsh truth: 'most of our sentimentalists, friends of humanity and protectors of animals have been evolved from little sadists and animal-tormentors.'[364]

Nor could this reality be altered by social reform or moral progress. Freud was certain that, however society was ordered, 'this indestructible feature of human nature will follow it there'.[365] He argued that although '[c]ivilization has been attained through the renunciation of instinctual satisfaction ... the primitive stages can always be re-established [because] the primitive mind is, in the fullest meaning of the word, imperishable'.[366] The 'consequence of this primary mental hostility of human beings' was that 'civilized society is perpetually threatened with disintegration ... [as] instinctual passions are stronger than reasonable interests'.[367]

The problem was not just the power of instinctual drives, but also that they were so difficult to access and so pervasive in their influence. A person's understanding of his or her own motives would always be limited, and there could be no such thing as a pure act. Intelligent self-knowledge could constrain and control the personality, but this was a lifelong and never-to-be-completed project, undertaken with serious intent only by a small number of people. Most were constrained from acting out their base passions by communal rules and expectations, including religious ones.

Scholars have noted that Freud's ideas in some ways resemble those of Thomas Hobbes, but Freud's focus on the divided self – in which even the most worthy action or good deed is corrupted by innate drives which are beyond the power of the will to fully control – is closer in theory and sentiment to Augustine.[368] The fundamental similarity of the two men is accentuated by the importance each placed on sex. Peter Gay has noted that, for Freud, the theory of infantile sexuality represented 'a kind of touchstone, separating those who truly accepted his libido theory from those who were unwilling to grant sexuality the prominent place he himself assigned to it'.[369] Augustine did not focus on the sexuality of children, but he did emphasise that sexual desire provided both the first cause and the final proof of the truth of his doctrine.

Freud's complex theory of the 'psychical consequences of envy for the penis' in girls, as well as the supposedly less damaging 'fear of castration' in men, is now rightly ridiculed, but this has not less-ened the cultural resonance of his findings about the defining role of the sex drive. Darwin, who influenced almost every major thinker at this time, shared this focus, but it was Freud who ensured that Dar-winian ideas become integral to people's sense of themselves not just as human animals, but as individual personalities. Darwin might have answered the question of who *we* are, but it was Freud who connected evolutionary theory with the Western quest to establish who *I* am.

Freud even provided a modern framework for the traditional Western belief that guilt was an integral part of the human condi-tion. While Freud considered an exaggerated sense of guilt to be a neurosis, he believed that there is also a 'normal, conscious sense of guilt' which emerged from the fact that the 'super-ego ... in the form of "conscience" is ready to put into action against the ego the same harsh aggressiveness that the ego would have liked to satisfy upon other, extraneous individuals'. It was this 'tension between the harsh super-ego and the ego that is subjected to it' which Freud called 'the sense of guilt'.[370]

The internal warfare between an unconscious human nature and the 'higher nature in man' meant that Freud's view of 'the sick' was as large and democratic as Augustine's or Luther's. He adopted a language of universal disease as freely as any prophet of original sin because, like them, he believed that the divided, selfish, aggressive, sexually perverse and self-destructive self was the imperishable core of human nature.[371] Even the journey to redemption began at the same point: with a brutally honest acknowledgement of the truth of one's inner life.[372]

The reason the continuity between Freudian thought and the Western Christian tradition took a long time to be recognised is that Freud always asserted that he was employing science to confront the 'universal neurosis' and 'illusions' of religion.[373] In *Moses and Monotheism*, Freud even provides an account of how religion arose. He postulates the existence of a leading male in a social group of primal humans or apes who, because he dominates the females and castrates his male competitors, is murdered by young males, who then feast on his body. They then feel remorse for their deed and place a taboo on murder and incest. In time, the sorrow, pain and guilt of the murder is forgotten and buried deep in the unconscious, and the dead male is deified as a heavenly father. The guilt of the murder is then passed on to every new person as a neurosis in the form of religion.[374] Freud describes the Christian Eucharist as 'essentially a fresh elimination of the father, a repetition of the guilty deed'[375]

While it might seem ironic that a creation story that begins with an original sin, the guilt for which is passed on to every subsequent person, would be employed to *undermine* Christianity, there can be no doubt that Freud believed he was taking a principled anti-religious stance.[376] He understood his theories to have emerged *only* from objective scientific study, and always maintained that 'there is no appeal to a court above that of reason'.[377]

Because Freud rejected religion so emphatically, the possibility that his own assumptions about human nature might have religious

roots was not considered during his lifetime. But now it is the assertion that his conclusions were reached only through empirical observation which seems improbable, and the relationship between
Freudian ideas and their cultural antecedents has come to the fore. In
1960 David McClelland, a Harvard psychologist, suggested that one
of the reasons for the considerable appeal of psychoanalysis to American intellectuals was that 'its insistence on the evil in man's nature,
and in particular the sexual root of that evil, suited the New England
temperament well' because it 'had been shaped by similar Puritan
emphasis'. McClelland pointed out that 'to hear Anna Freud [Freud's
daughter and a leading Freudian theorist] speak of the criminal tendencies of the one and two-year old is to be reminded inevitably of
Calvinistic sermons on infant damnation'.[378] In the 1980s Ernest
Gellner argued that 'the unconscious is a new version of original sin'
because every person is seen to be born 'with ever-renewable and
self-perpetuating debts to pay right from the start' and must address
this debt to have any 'hope of salvation'.[379] The following decade,
Richard Webster concluded after a comprehensive review of the history of psychoanalysis that Freud had 'succeeded in reinventing for a
modern scientific age the traditional Christian doctrine of Original
Sin'.[380] Most recently, Shadia Drury has suggested that 'far from
rejecting original sin as preposterous, chimerical and unfounded,
Freud provides it with a historical and psychological justification'.[381]

The continuity between the two understandings of human
nature might also explain why Freud's complex concepts have been
so readily absorbed into popular culture. Peter Gay believes that the
major reason why Freud's ideas are not fully appreciated is that his
'estimate of the human animal is far from flattering, and his message is sobering to the extreme ... Freud took some pride in disturbing the sleep of mankind, and mankind has responded by trivializing
him, watering him down, or finding reasons ... for disregarding
him altogether'.[382] But the greater mystery is not why Freud's seemingly inaccessible ideas were 'watered down', but why they resonated

so deeply. Freud's biographer Anthony Storr was close to the truth when he suggested that 'psychoanalysis has had such an inescapable influence upon our thinking that it must resonate with something deep within us'.[383]

The Freudian faith that human nature is rooted in two forms of instinct, the aggressive and the erotic, which are barely kept in check by the super-ego and civilisation, fitted easily into Western culture because Freud gave secular expression to something people already knew but had lost the language to describe. The traditional understanding of human nature had been without a conceptual framework since Darwin sidelined Adam and Eve. Freud restored to Western people a terminology that enabled them to continue debating and exploring what they had never ceased to believe, thus ensuring 'a deep cultural continuity was preserved'.[384]

Nor was this only a matter of the intellect. People's sense that there was something wrong with who they were, which remained a core component of their spiritual inheritance, was again given credibility and respect, and their dis-ease made normal. Reconnecting private suffering to a shared story was Freud's great therapeutic achievement. People did not need to read or agree with Freud to share his legitimisation of the sick self; all self-help and therapeutic advice relied on this premise.

Although Freud's perspective on human nature was remarkably consistent with original sin, his thought was radically severed from the doctrine's teaching on salvation. Freud was never further from Augustine than when he considered how people might be saved from their misery. He wrote that 'there is no golden rule which applies to everyone: every man must find out for himself in what particular fashion he can be saved'. Not even psychoanalysis offered much comfort. Freud confessed that, ultimately, he could offer 'no consolation', even though that was 'at bottom ... what they are all demanding – the wildest revolutionaries no less passionately than the most virtuous believers'.[385]

While psychoanalytic ideas would be packaged into optimistic frameworks, such as Dr Spock's consumer-friendly and bestselling child-rearing manual (in which even penis envy was normalised), Freud himself resisted easy solutions.[386] He had devoted parents and six children of his own, but one of his earliest conclusions was that 'children are completely egoistic; they feel their needs intensely and strive ruthlessly to satisfy them', and he never wavered from the conviction that few people progressed from this childlike state.[387] It took rare courage to confront the dark reality of the inner self. And even the select group who did so had to live with the fact that there could be no final redemption. Freud's failure to show how people can be saved explains the ambivalent response to psychoanalysis. After fifteen hundred years of immersion in original sin, Western people were ready to be told that they were sick, but their established expectation was that this would be accompanied by a pathway to salvation. When not even the most comfortable Freudian couch provided this, disillusionment soon set in.

In the aftermath of the First World War, the question of salvation from the destructive capacity of human nature was widely discussed. In 1932, as fascist and communist movements sought to replace liberal ideals with ideologies of collective certainty, Albert Einstein wrote to Sigmund Freud to seek his advice on the 'most insistent' question facing civilisation: 'Is there any way of delivering mankind from the menace of war?' Einstein was sure that the 'ill-success' of the League of Nations and related international projects to put an end to war left 'no room to doubt that strong psychological factors are at work, which paralyze these efforts'; he believed a solution could only be found by probing 'into the dark places of human will and feeling'. Einstein, a prominent pacifist, believed that 'only one answer was possible' to the question of why 'ordinary people who stand to lose, go along with those whose interests are served' through war: 'each man has within him a lust for hatred and destruction'. He asked Freud the question which he believed would decide the fate of the world: 'Is it possible to control man's mental evolution so as to make him proof against the psychoses of hate and destructiveness?'[388]

In reply, Freud, who also described himself as a pacifist, noted that there was 'a biological justification for all the ugly and dangerous impulses against which we are struggling', and since these 'stand nearer to Nature than does our resistance to them', there 'is no use in trying to get rid of men's aggressive inclinations'. The only hope was the imposition of a strong international authority and doing everything possible to restrain people's natural inclination to violence: 'one thing we can say: whatever fosters the growth of civilization works at the same time against war'.[389]

In the year following this exchange of letters, the Nazis were elected to power in Germany and the lives of both men were imperilled, not because of their ideas but because of their 'race' – both were of Jewish background. Einstein sought refuge in the United States in 1933, and Freud fled Vienna in 1938. He died in London in September 1939, three weeks after the Second World War had begun, no doubt more certain than ever of the truth of his grim conclusions concerning human nature and the fragility of civilisation.

20

STAYING POSITIVE: ORIGINAL SIN AND CONTEMPORARY CHRISTIANITY

DURING THE 1950S, three of America's most influential Christian thinkers made the cover of *Time*. Reinhold Niebuhr's caption read 'Man's story is not a success story'; Paul Tillich was pictured in deep thought, with a human skull resting on the table in front of him; while Billy Graham was accompanied by a picture of the Garden of Eden.[390] In this instance, each picture was worth a thousand words: Niebuhr and Tillich were central to a confrontation with the human condition spawned by war, Nazism and the Holocaust, while Graham, who seemed at first to embody a Third Great Awakening of American Protestantism, eventually caved in to the consumer preference for an upbeat, feel-good salvation message that would define the evangelical decades to come.

Reinhold Niebuhr was an exemplar of a breed of public intellectual that has now become history even in America: a serious thinker with a mass audience, reinterpreting the Christian tradition for the contemporary age. Niebuhr's books were bestsellers, frequently referred to in the mainstream media as well as in the three most influential Christian publications: *The Christian Century*, *Christianity and Crisis* and *Christianity Today*, which had a combined circulation of twenty million.[391] Like most twentieth-century theologians, Niebuhr did not believe that the doctrine of original sin depended on events in some real-life Garden of Eden; it was an essential human fact, a prophetic myth that was 'true in every moment of existence'.[392] The doctrine spoke to the true condition of humanity: human beings were in rebellion against God, with evil 'at the very centre of human personality – in the will'. The source of this evil, argued Niebuhr, was 'that man refuses to admit his "creatureliness" ... He pretends to be more than he is.'[393] Niebuhr therefore called on people to cease denying their 'own deepest and most essential nature', as only this would open 'the eyes of faith' and ensure that 'out of ... despair hope is born'.[394]

Like most of his generation, Niebuhr was influenced by the rise of totalitarianism, and he believed that renewing the doctrine of original sin was essential to saving democracy. He sought to challenge the liberal faith in human nature which, far from underpinning democratic government, led to cynicism and despair when its expectations were inevitably dashed. He explained that his 1944 book, *The Children of Light and the Children of Darkness*, 'grew out of my conviction that ... the excessively optimistic estimates of human nature and of human history ... are a source of peril for democratic society; for contemporary experience is refuting this optimism and there is danger that it will seem to refute the democratic ideal as well'. Niebuhr argued that the 'children of light ... must know the power of self-interest in human society without giving it moral justification ... in order that they may beguile, deflect, harness and restrain self-interest, individual and collective, for the sake of the community'.[395]

How distant the twenty-first century is from the public conversation of the postwar decades is even more clearly shown by the book sales and public profile of Paul Tillich, whose writings on original sin and the myth of the transcendent Fall (which he believed 'was replayed in every human life and in every human act') would now be considered to be inaccessible to all but the most enthusiastic theology buffs. Yet very few public intellectuals, before or since, have enjoyed the popularity that Tillich achieved in the decades after he came to America in 1933, having been dismissed from his position as professor of philosophy in Frankfurt by the Nazis.[396] Perhaps only in the widely caricatured religious revival of 1950s America could millions of people have pondered Tillich's convoluted conviction that '[s]in is a universal act before it becomes an individual act ... [as] freedom is imbedded in the universal destiny of estrangement in such a way in every free act the destiny of estrangement is involved'.[397]

Niebuhr and Tillich not only defined a religious subculture, they also helped to shape American society. Their influence continued through the upheavals of the 1960s; along with a distinguished group of Europeans, including Karl Barth, Emil Brunner and Dietrich Bonhoeffer, they made a dynamic Protestant contribution to politically charged debates on human nature.[398] Their legacy remains – Barack Obama claims both men as major influences – but from the 1970s their broader cultural influence declined. The change was most noticeable in Western Europe, where Christian thought and practice was marginalised with extraordinary speed, but it was also true in the United States, where the evangelicals successfully narrowed the religious conversation.

It was the third of *Time*'s Christian coverboys of the 1950s, Billy Graham, who did most to define contemporary Christianity. Graham conducted the first of his mass crusades in 1949, preaching to two hundred and fifty thousand people in Los Angeles over seventy-two days. Near the end of the crusade, Graham preached Jonathan Edwards' passionate 1741 sermon, 'Sinners in the Hands of an Angry God', an extended and vivid depiction of the brutal consequences of original sin.[399]

By connecting his crusade to the First Great Awakening, Graham seemed to suggest that postwar American Protestantism would return to its Reformation roots, but a truer indication of what was to come was that the young preacher only made it only halfway through

Edwards' sermon, stopping just before the section which graphically describes the fate which awaited every 'natural man'. Did Graham run out of time, or did he know his audience too well to risk depicting them as being like 'some loathsome insect' who was 'a thousand times more abominable in [God's] eyes than the most hateful, venomous serpent is in our ours'?[400] In Graham's 1952 book *Peace with God* (which sold more than two million copies), his *Hour of Decision* radio program (broadcast on more than seven hundred stations), his 'My Answer' nationally syndicated newspaper column and his various magazine ventures (which included *Christianity Today,* founded in 1956), it became clear that the focus would be on a benign Jesus and the comforting prospect of salvation, not on Edwards' piteous description of the human condition.

This emphasis was clear by the time of Graham's New York City crusade of 1957, in which more than two million people heard him live and ninety-six million more watched at least one broadcast of his services. The fires of hell were now well and truly dowsed.[401] It is not that Graham came to deny what he termed the 'disease of the soul' and the judgement owing on this, but that for him, and even more for the televangelists who would follow, selling Christianity meant downplaying the universal evil to be found within even the most decent and patriotic American.

The paradox of the postwar Christian revival is that it was those preachers who professed themselves faithful to the Reformation who ensured the doctrine of original sin was finally silenced in Western Protestantism. While original sin was always theologically vulnerable because no scriptural passages straightforwardly supported it, and because it made little rational sense to many other believers (such as the bestselling English apologist C. S. Lewis), it was the free market that hastened the doctrine's demise.[402] American Christians did not want to hear that they and their children were no better in God's eyes than any criminal or drug addict – and with real religious freedom of choice, they didn't have to. As consumers who had the freedom to attend whichever church they wanted – denominational loyalties were becoming ever weaker – evangelical Americans largely chose to listen to preachers whose upbeat message of salvation put them on the side of good in a drama-filled combat with an *external* enemy, and it was the flexible, tradition-free, 'seeker-sensitive' evangelical churches that were best able to meet this demand.[403]

The identification of evil with an external power complemented and sometimes combined with America's Cold War rhetoric against the menace of communism. When an evangelical preacher warned of an outside force that sought to corrupt American society, spread atheism and tempt good Christians to backslide, he might be speaking of communism or the devil or both. And with the end of the Cold War, the enemy shifted easily from the secular creed of communism to the religious one of Islam.

The theology of Franklin Graham, who has followed his father in conducting mass outreach across America and the world, is explicitly centred on Satan and enthusiastically employs the language of war. Graham believes that 'the battle America is fighting against terrorism is really just a skirmish in a war that began when Satan turned against God and made his declaration of independence' – which in turn required that 'God sent his Son to this earth on the ultimate commando raid'. While Franklin Graham allows that 'our nation is full of problems and much in need of repentance from sin', he maintains that 'America, at its core, is a symbol of the freedom purchased with the precious blood of the Lord Jesus Christ on the Cross – the freedom of men and women to choose to love and follow the Saviour of their souls'. Graham maintains that 'God has blessed the United States of America more than any other nation on this earth', and that Islam is a satanic force whose 'ultimate objective ... is world domination'.[404] Furthermore, the battle in which the American nation (and, in a confused apocalyptic sense, Israel) is engaged is now seen to be approaching the end times, which considerably raises the stakes for believers and non-believers alike.[405]

Franklin Graham's political theology was shared by his friend President George W. Bush, who appropriated his country's evangelical heritage in order, as he promised during a service in the National Cathedral in Washington, 'to rid the world of evil'. His 2003 State of the Union address spoke of the 'power, wonder-working power, in the goodness and idealism and faith of the American people', which, as Jim Wallis has pointed out, was a heretical arrogation of an evangelical hymn that emphasised the 'power, power, wonder-working power, in the blood of the Lamb'.[406]

In such a crowded evangelical marketplace, it is not difficult to find exceptions to every claim; there are literally thousands of evangelical groups and congregations, including some associated with the political left, such as Wallis' own Sojourners Community. But in today's America, secular and religious creeds have so overlapped, and taken American Protestantism so far from its Reformation roots, that even nineteenth-century evangelicals, let alone John Calvin or Martin Luther, might struggle to say 'yes' to the contemporary offer of salvation. Jonathan Edwards and John Wesley would be horrified that the radical spiritual equality that defined the Reformation, underpinned as it was by the conviction that every human being is innately sinful, has been lost.

Chauvinism is not new to evangelicalism, but the doctrine of original sin and salvation *by faith alone* has usually posed a challenge to it. The vigour of overtly nationalistic religion is thus a measure of the extent to which the doctrine of original sin has been abandoned in American evangelicalism.[407] The profound difference between what Jonathan Edwards preached in 1741, what Billy Graham preached in Los Angeles in 1949 and what his son preaches today can be measured by the extent to which believers have been freed from the traditional evangelical duty of probing the evil in their own hearts.

In Germany, in the aftermath of the First World War and liberal Lutheran theology's accommodation with the state known as *Kul-*

turprotestantismus, Karl Barth asserted that original sin was 'the doctrine which emerges from all honest study of history' because it made clear that '[t]here is none righteous, no, not one ... the way of peace they have not known. This is the final judgement upon the deeds and works of men.[408] Barth's determination to ensure that God was not appropriated by any government or society was underpinned by his Luther-like conviction that *every* person was equally and wholly in need of God's grace. In the twenty-first century, Barth's Reformation-style religion has come to pose as much of a challenge to the teachings of many of the evangelical churches in America as it did to the nationalised German church in the 1930s.

Original sin might have been marginalised in American evangelical Christianity, but what of the more than five hundred million Pentecostals, who comprise around a quarter of the world's Christians? Not one of the world's top twenty mega-churches by size is now in America or Europe. The largest Christian congregation in the world is Yoido Full Gospel Church in Seoul, where about two hundred and fifty thousand people attend one of the numerous Sunday services conducted by its five hundred pastors; the most Pentecostal city is Lagos, where hundreds of thousands of people attend all-night Friday meetings in places with names like Redemption Ground and Canaan Land; and the biggest Pentecostal groupings are the Han Chinese and African Independent churches, with eighty million and fifty-five million members respectively. It is probably already the case that the number of people attending a Pentecostal church on a single Sunday in China outnumbers the number of people attending *every* church service in Europe. Even India has thirty-three million Pentecostals.[409]

Most people assume that Pentecostals are similar to American evangelicals. But even though evangelicals were often responsible for the export of the faith, and Pentecostalism in its modern form began in America in the early twentieth century (with the best advertised version still the one seen on American television), most of these churches are now defined by their own customs, rituals and beliefs, of which there is an almost infinite variety.

The difficulty in assessing how the doctrine of original sin has fared in this trans-cultural migration is that Pentecostals put less focus on 'the word' (written and otherwise) and have little interest in setting out a Reformation-style confession. This means that what is distinctive about Pentecostal theology is not easy to define. The Assemblies of God, the Pentecostal group which comes closest to being a traditional Western denomination, does have a succinct statement of 'fundamental truths' – one of which acknowledges that 'man by voluntary transgression fell and thereby incurred not only physical death but also spiritual death, which is separation from God' – but little reference is made to this creed. The primary Pentecostal emphasis is on the believer's *experience* of salvation, which is made manifest by the presence of the Holy Spirit.

The Pentecostal understanding of evil is equally immediate and personal: since Satan and his demons interfere in every aspect of life, exorcism (usually called 'deliverance') is perceived as a necessary and standard practice. As it once was for the peasants of medieval Europe, salvation is not narrowly focused on gaining forgiveness for one's sins and avoiding hell, but is an all-embracing concept that relates directly to daily life; it is evidenced in freedom from sickness, poverty and misfortune *and* in deliverance from demonic power.[410] But Pentecostal Christianity is perhaps closer still to the spirit of the first three centuries of the Common Era, when there was little concern to impose a single set of beliefs on a diverse church, and the prevalence of sin and the need for repentance was more assumed than explained. There is little doubt, though, that most Pentecostals share the popular evangelical assumption that the *source* of evil is Satan and his auxiliaries, not the human heart.

The combined impact of the rapid secularisation of European countries, the shift away from original sin in American evangelicalism and the doctrine's irrelevancy in Pentecostalism means that the religious idea which defined the Reformation and the First Great Awakening has now all but vanished from Protestant Christianity. The theological divide imagined at the Council of Trent has belatedly eventuated, with the final religious stronghold of the doctrine developed by St Augustine being the institution that he fought so hard to secure against 'heretical' sects: the Catholic Church.

For over a century after the publication of *The Origin of Species*, the Vatican fiercely defended the historical existence of Adam and Eve, largely out of a determination to uphold the theological integrity of original sin. In 1909 the Pontifical Biblical Commission maintained that the relevant texts could not be called into doubt, and as recently as 1950 Pope Pius XII argued in his encyclical *Humani Generis* against 'certain false opinions which threaten the foundations of Catholic doctrine', including the idea that 'Adam was the name given to some group of our primordial ancestors', on the basis that it 'does not appear how such views can be reconciled with the doctrine of original sin'.[411]

In the wake of the Second Vatican Council (1962–1965), Catholic theologians sought to detach the doctrine from a literal reading of Genesis. The council itself made only minor adjustments to the dogma enunciated in the sixteenth century, but the culture of relative openness and inquiry it fostered encouraged theologians to provide original sin with a more believable foundation.[412] This work was given a degree of official blessing by Pope Paul VI, who convened a conference of experts on original sin at the Gregorian University in July 1966. In his address to the symposium, however, this 'reformist' pope made clear that the participants were not to question that 'the sin of the first man is transmitted to all his descendants by way of propagation, not of imitation … even in newborn infants'; and 'as to the theory of evolutionism, you will not consider it acceptable if it … does not regard the disobedience of Adam, the first universal parent, as of decisive importance for the destiny of humankind'.[413]

The most sensitive aspect of the Catholic debate remained the status not of Adam but of babies. In 1972 the Jesuit theologian Henri Rondet observed: 'In our days, the problem of infants who die unbaptized has become even more acute.'[414] The difficulties associated with sending babies to hell were accentuated by mixed messages regarding the doctrinal status of limbo. Such was the determination not to compromise original sin that it had not been until 1904 that Pope Pius X finally confirmed that limbo even existed.[415] But in 1992 Pope John Paul II had limbo removed from the catechism, and work resumed on the substantial issue of whether or not unbaptised babies could make it to heaven.

This work was a priority of Cardinal Josef Ratzinger, who in 2005 became Pope Benedict XVI. In 1954 Ratzinger had written his dissertation on Augustine, and in the 1980s he had noted that '[t]he inability to make original sin understandable is really one of the most difficult problems of present-day theology and pastoral ministry'.[416] His book *In the Beginning: A Catholic Understanding of the Story of Creation and the Fall* (1986), suggested that at the 'very heart of sin' is a human being's denial of his or her 'creatureliness'; people 'cannot save themselves ... We can only be saved ... when we stop wanting to be God and when we renounce the madness of autonomy and self-sufficiency'. Sounding more like Meister Eckhart than a dogmatic defender of orthodoxy, Ratzinger proposed that people inherit sin only in the sense that they 'enter into a world that is marked by relational damage'.[417] While he never stated it precisely, in *Creation and the Fall* Ratzinger renounced the Catholic Church's official teaching on original sin.

However, when it came to formulating dogma as the prefect of the Vatican's Congregation for the Doctrine of the Faith (the institution formerly known as the Office of the Holy Inquisition), Ratzinger forwent his mystical side. In the wake of the theological exploration unleashed by Vatican II, Pope John Paul II sought an all-encompassing catechism which would set out the non-negotiable teachings of the church. This document, prepared by a commission presided over by Ratzinger and released in 1992, largely restated the position reached at Trent, on the basis that '[t]he Church, which has the mind of Christ, knows very well that we cannot tamper with the revelation of original sin without undermining the mystery of Christ'. The Catechism maintained that the Fall 'affirms a primeval event, a deed that took place at the beginning of the history of man'. It reiterated that Adam has 'transmitted us a sin with which we are all born afflicted, a sin which is the "death of the soul"'; 'because of this certainty of faith, the Church baptizes for the remission of sins even tiny infants who have not committed personal sin'. It is 'revelation', the Catechism stated, that 'gives us the certainty of faith that the whole of human history is marked by the original fault committed by our first parents'. One of the document's few innovations was to directly critique the liberal understanding of human nature. Citing John Paul II, the Catechism noted: 'Ignorance of the fact that man has a wounded nature inclined to evil gives rise to serious errors in the areas of education, politics, social action, and morals.'[418]

As Pope Benedict XVI, Ratzinger did accept the findings of the International Theological Commission that 'there are reasons to hope that infants who die without baptism may be saved and brought into eternal happiness'. However, there was a major qualification to this historic concession which simultaneously preserved the necessity of baptism: 'there are reasons to hope that God will save these infants precisely because it was not possible [to baptise them]'. Those babies who *could* have been baptised, but were not, continued to face a very uncertain eternity.[419]

Perhaps Ratzinger's discomfort with church teaching on this issue is reflected in the fact that in the last of his weekly public audiences before he announced his resignation, in February 2013, he chose to return to the themes of *Creation and the Fall*. The pope reaffirmed that all human beings carry within them 'God's life-giving breath', and said that sin was succumbing to the temptation of 'building a world of one's own without accepting the limits of being a creature'. Original sin, noted the pontiff, simply meant that 'sin begets sin and the sins of history are related'.⁴²⁰

Whether Pope Francis will shift the formal position of the church closer to the spirit of his own convictions is not yet clear. His suggestion early in his pontificate that Christ saves even non-believers suggests such a possibility, but it seems equally likely that the bottom line will remain, as it did for Pope Benedict XVI and all his predecessors since the sixth century, a version of original sin that guarantees that parents cannot be absolutely certain of their children's salvation until they have them baptised in the Catholic Church.⁴²¹ For popes and parish priests, there is freedom to debate original sin but not to abandon it. Matthew Fox, a Dominican monk who in 1983 published a bestselling book, *Original Blessing: A Primer in Creation Spirituality*, claimed that 'Cardinal Ratzinger called this book "dangerous and deviant" and was so blinded in his fury that he had me expelled from the Dominican Order ... saying that I deny the doctrine of original sin'.⁴²² Many other Catholic scholars had gone as far in their theological explorations – arguably even Ratzinger himself – but had escaped censure by focusing on finding a new meaning for original sin rather than denouncing the old one.

Nevertheless, it is characteristic of most recent theology that its explanation of how original sin is transmitted – which is often linked to social injustice – quarantines human nature from indelible corruption.⁴²³ The principal exception to this is, ironically, the work of those theologians who appropriate Darwin to explain the consequences of the Fall. But even this innovative theology cannot preserve the integrity of the *doctrine* of original sin.⁴²⁴ Seemingly now abandoned by all but the most loyally conservative theologians, only in the formal pronouncements of the Vatican is the purity of the doctrine preserved. But how many people still listen to these edicts? There is considerable evidence that the laity, priests and members of religious orders in Europe, North America and Australia pay increasingly scant attention to the decrees of Rome. But what the doctrine of original sin means to the majority of the world's practising Catholics, who now live outside the West, is less certain. The faithful of these countries have customs and rituals almost as diverse as those of the Pentecostals, but they can sometimes seem comparatively more receptive to an official ukase.

Although the global situation is complex, there can be little doubt that the doctrine of original sin now has little relevance in Christianity. Despite the strength of conservative impulses, popular piety, in both its Protestant and Catholic forms, has effectively renounced Western Christianity's defining dogma. It is all the more extraordinary, therefore, that the anthropology associated with original sin seems to be enjoying another revival in secular culture. In the twenty-first century, the task of confronting Western people with the dark truth of their own nature has largely passed from Freudian psychologists to passionate polemicists of genetic evolution.

21

THE SELFISH GENE

RICHARD DAWKINS PUBLISHED *The Selfish Gene* in 1976, the
book that established his reputation and which, his closest support-
ers maintain, 'takes pride of place among his achievements'.[425] With
it, he helped popularise the idea that not only the human body but
all behaviours, beliefs and emotions are, to a large extent, products
of evolution.[426]

Dawkins came to believe that his argument – that the 'predominant quality to be expected in a successful gene is ruthless selfishness', and that 'gene selfishness will usually give rise to selfishness in
individual behaviour' – might have been expressed differently. But
his frustration with the 'selfish' metaphor arose from the way it was
misrepresented and misunderstood, rather than because of any
error in the theory itself.[427] Dawkins' point was not that human
beings are *always* selfish, but that altruistic behaviour remains the
unlikely act which goes against humanity's essential nature:

> ... we must expect that when we go and look at the behaviour of
> baboons, humans, and all other living creatures, we shall find it
> to be selfish. If we find that our expectation is wrong, if we
> observe that human behaviour is truly altruistic, then we shall
> be faced with something puzzling, something that needs
> explaining.[428]

This perspective on human nature seems similar to Augustine's – but given that Dawkins is one of the world's most prominent atheists, how does his teaching relate to the Western spiritual tradition? Dawkins is certain that his claims are based on empirical science alone. But is he right? Has his expertise in evolutionary biology meant that he has achieved what Darwin and Freud could not: culture-free knowledge about what it means to be a human being?

Dawkins' conclusions in his field of ethology – the study of *animal* behaviour, especially under natural conditions – are not under scrutiny, but the scientific status of his explanation for *human* behaviour in the post-Pleistocene age is. To his credit, Dawkins, unlike some of his colleagues in evolutionary psychology, has never claimed that gene-driven evolution could explain the rapid changes in human society over recent millennia. In *The Selfish Gene*, he openly acknowledged that: 'Among animals, man is uniquely dominated by culture, by influences learned and handed down.'[429] However, this was not, as one might expect, a diminution of the role played by evolution. Instead, Dawkins maintained that:

> ... a new kind of replicator has recently emerged on this very planet. It is staring us in the face. It is still in its infancy, still drifting clumsily about in its primeval soup, but already it is achieving evolutionary change at a rate that leaves the old gene panting far behind. The new soup is the soup of human culture. We need a name for the new replicator, a noun that conveys the idea of a unit of cultural transmission, or a unit of *imitation*.

The term Dawkins chose for the new replicator was 'meme'. He argued that memic evolution is now more influential than the 'old gene-selected evolution'. Just as 'genes propagate themselves in the gene pool by leaping from body to body via sperms or eggs, so memes propagate themselves in the meme pool by leaping from brain to brain via a process which, in the broad sense, can be called imitation'.[430]

Examples of memes include 'tunes, ideas, catch-phrases, clothes, fashions, ways of making pots or building arches'. In fact, almost everything that can be called a shared idea (and what idea isn't to some degree shared?) is seen to be a meme, including Darwinian science itself:

> [M]eme transformation is subject to continuous mutation, and also to blending ... when we say that all biologists nowadays believe in Darwin's theory, we do not mean that every biologist has, graven in his brain, an identical copy of the exact words of Charles Darwin himself. Each individual has his own way of interpreting Darwin's ideas. He probably learned them not from Darwin's own writings, but from more recent authors. Much of what Darwin said is, in detail, wrong. Darwin if he read this book would scarcely recognise his own original theory in it ... Yet, in spite of all this, there is something, some essence of Darwinism, which is present in the head of every individual who understands the theory ... The meme of Darwin's theory is therefore that essential basis of the idea which is held in common by all brains that understand the theory.[431]

Except insofar as Dawkins presented the meme as analogous to the gene in the way that it behaves and mutates, this was not a controversial or novel explanation of cultural transmission. But nor was Dawkins' memetic/genetic explanation of human development *scientific*, in the usual sense of the term. There is no observational evidence that memes exist, and the transmission of culture can be explained equally effectively without them.[432] Furthermore, there is no conceivable way that the claims he makes can be proved or disproved – the same objection that is made to the science of Freud.

It is ironic, given Dawkins' respect for the ideas of Karl Popper, the philosopher of science who argued that a scientific theory had to be falsifiable, that there is no imaginable human behaviour that would bring Dawkins' theory into question.[433] For example, the fact that gender-based sexual mores have changed markedly since they were explained in *The Selfish Gene* does not challenge the original theory, because an explanation for the change can readily be provided. Indeed, *any* human action can be explained by reference to an evolving gene or meme. All contradictory evidence that might throw doubt on the explanatory power of either replicator can be dealt with either by reimagining the lives of our Pleistocene ancestors (of which very little is known), or by employing the highly adaptable, rapidly evolving concept of the meme. The same criticism can thus be made of Dawkins that Darwin levelled at Herbert Spencer: 'His fundamental generalisations ... are of such a nature that they do not seem to me to be of any strictly scientific use ... They do not aid one in predicting what will happen in any particular case.'[434] Like the all-explaining God of scholastic theologians, this, as Mary Midgley has pointed out, 'is a game where it's impossible to lose'.[435]

Dawkins' discussion of memes is largely confined to one chapter in *The Selfish Gene*, but in 2013 he emphasised that the concept was critical to his objective to 'push Universal Darwinism'. In his memoir, Dawkins explained that precisely because 'the rest of the book thrust the gene to centre stage as the starring replicator in the evolution of life, it was important to dispel the impression that the replicator had to be DNA'. A distinctive feature of Dawkins' thought, highlighted by this commitment to Universal Darwinism, is that he is as eager as any medieval theologian to develop a unified understanding to life. He is certain that evolution can potentially explain everything, but for it to do so, the meme, and probably other replicators as well, are essential. So it is not surprising that, thirty-five years after he invented the term, Dawkins was 'delighted that the philosopher Daniel Dennett, the psychologist Susan Blackmore and others have run, so productively, with the meme ball'; he noted that 'more than thirty books have now been published with the word "meme" in their title, and the word has made it into the *Oxford English Dictionary*'.[436]

Dawkins has conceded 'that we don't know what memes are
made of, or where they reside' (they have 'not yet found their Watson
and Crick, they even lack their Mendel').[437] But the speculative status of memes, and Dawkins' admission that human behaviour is
largely determined by cultural influences, mean that the question of
where his understanding of human nature comes from has been left
unanswered. He gives no suggestion that this is an argument based
on historical or anthropological knowledge. The idea of the meme as
a *selfish* replicator is assumed rather than explained.

Dawkins is well aware of the doctrine of original sin, which, as the
'main doctrine of Christian theology', he employs to open people's
eyes to the 'mental illness' of religious faith.[438] But despite, or perhaps
because of, his conviction that the 'belief that everyone is born in sin,
inherited from Adam ... is one of the very nastiest aspects of Christianity', he seems unaware of the continuity between his own understanding of human nature and the ancient teaching of Augustine.[439]

The memic similarity is most obviously manifest in Dawkins'
assertion of the selfishness innate to human beings, but it is equally
evident in his hope that we might transcend the nature that we are
born with. Dawkins is as anxious as John Wesley to deny predestination (in the form of brute genetic determinism), and presents two
grounds for his 'qualified hope' that human beings can choose to be
independent of their selfish nature. The first is 'conscious foresight',
or 'our capacity to simulate the future in imagination', which provides 'the power to defy the selfish genes of our birth and, if necessary, the selfish memes of our indoctrination' and pursue long-term
interests.[440] The second basis of hope might be called a matter of
'faith', defined by Dawkins as a 'blind trust, in the absence of evidence, even in the teeth of evidence':

> We can even discuss ways of deliberately cultivating and nur-
> turing pure, disinterested altruism – something that has no
> place in nature, something that has never existed before in the

whole history of the world. We are built as gene machines and cultured as meme machines, but we have the power to turn against our creators. We, alone on earth, can rebel against the tyranny of the selfish replicators.[441]

But why would the human brain 'rebel' against its meme- and gene-given nature? Is the brain also not part of who we are? Dawkins rejects the dualist implication of his argument, but nevertheless seems to have absorbed the idea that there is a dimension to human beings, traditionally called *mind, consciousness* or *soul*, which exists independently of the biologically and culturally derived side of human nature.[442] Dawkins can surely be excused for not being clear about what this is, but it leaves him with the challenge of either admitting to the limits of the capacity of evolutionary theory to explain the human condition, or explaining on what basis readers can be expected to share his speculative hope that the limits of human nature might be transcended.

There is another, more definitive source of hope presented in *The Selfish Gene*: death is not the end of life because the human body is but a temporary carrier of the potentially immortal gene. Indeed, Dawkins now believes that the title *The Immortal Gene* would have conveyed the meaning of his book more clearly. Is this another mutation of the meme of original sin? Human bodies are flawed and limited, with an inherent tendency to selfishness and decay, but what is most essential to a person can potentially live forever.[443]

The final way in which Dawkins' thought seems to echo his culture's spiritual tradition is his certainty that there is only one legitimate way of understanding the purpose of existence. Original sin provided an ideological foundation for the Catholic Church's monopoly claim on the meaning of human life. In the revised edition of *The Selfish Gene*, published in 2006, Dawkins vigorously upheld his equally exclusive counter-claim. He asserted that, until Darwin published *On the Origin of Species*, 'all attempts to answer' questions on the 'meaning to life', such as 'What are we for?' and 'What is man?', were 'worthless'. He concluded that 'we will be better off if we ignore them completely'.[444] In *The God Delusion* (2006), which has sold more than two million copies, Dawkins set out the implications of this. His judgement on Australian Aboriginal culture, for example, was unambiguous:

> On the one hand aboriginals are superb survivors under conditions that test their practical skills to the uttermost ... [but t]he very same peoples who are so savvy about the natural world and how to survive in it simultaneously clutter their minds with beliefs that are palpably false and for which the word 'useless' is a generous understatement ...

At least Aborigines were not singled out: 'Though the details differ across the world, no known culture lacks some version of the time-consuming, wealth-consuming, hostility-provoking rituals, the anti-factual, counter-productive fantasies of religion.[445]

Few people, atheist or not, would be so certain that Australia's fifty-thousand-year-old culture, not to mention those of the Chinese and Indian civilisations and of myriad other nations and peoples, have been 'useless' at grappling with questions of meaning. Indeed, it is the manifest falsity of Dawkins' claim here which tells us that, at some point, his logic has gone terribly wrong. In the thirtieth anniversary edition of *The Selfish Gene*, Dawkins acknowledged that some people were concerned by his assertion that all attempts to answer questions on the purpose of existence before 1859 were 'worthless', but his response – a demand to 'show me' examples where this was not the case – only highlighted how culturally constrained was his conception of truth. Church history provides proof enough that when you insist with non-negotiable certainty that there is only one way of understanding what life is about, it is then not possible to be shown any other.

Through their determination to expose and transcend the dark hidden truth of human nature and to proclaim a single way to inquire into the meaning of life, Dawkins' ideas are related to those of Augustine in much as the same way as they are to those of Darwin. Obviously, Dawkins' thought is not an 'identical copy' – if Augustine were to read Dawkins, he 'would scarcely recognise his own original theory in it' – and yet 'in spite of all this, there is something, some essence' of Augustinianism clearly evident in the 'essential basis of the idea'.

Given the evident continuity in the approach to human nature upheld in the Western Christian tradition and that expressed in *The Selfish Gene*, how can Dawkins and his colleagues in evolutionary psychology be so certain that they owe nothing to pre-Darwinian ideas? There are two likely reasons for their blind spot: the first relates to a misunderstanding of history, the second to their hostility to 'God'.

Evolutionary psychologists share a view that Western thought has always been defined by its denial of the existence of human nature; hence their mistaken assumption that their own ideas represent a radical break with the past. Steven Pinker's bestselling book *The Blank Slate* focuses on this subject. Pinker presents Western intellectual history as the triumph of John Locke's 'blank slate', which is defined as 'the idea that the human mind has no inherent structure and can be inscribed at will by society or ourselves' – an idea that, as we have seen, was not even accepted by Locke himself.[446] Pinker believes this denial of human nature and the long celebration of free will started with the story of Adam and Eve, and because he is ignorant of the meaning of the Fall in the Western Christian tradition – in which the nature of every human being is distorted and free will is, to a large extent, *lost* – he cannot see the parallels between the perspective on human nature found in evolutionary psychology and that in the creation story of the Western world. His misunderstanding of Christianity continues through the rest of the book, even though his main target seems to be what evolutionary psychologists derisively call the 'Standard Social Science Model' of human nature.[447]

Pinker documents how from the 1930s, and accelerating after the war, there was a shift in disciplines such as psychology, anthropology, sociology and political science in the rapidly expanding universities towards a belief that environmental factors could explain human behaviour, but he overlooks that this was a reaction to the tragic consequences of a decades-long fascination with biology. It is also wrong to assume that the postwar trend always involved a denial of human nature. To take psychology as an example, while in B. F. Skinner's *Science and Behaviour* (1972) human beings are seen to be almost completely products of their environment, the more influential humanistic psychologists, such as Carl Rogers and Abraham H. Maslow, focused on an individual's growth towards 'self-actualisation' – the term employed for the revelation of a true or innate nature. Because Rogers and Maslow emphasised how few people were able to realise the highest stage of emotional and spiritual development, their understanding of human nature (and the path to salvation) was closer to that of Pelagius, Celtic monks and Ignatian spiritual guides than to the blank slate of Skinner and his colleagues.[448]

At any rate, a bias in postwar academia does not establish Pinker's case that the 'blank slate' has historically dominated Western thought. Indeed, the most perplexing historical question is why liberal academics' extensive research output had such a limited impact on how human nature was popularly understood, while the marginal discipline of evolutionary psychology is having such a defining influence. Why have people been so open to hearing that a tendency to violence, selfishness, greed and looking after their own – whether family, tribe or nation – is inherent to their evolutionary nature? What is the source of the broad cultural acceptance of the idea that the way human beings feel, respond and act – even to the extent of their choice of mate – has been significantly shaped by evolution, given that the scientific consensus remains, as the former director of the National Center for Human Genome Research put it, that 'genetic influences on behaviour are in most instances relatively modest'?[449]

Part of the answer to this question is very likely to be that evolutionary psychologists, like Freud before them, are actually elucidating traditional knowledge. Far from being revolutionaries confronting the religious and social scientific dogmas that have imprisoned the Western world, Dawkins and Pinker provide a contemporary terminology for what people already think. In offering a quasi-scientific explanation of existing beliefs and intuitions, their theories connect contemporary people to ideas of human nature that have defined Western culture for over fifteen hundred years. Evolutionary psychology is less a product of new discovery than of intellectual amnesia, and its self-proclaimed break with the religious past reflects less the progress of science than the extent to which Western people have forgotten the source of what they have always believed to be true.[450]

None of this is meant to imply that Dawkins' well-known atheism is irrelevant to the popularity of his ideas. Indeed, the other reason why the parallels between the central doctrine of Western Christianity and evolutionary psychology are rarely recognised is precisely because a primary purpose of Dawkins' work, shared by many of his colleagues, is to make God redundant.[451] Taking science into questions of human existence is *meant* to provoke a confrontation with Christianity. And from inside the boxing ring, with the fight underway, few onlookers see the tent in which the contest is occurring.

Dawkins' determination to defeat religion arises because his science is ultimately less concerned with human nature than with redemption. He is rightly proud that all his books seek not only to 'persuade' but also to 'inspire' his readers with what he terms 'a vision of our own existence'; but as with Augustine, Calvin and

Freud, this requires that people first know the truth of who they really are.[452] It is ironic that at a time when Western Christianity has largely abandoned its ancient project to confront people with the evil in their hearts, atheistic prophets have emerged who seek to make people face the reality of human nature before allowing them to choose to accept or deny the only salvation available to them. People must understand and accept how genes, memes and evolution work if they are to achieve any control over what nature and culture have bequeathed them. Only after accepting the truth of their innate selfishness can people practice altruism, celebrate and honour nature, and influence the future evolution of the human race.[453]

Recently, Dawkins reflected that in a previous age he might have been a priest, given that his interest was always in the 'deep questions of existence'. He admitted that his 'interest in biology has been largely driven by questions about origins and the nature of life, rather than – as is the case for most young biologists … by a love of natural history'. Even as a child, Dawkins recalled, he 'was drawn to questions that grown-ups would have called philosophical. What is the meaning of life? Why are we here? How did it all start?'[454] Dawkins' approach to biology is commendable and at times awe-inspiring, but when he presents all attempts to consider the meaning of life from a non-evolutionary perspective – pre- and post-Darwin, and in both in Western and non-Western cultures – as dangerous distractions which deny people access to the single source of salvation, he sounds more like a missionary than a scientist.

In the writings of Richard Dawkins the creation story has come full circle, with the uncomfortable reality of human nature again speaking directly to the purpose of existence. Perhaps it is not surprising, with so much of Western society now proclaiming an easy salvation, that an evangelical philosophy which restates the hard 'truth' of the creation story has emerged once more, and that in a secular age it has been cast in the language of science.

Christian de Duve argued in 2010 that nothing less than the future of life on earth is dependent on genetic self-knowledge, and that the only chance of redemption from the impending environmental catastrophe comes from the human ability to know our true selves and then act against our innate nature:

> If we wish to escape the fate that awaits us, we must take advantage of our unique ability to consciously and deliberately act against natural selection. But to exercise this power, we will have to find in the resources of our minds a wisdom that is not written in our genes.[455]

For both de Duve and Dawkins, human beings are the problem *and* the only available solution, and herein lies the critical difference between them and Augustine, Luther, Calvin, Edwards and Wesley. Yet might these apologists for the doctrine of original sin have applauded the fact that, in the twenty-first century, the focus is back where they wanted it – not on the universality of human evil, but on the means of salvation?

22

WHERE TO FOR SALVATION?

Wilt thou forgive that sin where I begun,
Which was my sin, though it were done before?
—JOHN DONNE, 'A Hymn to God the Father', 1633

THE COMMITMENT NOT JUST to *do* good but to try to *become* a 'good person' is probably as prevalent as it has ever been in the Western world. This longing is consistent with the West's singular spirituality, which taught that people face divine judgement merely for being who they are. The doctrine of original sin only emphasised the universal corruption of humanity in order to stress the universal need to rely on God's forgiveness alone; because *everyone* was born bad, *everyone* needed to be redeemed. Modern history suggests that disbelief in a saviour might not have removed Western people's deeply ingrained need to be saved. But with grace sidelined by secularism, salvation has become solely dependent on the forces of *this* world: the market, technology, politics and self-help movements, all of which share a language of redemption.

Of these worldly entities, none has judged and redeemed as readily as 'market forces'. It is often observed that faith in the market has many characteristics formerly reserved for the deity: it punishes and rewards individuals, organisations and communities, and requires that citizens and governments trust in it as an ultimately beneficial power, despite the suffering and sacrifice that must be implemented in

188

its name. But since the failure of communism – itself popularly understood to be due to its failure to accept the reality of human nature – and the recent Global Financial Crisis, market-faith has seemed to rest more on monopoly power than on genuine conviction.[456]

Liberal democracy, the other central creed of modernity, has suffered a similar crisis of faith. In the first half of the twentieth century, totalitarian regimes promulgated an ideology of salvation which, aided by the destructive capacity of new technologies, led to persecution, violence, genocide and war on a scale never before imagined.[457] But the problem of subsequent decades was that it was not only extremist political ideologies that were widely discredited, but politics itself. Democracy's biggest danger remains what Reinhold Niebuhr warned against: a pervasive disenchantment created by unfulfilled and often unfulfillable expectations.

Even technology, which has been central to the salvation project of the modern West, has been somewhat discredited.[458] While there remains a widespread hope that personal, environmental, social and economic challenges can be transcended through technological innovation, faith in big technology to solve and to save has been increasingly questioned. It is noteworthy that the archetypal symbol of the new millennium is an intimate personal device that both connects the individual to the world and increasingly defines, through social media, his or her place in it. Through this technological reformation, the individual has been given direct access to technology's redemptive power without the intermediary of the discredited state.

The focus on a personalised redemption has been gathering strength since the 1950s, but it does not, as is widely assumed, represent a rejection of communal tradition. While Augustine (when he was not raving against the Pelagians) stressed the authority of the church, the doctrine of original sin was never easily reconciled with an institutional monopoly over salvation. The sentiment which exploded in the Reformation – that the individual needed no intermediary to be saved – was latent in the Bishop of Hippo's teaching that sin was personally received at conception, and that Christ saved one soul at a time. The West's self-obsession began with its creation story.

What *is* new is for there to be so little consensus on the path to salvation. Over a century ago, Friedrich Nietzsche welcomed the fact that 'God is dead', but far from accepting human nature, he saw it as something that must be overcome, not by trying to escape the reality of *Selbstsucht* (innate selfishness) but by harnessing its power to create a new being. Nietzsche did not expect that most people would have it in them to undertake this heroic act of will, and was himself prevented from doing so by the onset of mental illness, but his starting point – that God is dead but humanity is still broken, and each person must find his or her own path to redemption – was reproduced by many less confronting self-help creeds.[459]

Yet by the late twentieth century, even the reassuring promise that everyone could become 'whoever they want to be', if only they abandoned self-doubt and believed in themselves, had been discounted by decades of disappointment. Norman Vincent Peale's influential thesis of the 1950s never eventuated: power did not come with positive thinking.[460] People were instead offered a smorgasbord of hope, in which wholeness, happiness and communal affirmation could be theirs if only this product was consumed or that piece of advice accepted. The goal of overcoming personal limitations, whether these be physical, emotional, sexual or relational, became a major driver of the economy, used to sell goods, services, people, places and ideas. But not even the iconic image of the information-technology reformation – Steve Jobs' once-bitten apple, which is reproduced on each personal appliance his corporate creation spawns (Adam's bite has never been so well publicised) – seemed to satisfy.[461]

If seeking salvation has been such a wide-ranging project, why has a solution never been found? Original sin suggests an answer to this question. The doctrine teaches that human beings are born not just bad, but also *guilty*. The market theorist, advertising baron, technology guru, self-help counsellor and charismatic leader all speak to the desire to fix human brokenness, but they cannot forgive people for being who they are. Even when the legitimacy of these feelings is angrily rejected (and Christianity is named as their source), people often denounce what they personally experience: a deep-seated sense of guilt that is seemingly unrelated to actions or deeds.

The discontent that is spawned by original sin remains both a creative and a destructive influence in Western culture, as it has always been. The determination to remake people and places, which, for good and ill, has transformed life everywhere on earth, is unlikely to have been as vibrant or damaging if Western Christianity had emphasised the innate goodness within every person. Of course, there have been many factors contributing to both the neurosis and the vigour of the West, but the searing energy of its people becomes more explicable when we remember their extraordinary creation story.

Facing up to the legacy of original sin provides neither a diagnosis nor a cure for personal and social challenges. It does, however, help illuminate one aspect of the pain: the aching and never satisfied self, and one danger of which to beware in any solution: the promise to provide a 'fix' for being human. Perhaps the first step towards healing our relationship with ourselves, each other and the natural world is just to accept that, after fifteen hundred years, the idea that 'there is something wrong with me' might be so internalised that it has become part of who we are. A newborn baby is no longer 'born bad', but one component of her most intimate cultural inheritance remains the scar that suggests otherwise.

23

BEYOND GOOD OR BAD: A FINAL JUDGEMENT ON ORIGINAL SIN

I was in darkness because I knew nothing – not even my very self … The weight of original sin was dragging me down.
—ANSELM OF CANTERBURY[462]

ALL WESTERN PEOPLE ARE BORN with the legacy of original sin, but this does not make it 'true'. It is easy to identify a discontent in the psyche so deeply rooted that it seems innate, but what if the creation story has spawned the symptoms cited to prove its existence? Face the truth of yourself, preached the fifth-century Bishop of Hippo, sixteenth-century reformers and twenty-first-century evolutionary psychologists alike, but does the search within reveal objective truth or attest to the power of proclamation? Blaise Pascal believed that 'nature points everywhere – both within the human being and outside of him – towards a God who has been lost and a nature that has been corrupted', but have our centuries of conditioning meant that original sin is, to use the contemporary expression, 'in our DNA'?[463]

A similar point can be made about a parallel 'proof' for the doctrine, first advanced by Augustine, which enjoyed a renaissance in the battle-scarred twentieth century. G. K. Chesterton believed that original sin was the only Christian creed that could be empirically proven to be true. Yet the truth of the doctrine's perspective on human nature cannot be established by the indisputable prevalence of malevolence in every age. While evil is pervasive in human history, so is the bias to sin in writing history. Documentary sources are largely produced by those with riches, honour, power and scribes. There are relatively few records of the 'small' acts of kindness, compassion and self-sacrifice which, almost by definition, seek no recognition but keep children, communities and cultures alive. Honest history must admit that human beings seem to be capable of all things, and acknowledge that the history of original sin is not concerned with who we are, but who we *think* we are.

It is true, though, that it is those ideas and movements that are consistent with the doctrine of original sin which have endured in the West. While belief in an innate core of incorruptible goodness never disappeared, Augustine has towered over Pelagius and other carriers of the alternative Christian tradition, including the mystics, for centuries. Luther's and Calvin's branches of the Reformation dominated groups which took a more positive view of human nature. The principles of the 'realistic' American Founding Fathers continue to change the world, while the leaders of the French Revolution are studied for where they went wrong. Freudian concepts have entered everyday language, while strict behaviourists are confined to first-year university courses. The postwar social scientists struggled to find an audience beyond the academy, while the books of eccentric evolutionary psychologists have become bestsellers. Edmund Burke's letter to the most influential moral philosopher in history, Adam Smith, has proved prophetic: 'A theory like yours founded on the Nature of man, which is always the same, will last, when those that are founded upon his opinions, which are always changing, will and must be forgotten.'[464]

But was Burke's prophecy fulfilled because Smith had human nature right, or because, after centuries of inculcation in original sin, most Western people thought he did? The most effective critique of mystics and Marxists alike has always been not that they are wrong but that their faith in human goodness is not *realistic*.[465] When dreamers and radicals were seen to deny the reality of human nature, most Western people stopped listening to them.

Once we recognise that this heritage is a component of every Westerner's intellectual and emotional ancestry, we can see that a guilt-ridden people has been both freed and subjected by being brought up in original sin. In postulating a 'religion for atheists', Alain de Botton points to the paradox that 'Christianity never sounds more beguiling than when it ... acknowledges that we are all in the end rather infantile, incomplete, unfinished, easily tempted and sinful'. He suggests, much as Augustine did to Julian, that 'being repeatedly informed of our native decency can cause us to become paralysed with remorse over our failure to measure up to impossible standards of integrity'. This non-believing apologist for Christian wisdom finds a 'relief, which can explode into bursts of laughter, when we finally come across an author generous enough to confirm that our very worst insights, far from being unique and shameful, are part of the common, inevitable reality of mankind'.

And yet, against this benign reflection on the 'ongoing charm and utility of the idea of Original Sin', one might cite the numerous testimonies of the paralysing long-term damage caused by church, school and families obsessed with the innate sinfulness of the children in their charge.[466]

A similarly complex legacy can be seen in the impact of original sin on politics and society. A widespread view is that 'doctrines about original sin ... seem to offer a prescription for passivity in politics and an acceptance, however reluctant, of the way things are'.[467] Hence original sin's postwar popularity with conservative culture warriors attacking liberal thought, a tradition that goes all the way back to the doctrine's formative years.[468] Nevertheless, the doctrine has also been a central idea underpinning political reform because of its inherent egalitarianism.[469] It required a profound shift in consciousness for ordinary people to see themselves as 'fundamentally equal to the clergy in the sight of God'.[470] It is true that spiritual equality did not lead directly to a commitment to political or social equality, but it was surely part of the journey. The demand made on the rebellious American colonists by the British Parliament's *Declaratory Act* of 18 March 1766 could be resisted by a reformed Protestant people only because they understood that the external power was not made up of divinely appointed rulers, but of sinful men.[471] In 1776 the authors of the Declaration of Independence invoked one of the Biblical accounts of creation to declare that 'we hold these truths to be self-evident, that all men are created equal', but it was original sin which ensured that, in a fallen world, they had remained so. Even today, the teaching of one of the first Puritan ministers in Massachusetts, Thomas Shepard, that in God's eyes every person is equally guilty of 'heart whoredom, heart sodomy, heart blasphemy, heart drunkenness, heart buggery, heart oppression [and] heart idolatry' subverts the status quo.[472] No wonder churches have often been as concerned to soften the teaching of original sin as to uphold it.

Even progressive thinkers who have critiqued the doctrine have often wanted to hold on to what Aquinas termed 'the unity of original sin', which results from all people sharing 'the nature which they have received from the first man'. Martin Luther King, influenced by Reinhold Niebuhr, was one of these.[473] He understood, as generations of reformers had before him, that human solidarity was on more solid ground when it was premised on seeing everyone as a sinner, rather than in seeking out the saints.

The too rarely realised potential of original sin has been to undermine all attempts to separate not just 'us' and 'them', but 'me' and 'you'. Xenophobic creeds become vulnerable when it is acknowledged that 'the line separating good and evil runs ... inside every human heart'.[474] For all its grotesque limitations, God's view of humanity in the Western Christian tradition was remarkably democratic.

In the end, whether original sin has been a conservative or progressive doctrine has largely come down to where you sit. Kings and popes have emphasised the need to maintain order among inherently sinful subjects, while oppressed peoples have pointed out that the doctrine says that their rulers are sinners too. Probably the doctrine's most notable legacy has not been in inhibiting or inspiring change, but in humbling all who pursue either. As John Calvin argued, destruction 'must be the fate of all who confide in the efficacy of their own virtue'.[475]

I suspect that the suffering undoubtedly associated with original sin has been less the result of its forlorn view of human nature than its failure to imagine a God who could accept this. Original sin unfavourably compares *actual* human nature with the supposedly *true* human nature of paradise. In presenting perfection as God-given, and the Fall as a distortion of created reality, not only did sin become universal, but grace became restricted.

The creation story of the Western world does not primarily concern humanity's exile from Paradise but God's exodus from earth. The allegory aims to explain not a lost Eden but an absent God. In *Paradise Lost*, Milton recognised that after the forbidden fruit was eaten, it was 'on the part of *heaven*' that there arose 'alienat[ion], distance and distaste, anger and just rebuke and judgement given'.[476] Because God departed their earthly home, Adam and Eve were left, isolated and guilty, to pass on their burden of sin to every human being. No theological trick to quarantine the concept of a loving, transcendent God from the implications of the story can overcome the fact that the doctrine of original sin proclaimed the self-exile of the divine from the world.

It was no small matter when the Roman church constructed a God who scorned a fallen world and condemned its inhabitants because of a primeval sin. It is embarrassing for a secular people to admit it, but the West's unique spiritual tradition has shaped its history. Empirical historians have avoided this subject for legitimate reasons (spiritual experience is hard to pin down), but their neglect has left a gaping hole in our understanding of the past. I have not sought to fill this, but I hope others do.

For in a sense, the history of the West is an account of what happened when a people were brought up to believe that their deity had turned his back on his own creation. It is impossible to know what would have been had Pelagius triumphed over Augustine, the Celtic church survived, mystics infiltrated Rome, or the Catholic Catechism and Protestant Confessions remembered the ancient teaching that Christ was 'united to every human being without exception' – but Western people would certainly have had a very different experience of what it means to be human.[477]

If the West is ever to move beyond original sin, history suggests this will not begin with the discarding of the doctrine's view of human nature, which is now so ingrained that even atheists promulgate it. Rather, it may involve rejecting the caricature of a God who can only be at home in a sanctified soul or lost paradise. As the present environmental crisis brings the question of salvation once more to the fore, perhaps it is time to complete the journey that Western people embarked on when God was exiled to heaven. Freedom from the bondage of original sin has not come from throwing off the chains of religion, but it might yet come by bringing grace back to earth.

APPENDIX

WHERE DID ORIGINAL SIN COME FROM?

Who can quickly explain everything which makes the yoke heavy upon the children of Adam?

—St Augustine[478]

THE MISTAKEN ASSUMPTION THAT original sin is 'in the Bible' explains why its distinctively Western heredity is rarely recognised. Although the doctrine's zealous defenders have usually denied it, the core elements of the creation myth which gradually emerged in the first four centuries of the Common Era have no scriptural precedent.

There are two creation stories in Genesis, and each underpinned a rival spiritual stream in the nascent religion of Christianity.[479] In the first, God 'created man in his own image, in the image of God he created him; male and female he created them', and 'God saw all that he had made, and it was very good'.[480] In the second, man is created first, and the woman is made from a man, and she, after a conversation with a snake, defies God's instruction not to eat from the tree of knowledge of good and evil and shares the forbidden fruit (not yet defined as an apple[481]) with her husband. An angry God then banishes the couple from the Garden of Eden.[482]

In the spirit of Genesis 1, leading theologians of the Eastern tradition, such as Irenaeus, Clement and Origen, emphasised that human beings were made in the image of their maker, with Christ

198

revealing and restoring what had been obscured by sin.[483] In contrast, relying on Genesis 3, Catholic writers of the third and fourth century focused on the Fall from God's created paradise, and the need for redemption from a corrupt world.[484]

Nevertheless, not even the most pessimistic Latin yet professed what became the doctrine of original sin.[485] This is unsurprising, given that in neither creation story is the word 'sin' ever used. The punishment for disobeying God was, for Eve, labour pains and submission to her husband; for Adam, it was toil and work. No one was damned. And nowhere in the Old Testament was there any suggestion that the wrongdoing of the very first humans was transmitted to their descendants.[486]

The idea of original sin arose from centuries of discussion and debate on the meaning of the life, death and resurrection of Jesus, rather than from any literal reading of scripture. The challenge for early Christians was to explain in what sense Christ was a universal saviour: from what, exactly, did *everyone* need to be saved? Christianity's conundrum was how to answer this question without compromising its message of an all-loving and all-powerful creator.

Part of the solution was provided by St Paul, who imagined Christ as the new Adam, who had come to put right humanity's fractured relationship with God that started with the first Adam.[487] However, Paul suggested that the permanent punishment for Adam's sin was physical death – which Jesus had overcome. He never wrote that all humans had inherited the sin of Adam and faced the wrath and judgement of God because of this.

Reinterpretation of Paul occurred in the context of an extreme distrust of sex, which was part of a wider neo-Platonic distrust of the body.[488] Some among the expanding number of professed celibates within the early Christian community believed that the knowledge the first humans gained from eating the forbidden fruit was specifically carnal, and that this had separated people from God ever since. Extreme views on the evil of sexuality were associated with Jesus having being born of a virgin (even though no link between the holiness of Jesus and his conception was made in the Gospels). It was increasingly assumed that anyone who experienced lust, married or not, was participating in sin, and this encouraged the idea that since all people had sexual desires, all must be innately sinful.

But the most significant popular foundation to the doctrine of original sin was a custom that initially lacked any theological justification: infant baptism. Jesus himself had been baptised as an adult, and early Christians followed this example. Yet from the second century the baptism of babies became widespread. It was not surprising, given the high infant mortality rates, that parents embraced a ceremony which proffered a blessing on their newborn, but baptism was meant to wash away sin – and what sin could a baby have committed, other than one that was innate to human nature?

Linking original sin to baptism had the added advantage of allowing the Catholic Church to assert a monopoly over salvation. At a time when the competition for souls was rife within and beyond Christianity, there was a competitive advantage in depicting Catholic baptism, the rite of entry to the 'universal' church, as the only sure path to salvation. Many a loving but doubting parent would come to accept that it was better to be safe than eternally sorry.

Nevertheless, those who justified infant baptism before the fifth century retained diverse views on its precise meaning, none of which *directly* corresponded with the doctrine of original sin.[489] The point is that while the three factors discussed – a concern to explain the necessity of universal salvation through Christ, a distrust of sexual desire and the popularity of infant baptism – suggested that human beings were innately bad, there was as yet no direct link between these matters and the doctrine of original sin.

Indeed, because Greek and Roman philosophy emphasised a person's inability to avoid sin or evade his or her destiny, most early Christian thinkers emphasised the alternative to pagan fatalism: free will and responsibility.[490] Furthermore, Gnostic critics of

Orthodox Christianity articulated an acute dilemma: if human beings are created good, how can they have sinned; if they are flawed, how can the creator be wholly good? The Gnostics argued that the Fall had made the whole material universe – including physical bodies – evil, and sin inevitable. Christian apologists countered that there had been no corruption of creation, and emphasised people's capacity to *choose* good or evil.[491]

For these and other political and theological reasons, for more than three hundred years after the death of Jesus church teaching on human nature and divine salvation was the subject of widespread debate across a far-flung empire. None of the questions to which the doctrine of original sin would respond had a settled answer.

Such was the legitimate diversity of opinion that it was not until the fourth century that serious attempts were made to impose a consistent set of teachings on the whole church. By now Christianity was the dominant state religion of the Roman Empire, and interpretation of the faith was tied to questions of political and social order.[492] In the third century, Clement of Alexandria could point to the political radicalism latent in Adam and Eve to encourage Christians to stand firm in the face of persecution: 'Since God had made every human "in his image" [then] I would ask you, does it not seem to you monstrous that you – human beings who are God's own handiwork – should be subjected to another master, and, even worse, serve a tyrant instead of God, the true king?'[493] By the late fourth century, the number and status of Christian citizens meant such sentiments posed a potent threat to imperial order.

As theology and politics intertwined, an anonymous Latin, referred to as Ambrosiaster, fatefully popularised a mistranslation of Paul's letter to the Romans. The original Greek text had Paul saying that, after Adam, death spread to all *because all have sinned*. The Latin Vulgate version was that death spread to all through Adam, *in whom* all sinned. Ambrosiaster's logic was extended by Ambrose of Milan, who linked Christ's sinlessness to the virginal conception.[494]

Poor Greek and a pragmatic theology had ensured that the final building blocks of the doctrine of original sin were in place.

But why was it only in the West that emperors and popes would proclaim that human beings were born bad and guilty, and thus subject to the just condemnation of God? It is unlikely to be a coincidence that this gloomiest of perspectives on human nature received official backing in the increasingly chaotic Western empire of the early fifth century, even as a more optimistic analysis persisted in the comparatively secure East. Perhaps it was only in the context of a crumbling state that the need to assert ecclesiastical authority over sinful human beings became pressing. Certainly, it was only after the sack of Rome in 410, when the aristocracy of the ancient world was exposed to the horror of which human beings were capable, that the idea of original sin become a doctrine of the church. And even then it took a theological genius, Augustine, Bishop of Hippo, to formulate from the Latin tradition and from his own inner anguish a doctrine that would buttress believers as the ancient order collapsed.

Acknowledgements

My great-great-grandfather, Major Flintham Peet, was a Wesleyan minister who, in the evangelical custom of his day, kept a journal. In 1863 the young man was 'reading Wesley on Original Sin' but reported that he had 'got on very slowly with it so far'. That the book was hard work was not wholly the fault of John Wesley, who was a fine writer with too little time for editing. Original sin is a strange doctrine that makes for idiosyncratic books. While reading them, I have often felt in solidarity with Anselm, the twelfth-century Archbishop of Canterbury, who testified that he 'knew nothing' because 'the weight of original sin was dragging me down'.

But immersion in original sin has also had a surprising upside. I began this book scornful of a barbaric doctrine which I suspected was integral to what had gone wrong in Western Christianity. I finish it with an undiminished conviction that to see a newborn baby as a sinner who has inherited the guilt of a mythical first parent is closer to mental illness than to healthy religion, but more aware than ever what a fine line it is between madness and truth. I owe much to those who believed in the doctrine, but my debt is greater still to those courageous souls who upheld the tradition which resisted it. I am equally indebted to those fine contemporary scholars, such as Euan Cameron and Diarmaid MacCulloch, whose books make the culture of Christendom accessible.

Many other people have helped me navigate sin's troubled waters. I thank those who read drafts of the manuscript in part or in full:

Keith Jacobs, David Treanor, Aidan Davison, John Armstrong and Paul Hazel. Information and support on the journey was provided by Angela Marquis, Andreas Loewe, Andrew Harwood, Peter Ryan, Grant Finlay, Penny Edman, Don Pitcher, Jo Flanagan, Rick Tipping, Remo Di Benedetto, Dennis Blachford, Chris Tomlinson, June Pattinson, Hans-Jakob Pfenninger, Tony Spandler, Peter Millar, Fran Reams, Gary Fox and Mark Danner. Staff at the then School of Geography and Environmental Studies at the University of Tasmania, where I am an honorary associate, have provided critical support, as have the staff of the university library. I thank especially the efficient and friendly team in Document Delivery.

I am a writer who needs solitude, and Mark Delaney, David Fulton and Mark Caswell helped create a beautiful writing space out of an old caravan. Down at Eggs and Bacon Bay, Wendy and Casey Overeem, Anne Le Fevre and Terry Dyer kept a caring eye on head office and were good friends to me and Henry, a Jack Russell denier of original sin.

Immersion in sin also requires that there be regular distractions, and my Friday BBQ friends, especially Adge Ashcroft, Trevor Bramich, Heather Nielsen and Suzanne Vincent, have helped keep the project in perspective, as have my creative sisters, Catherine Campbell and Margaret Boyce, and their respective clans. My parents, Peter and Lorinne Boyce, provided support in many different ways – without them the writing would have stalled – as did my parents-in-law, Mary Bingham and Bill Bingham.

My children, Clare and William, provide evidence every day of the truth of original blessing, and are proof that, whatever truths were revealed by original sin, it got the essence of human beings profoundly wrong.

My wife, Emma Bingham, provided the foundation for the writing of this book through her faith, her openness to life's surprises and her hard work as a neonatal intensive care nurse. She also has Methodist ministers in her ancestry, and we share a spirituality which, although it bears very little resemblance to theirs, honours its inheritance. Like our love, it is largely beyond words.

As with my previous two books, *Born Bad* has been very much a joint project with Black Inc., and especially with my friend and publisher, Chris Feik. The book's ambitious reach and the limits of its author meant that whatever clarity has been achieved is in large measure due to his scholarship and skill. It was also a privilege to work with Julian Welch for the first time – a wise wordsmith in a talented team. I thank everyone at this wonderful publishing house, including its courageous founder, Morry Schwartz, who is doing more than any other person in Australia to free our nation's public conversation from the shackles imposed by self-interested moguls.

I also want to acknowledge everyone who has purchased one of my previous books. I received no grant or wage to support the research and writing of *Born Bad*, and without the generosity of book buyers it could not have been written. I owe a special thanks to those who have visited me at Salamanca Market; your words and presence encouraged me to keep writing. As with the end of original sin, both the death of the book and the collapse of community have been called much too soon.

James Boyce
Hobart, April 2014

NOTES

1 Cited in William Poole, *Milton and the Idea of the Fall*, Cambridge University Press, Cambridge, 2005, p. 310.

2 Eastern theologians sometimes refer to Adam's sin as the 'original' sin, meaning the *first* sin, but their theological teaching concerning this is quite distinct from the Western doctrine of original sin, which uniquely concerns an inherited guilt passed on to every human being.

3 No theologian, from the sixth century to the present day, would say that there is evil in created human nature; that *would* be a slight on a loving God. Strictly speaking, original sin is more akin to a disease or injury which is solely the fault of Adam, not the creator. But given that it is a disease with which *every* individual is born, and that there is no possibility of prevention, it becomes a semantic technicality to deny that human nature itself has not been corrupted. The language of most discussion on original sin has always accepted this. As John Calvin put it: 'We say ... that man is corrupted by a natural depravity, but which did not originate from nature' (John Calvin, *Institutes of the Christian Religion, In Two Volumes*, Presbyterian Board of Christian Education, Philadelphia, 1936, p. 227).

4 Carl Jung, Basel Seminar 1934, cited in Richard Webster, *Why Freud Was Wrong: Sin, Science and Psychoanalysis*, The Orwell Press, Oxford, 2005 [1995], p. 387. Webster has been one of the few writers to document how the 'immense historical significance' and 'deep psychological appeal' of original sin has made it 'an essential part of the heritage of modern intellectual culture' (Webster, *Why Freud Was Wrong*, p. 315).

5 Augustine, 'Unfinished Work in Answer to Julian', in *Answer to the Pelagians III (The Works of St Augustine: A Translation for the 21st Century*, volume I/25), introduced, translated and with notes by Roland J. Teske, New City Press, New York, 1999, p. 356.

6 Readers who are particularly interested in the theological and cultural context in which Augustine's doctrine of original sin was formulated might prefer to read the appendix of this book first.

7   Augustine does not give his partner a name but this may have been from a concern to protect her reputation, as she was a Catholic also living in North Africa.

8   Augustine, *The Confessions of St Augustine*, translated by Tobie Matthew, revised by Dom Roger Hudleston, Fontana Books, Glasgow, 1957 [1923], pp. 160–61. I use this ninety-year-old translation because, despite (or perhaps because of) its archaic language, it captures the spirit of the personal struggle more effectively than more modern versions of *Confessions*.

9   Augustine, *The Confessions of St Augustine*, translated by Tobie Matthew, pp. 166–79.

10 During his twenties, Augustine had been for a few years a follower of Mani, who taught that all dimensions of the physical world were the domain of an evil power, but by now he was sure that such beliefs were irreconcilable with the Christian belief in the goodness of a creator God.

11 Augustine, *The Confessions of St Augustine*, translated by Tobie Matthew, pp. 167–88.

12 Augustine, *The Confessions of St Augustine*, translated by Tobie Matthew, pp. 201, 189–90.

13 Augustine, *Confessions of a Sinner*, Penguin, London, 2004, pp. 14–16.

14 Adeodatus appears as the interlocutor in a dialogue between father and son in *The Blessed Life* and was a significant contributor to *The Teacher*. Augustine once wrote that 'the grandeur of his mind filled me with a kind of terror'.

15 The theological and customary context from which Augustine formulated the doctrine of original sin is set out in the appendix of this book.

16 Peter Brown, *Augustine of Hippo: A Biography* (new edition with an epilogue), University of California Press, Berkeley & Los Angeles, 2000, p. 258.

17 Augustine, *Confessions of a Sinner*, Chapter X.

18 Augustine, *A Treatise on the Grace of Christ*, p. 255.

19 Augustine, *On Christian Teaching*, translated, introduced and with notes by R. P. H. Green, Oxford University Press, Oxford, 2008, p. 19.

20 Augustine, *On Christian Teaching*, p. 19.

21 Peter Brown, *Through the Eye of a Needle: Wealth, the Fall of Rome, and the Making of Christianity in the West, 350–550 AD*, Princeton University Press, Princeton and Oxford, 2012, p. 33.

22 Brown, *Augustine of Hippo*, pp. 232–35.

23 Although by the time he wrote *Confessions* Augustine was clear that human beings had inherited the sin of Adam and were thus inherently attracted to sin, for the first decade after his conversion he had remained resolute in affirming that people retained the free will to *choose* good or evil. In *On Free Will*, drawing on his own sexual history, he linked sin to

the 'compulsive force of habit' (or 'the pleasure of past actions amplified in memory to the point where compulsion sets in'); see Brown, *Augustine of Hippo*, p. 143.

24 Brown, *Augustine of Hippo*, pp. 409–10; Charles Hill, *Making Sense of Faith: An Introduction to Theology*, E. J. Dwyer, Alexandria, 1995, p. 14.

25 The other two tracts known to have been written by Pelagius were a profession of faith he published to reassure the Catholic authorities of his orthodoxy, and a commentary on the epistles of Paul.

26 Pelagius, 'Letter to Demetrias', in Robert Van de Weyer (ed.), *The Letters of Pelagius: Celtic Soul Friend*, Arthur James, Eversham, 1995, p. 3.

27 Ibid., p. 4.

28 Ibid., p. 11.

29 Ibid., p. 19.

30 As R. A. Markus has observed, Pelagius did not reject 'an established and recognized "orthodoxy" but was "breaking rules not yet made"' (R. A. Markus, *Sacred and Secular: Studies on Augustine and Latin Christianity*, Ashgate Variorum, Farnham, 1994, p. 215.

31 John Ferguson, *Pelagius: A Historical and Theological Study*, W. Heffer & Sons, Cambridge, 1956, pp. 44–47.

32 Augustine initially published two books, *Merit and the Forgiveness of Sins* and *On Nature and Grace*. The latter, written in 415, was a direct rebuttal of Pelagius' work *On Nature*. Augustine brought his responses together in *A Treatise on the Grace of Christ, and On Original Sin Written Against Pelagius and Caelestius in the Year 418*.

33 Augustine, *A Treatise on the Grace of Christ, and On Original Sin*, Kessinger Publishing, Whitefish, pp. 245–50.

34 Lewis Ayres, 'Articulating Identity', in Frances Young, Lewis Ayres and Andrew Louth (eds), *The Cambridge History of Early Christian Literature*, Cambridge University Press, Cambridge, 2004, pp. 414–63, 455–56; Augustine, 'Unfinished Work in Answer to Julian', in *Answer to the Pelagians III* (*The Works of St Augustine: A Translation for the 21st Century*, volume I/25), introduced, translated and with notes by Roland J. Teske, New City Press, New York, 1999, p. 13.

35 Julian was born between 380 and 386, and had studied in Rome while Pelagius was probably teaching there. He married a bishop's daughter and came to prominence through his efforts to combat the famine that came in the wake of the Gothic plunder of southern Italy; he sold most of his own estates in the process. After he was exiled from Italy, Julian lived with Theodore, Bishop of Mopsuestia (who wrote a treatise called *Against the Defenders of Original Sin*). After Theodore's death, Julian moved to Constantinople, where he lived with some of the other deposed Italian bishops until he died

around 454. See Brown, *Augustine of Hippo*, p. 352; Frances Young, Lewis Ayres and Andrew Louth (eds), *The Cambridge History of Early Christian Literature*, pp. 347–48; Jaroslav Pelikan, *The Christian Tradition: A History of the Development of Doctrine. Volume 1: The Emergence of the Catholic Tradition (100–600)*, University of Chicago Press, Chicago, 1971, p. 285.

36 Peter Brown has pointed out that 'both Augustine and Julian ... knew that imperial laws were only the opening shots. A bitter war of words to sway public opinion was bound to follow' (Brown, *Through the Eye of a Needle*, pp. 376–77).

37 Augustine, 'The Punishment and the Forgiveness of Sins and the Baptism of Little Ones, the Spirit and the Letter ... The Grace of Christ and Original Sin, The Nature and Origin of the Soul', in *Answer to the Pelagians I (The Works of St Augustine: A Translation for the 21st Century*, volume I/23), introduced, translated and with notes by Roland J. Teske, New City Press, New York, 1997, pp. 50, 53.

38 Augustine, 'Marriage and Desire: Answer to the Two Letters of the Pelagians, Answer to Julian', in *Answer to the Pelagians II (The Works of St Augustine: A Translation for the 21st Century*, volume I/24), introduced, translated and with notes by Roland J. Teske, New City Press, New York, 1998, p. 93.

39 Augustine, 'Unfinished Work in Answer to Julian', in *The Works of St Augustine*, 1999, p. 420.

40 Ibid., pp. 420, 393.

41 Ibid., pp. 362–63, 415–16, 424–25.

42 Ibid., pp. 432, 436.

43 Peter Brown, *Augustine of Hippo*, p. 390.

44 Julian saw Adam's sin as a representative example of the consequences of free will: 'Who told you that the sin of Adam was much greater than that of Cain?' he asked (Augustine, 'Unfinished Work in Answer to Julian', pp. 119, 661).

45 Augustine, 'Unfinished Work in Answer to Julian', pp. 354–55, 360, 683.

46 1 Timothy 2:4; Pelikan, *The Christian Tradition*, p. 325.

47 Augustine, 'To the Monks of Hadrumetum and Provence' and 'A Letter of Hilary to Augustine', in *Answer to the Pelagians IV (The Works of St Augustine: A Translation for the 21st Century*, volume I/26), introduced, translated and with notes by Roland J. Teske, New City Press, New York, 1999, pp. 60–64.

48 Diarmaid MacCulloch, *Christianity: The First Three Thousand Years*, Viking, New York, 2010, p. 317; Michael W. Herren and Shirley Ann Brown, *Christ in Celtic Christianity: Britain and Ireland from the Fifth to the Tenth Century*, The Boydell Press, Woodbridge, 2002, p. 79; Pelikan, *The Christian Tradition*, pp. 323–24. As a direct response to Cassian's critique, in 432 a

local disciple of Augustine, Prosper of Aquitaine, wrote *Contra Collatorem* (*Against the Sermonizer*). Prosper, who would be closely connected with the suppression of Pelagianism in Britain and Ireland, accused Cassian of sympathy with the heretic Pelagius (Cassian was not named directly, but it was clear that he was Prosper's target). Nevertheless, the 'semi-Pelagian' views (as they came to be called) described by Hilarius seemed to have remained widespread in Gaul for the next century. From 433 until about 460, the monastery at Lérins was headed by a Briton, Faustus, whose sympathy for Cassian did not stop him becoming an influential bishop of Riez until his death in about 495. See Herren and Brown, *Christ in Celtic Christianity*, p. 69; Brown, *Through the Eye of a Needle*, pp. 426–27.

49 Tatha Wiley, *Original Sin: Origins, Developments, Contemporary Meanings*, Paulist Press, New York, 2002, p.73; G. Vandervelde, *Original Sin: Two Major Trends in Contemporary Roman Catholic Interpretation*, Rodopi NV, Amsterdam, 1975, pp. 22–26.

50 Phillip Newell, *Listening to the Heartbeat of God: A Celtic Spirituality*, SPCK, London, 1997, p. 34.

51 John 3:3; my emphasis.

52 MacCulloch, *Christianity*, p. 338.

53 The ritual Patrick may have experienced in place of baptism was proscribed in the canon of the Penitential of Cummian in seventh-century Ireland: 'One who instead of baptism blesses a little infant shall do penance for a year ...' Even the seemingly trivial argument over the date of Easter was much more significant than it appears. The Roman authorities recognised that the Celtic custom of dating Easter by the Jewish celebration of Passover characterised Easter primarily as an observance of Christ's suffering rather than of his resurrection. The Celts put comparatively less emphasis on the resurrection precisely because this could not be imitated by other human beings, preferring to focus on Christ's determination to follow God even to the point of death, a choice which all Christians were called to emulate. See Herren & Brown, *Christ in Celtic Christianity*, pp. 122–23, 87–88.

54 More certain is Herren and Brown's conclusion that although there was a wide diversity of theological opinion within Britain (as elsewhere), 'one is very hard pressed to find representatives of Augustinian theology ... much before the middle of the seventh century, and then, primarily in the south of Ireland' (ibid., p. 278).

55 Bede, *Ecclesiastical History of the English Nation*, translated by the Rev. Lewis Gidley, James Parker and Co., Oxford, 1870, pp. 43–44.

56 Bede, *Ecclesiastical History of the English Nation*, pp. 68–70.

57 Bede, *Ecclesiastical History of the English Nation*, p. 180.

58 Despite papal intervention, Pelagian texts continued to circulate widely in

Britain. In the preface of his *Commentary on Canticles*, Bede warned readers to 'take great care when they read some short works by Julian of Eclanum, a bishop from Campania, which he composed on the same book ... lest on account of his abundance of seductive eloquence they fall into the point of baneful doctrine'. Bede also discussed Julian's *On Love* in some detail, and quotes extensively from another of Julian's works, *On the Good of Constancy*, as well as from Pelagius' *Letter to Demetrias*. Pelagius' commentary on Paul was also well known in the eighth and ninth centuries, and was cited a number of times in Irish writing of the period. Significantly, Pelagius' writings were cited under his own name rather than anonymously. See Herren & Brown, *Christ in Celtic Christianity*, p. 98.

59 Herren & Brown, *Christ in Celtic Christianity*, pp. 88–89.

60 Herren & Brown, *Christ in Celtic Christianity*, pp. 99–100.

61 Newell, *Listening to the Heartbeat of God*, pp. 31–32; Bede, *Ecclesiastical History of the English Nation*, pp. 263–271.

62 When Bede finished writing his history in 731, he was able to record that 'Catholic peace and truth with the universal church' had been established with the Picts and the Scots, but that the Britons were still 'for the most part, through their cherished hatred ... hostile to the nation of the Angles, and wrongfully, and from evil customs, oppose the appointed paschal feast of the whole Catholic Church' (Bede, *Ecclesiastical History of the English Nation*, p. 497).

63 Those that survived into the nineteenth century were documented by Alexander Carmichael and are collated in *Carmina Gadelica: Hymns and Incantations* (Floris Books, Edinburgh, 1992).

64 The quotations from St Francis are given in *The Message of St Francis*, Frances Lincoln, London, 1998, pp. 10, 22, 36.

65 As a young woman, Heloise got pregnant and had a son to Abelard, her tutor, while still living in her uncle's house. The couple were secretly married, but Heloise was subsequently placed in a convent and her influential uncle had Abelard castrated. The emasculated lover withdrew to a monastery, where he moderated not just his lifestyle but also, to some extent, his theology to better to fit the times. Heloise maintained her love for Abelard and refused to see her relationship with him as a sin or a cause for shame, even after she became an abbess.

66 Abelard argued that, through faith in Christ, the 'love of God who first loved us is awakened in our hearts so that we are freed from the power of sin and the Devil'. See Leif Grane, *Peter Abelard: Philosophy and Christianity in the Middle Ages*, George Allen and Unwin, London, 1970, pp. 102–04; Constant J. Mews, *Abelard and Heloise*, Oxford University Press, Oxford, 2005, pp. 191–93.

67 Abelard asserted: 'If the marriage bed or the eating of delicious foods was permitted from the first day of our creation, when we lived in Paradise without sin, who can prove that we sin in these pleasures as long as we do not pass the permitted limits?' See Roberta Anderson and Dominic Aidan Bellenger, *Medieval Worlds: A Sourcebook*, Routledge, London and New York, 2003, pp. 193–94.

68 Jeffrey B. Russell, *Religious Dissent in the Middle Ages*, John Wiley & Sons, New York, 1971, pp. 79–82.

69 Gary Anderson has pointed out that during the Second Temple period, an era in which some of the more recent books of the Hebrew scriptures were written, the metaphor of sin as a 'burden' was replaced by that of sin as a 'debt'. The key influence here, he suggests, was the wide use of Aramaic, because in this language 'the word for a debt that one owes a lender ... is the standard term for denoting sin'. While the general conception of sin as a debt owed to God can be found in the later Hebrew scriptures, Anselm was the first writer to integrate this understanding of sin with a theory of atonement. See Gary A. Anderson, *Sin: A History*, Yale University Press, New Haven, 2010, pp. 27, 189–99.

70 Anselm of Canterbury, *Monologion, Proslogion, Debate with Gaunilo, and a Meditation on Human Redemption*, edited and translated by Jasper Hopkins and Herbert Richardson, The Edwin Mellen Press, Toronto and New York, 1975, pp. 139–43. Whereas Augustine had understood the consequence of original sin to be an innate human desire to sin, Anselm defined it as the absence of 'owed' justice. In *Why God Became Man*, Anselm explains that the 'justice' that has been lost because of Adam's rebellion was the conformity of the human will to God's will, meaning that sin was now 'natural' or integral to the human condition (Anselm used the terms 'original sin' and 'natural sin' interchangeably). There was no possibility that human beings could repay the debt they owed to God, since, as a result of original sin, the will of human beings had been disconnected from that of God, but Christ's death on the cross had paid this debt in full for all who believed in him through the agency of his church. Because Christ died *for* (or *in place of*) each human being, this theory is sometimes called the penal substitution model of atonement.

71 Anselm of Canterbury, *Monologion, Proslogion, Debate with Gaunilo, and a Meditation on Human Redemption*, p. 143.

72 Diarmaid MacCulloch, *Reformation: Europe's House Divided 1490–1700*, Penguin, London, 2003, pp. 412–13.

73 Thomas Aquinas, *On the Power of God, First Book*, Burn Oates & Washbourne, London, 1932, p. 123.

74 John Hick, *Evil and the God of Love*, Macmillan, London, 1977, p. 94.

75 See Rudi A. Te Velde, 'Evil Sin and Death: Thomas Aquinas on Original Sin', in Rik Van Nieuwenhove and Joseph Wawrykow (eds), *The Theology of Thomas Aquinas*, University of Notre Dame Press, Notre Dame, 2005, pp. 145–166.

76 Recent scholarship has argued that Augustine remained important to Aquinas, but, as Norman Powell Williams pointed out over eighty years ago, it remains true that 'such a highly artificial and abstract notion as that of the mere non-possession of certain splendid endowments, which were believed to have for a brief space belonged the remote ancestor of human-kind, had little power to weigh upon men's consciences or even to excite their intellectual interest' (Williams, *The Ideas of the Fall and of Original Sin: A Historical and Critical Study*, Longmans, Green and Co, London, 1927, p. 418). For a discussion on the relation between the theology of Aquinas and Augustine, see Michael Dauphinais, Barry David and Matthew Levering (eds), *Aquinas the Augustinian*, The Catholic University of America Press, Washington DC, 2007.

77 Peter S. Eardley and Carl N. Still, *Aquinas: A Guide for the Perplexed*, Continuum, London, 2010, pp. 3–5.

78 Nominalist beliefs broadened into a practice of personal piety in the fifteenth century known as *Devotio Moderna*. Its most famous adherent was Thomas a Kempis, who wrote the spiritual classic *The Imitation of Christ* (see MacCulloch, *Reformation*, pp. 111–12; 564–67

79 Richard Tarnas, *The Passions of the Western Mind: Understanding the Ideas that Have Shaped Our World View*, Pimlico, London, 2010, pp. 212–218.

80 Euan Cameron, *The European Reformation* (second edition), Oxford University Press, Oxford, 2012, p. 15.

81 R. N. Swanson, *Religion and Devotion in Europe, c.1215–c.1515*, Cambridge University Press, Cambridge, 1995, p. 217.

82 MacCulloch, *Reformation*, pp. 555–57.

83 Sir Richard Southern's thesis concerning the consequences of the developments of parishes is discussed in MacCulloch, *Christianity*, pp. 369–70. It was the Fourth Lateran Council that imposed on all Catholics an obligation of penance or confession to their parish priest once a year, and communion at least at Easter (see Swanson, *Religion and Devotion in Europe c.1215–c.1515*, pp. 33–41).

84 Elizabeth Alvilda Petroff, *Body and Soul: Essays on Medieval Women and Mysticism*, Oxford University Press, Oxford, 1994, p. 166.

85 The giants of Eastern Christianity had not challenged a gender stereotype that reflected the norms of Jewish, Roman and Greek culture. Unconstrained by the doctrine of original sin, in contrast to Augustine, they enthusiastically blamed Eve for the Fall. Irenaeus argued that, 'having

become disobedient, [Eve] was made the cause of death, both to herself and to the entire human race'. Origen believed that 'what is seen with the eyes of the creator is masculine, and not feminine, for God does not stoop to look upon what is feminine and of the flesh'. John Chrysostom claimed that 'the women taught once, and deceived all'. And Tertullian, in his exhortation to Christian women (c. 202), directly warned his female readers that because 'you are ... Eve [and] the sentence of God on this sex of yours lives in this age ... *you* are the devil's gateway: *you* are the unsealer of that (forbidden) tree: *you* are the first deserter of the divine law: *you* are she who persuaded him whom the devil was not valiant enough to attack. *You* destroyed so easily God's image, man. On account of your desert – that is, death – even the Son of Man had to die.' See Grace M. Jantzen, *Power, Gender and Christian Mysticism*, Cambridge University Press, Cambridge, 1995, pp. 45–47; Tatha Wiley, *Original Sin: Origins, Developments, Contemporary Meanings*, Paulist Press, New York & Mahwah, pp. 155–58.

86 Aristotle's perspective on women was grounded in physiology: when the male seed reached its full expression, a boy was born, but when a defect occurred and the seed did not fully develop, a female resulted. This perspective on the character of women underpinned the determined witch-hunts of the Dominican inquisitors. Their fifteenth-century manual, *Malleus Maleficarum (The Witches' Hammer)*, states: 'There was a defect in the formation of the first woman, since she was formed from the bent rib, the rib of the breast which is bent in the contrary direction to a man ... And since through the first defect in their intelligence they are always more prone to abjure the faith, so through their second defect of inordinate passions, they search for, brood over and inflict various vengeances, either by witchcraft or some other means. Wherefore it is no wonder that so great a number of witches exist in this sex' (cited in Rosemary Radford Ruether, 'Women in Christianity', in John Bowden (ed), *Christianity: The Complete Guide*, Continuum, London, 2005, p. 1234).

87 Ruether, 'Women in Christianity', p. 1223. Even a woman's fertility, a power honoured in almost every spiritual tradition in human history, was removed when the church accepted that the womb was only a passive receptacle for the male seed, which contained all that was needed for a new life.

88 The resurrection of Eve was associated with the worship of Mary, the now permanently virginal mother of God, who was understood to have redeemed the sin of her sexually active ancestor. This left earthly women to oscillate between the pit (of Eve) and the pedestal (of Mary). Nuns might aspire to imitate the latter, but for married women, sex bound them in chains to the ever-dangerous Eve. The co-dependence of Eve and Mary was

reflected in medieval art. In the early Christian catacombs, Eve, depicted as a beautiful nude woman with long hair who held up an apple as the sign of her disobedience, had usually been placed alongside Adam in scenes of Paradise. But in the Middle Ages, Eve is often depicted without her husband but alongside the Madonna, with the image aiming to compare the two women. In late medieval and Renaissance art, Eve and the Devil become so intertwined that the Serpent sometimes has her head and torso. See Christine Peters, *Patterns of Piety, Women, Gender and Religion in Late Medieval and Reformation England*, Cambridge University Press, Cambridge, 2003, p. 130; Diane Apostolos-Cappadona, *Dictionary of Christian Art*, Continuum, New York, 1994, pp. 125–29.

89 Sandy Bardsley, *Women's Roles in the Middle Ages*, Greenwood Press, Westport, 2007, pp. 172–73.

90 Moreover, because Eve's starring role in the Fall was intertwined with the divinisation of Mary, the creation story helped foster belief in a *female* propensity for piety. Celibate women actively established centres of comparative freedom in convents and hermitages, but it was also increasingly believed that a woman's focus on the home predisposed her to God. This shift was reflected in the increasing numbers of women who were married by a priest (although canon law at this time still acknowledged that this was not necessary for a marriage to be valid). In the Sarrum wedding liturgy, which gradually spread throughout the British Isles from the mid-eleventh century, there is a blessing on the woman alone, reflecting perhaps *both* her vulnerability to sin and her special status in the household: 'O God by whom woman is joined to man, and the union, instituted in the beginning, is gifted with that blessings, which alone has not been taken away either through the punishment of original sin … look graciously, we beseech thee, on this thy handmaiden' (see Christine Peters, *Patterns of Piety, Women, Gender and Religion in Late Medieval and Reformation England*, Cambridge University Press, Cambridge, 2003, pp. 346–49; Emilie Amt (ed.), *Women's Lives in Medieval Europe*, Routledge, London and New York, 1993, pp. 83–88.

91 *Women's Bible Commentary*, pp. 17–18; Elisabeth Gossmann, 'The Construction of Women's Difference', in Elisabeth Schussler Fiorenza (ed.), *The Power of Naming: A Concilium Reader in Feminist Liberation Theology*, Orbis Books, Maryknoll, and SCM Press, London, 1996, p. 204. Christine de Pizan (1365–1429) defended women's characters in *The Book of the City of Ladies* (c. 1404–05), which became the catalyst for hundreds of works on the nature of women over the next three centuries. Such was the reactionary response to this book that, two hundred years later, Lucretia Marinella was still disputing 'the most frivolous arguments' of men who 'argue that

Eve was the cause of Adam's sin and consequently of our fall and our misery'. The most common point of resistance to orthodox misogyny was to point out that even the path of redemption suggested by the author of the purportedly Pauline biblical epistle known as 1 Timothy – having children – at least implied that women were not an unfortunate accident of creation. This argument was integral to the slow sacralisation of motherhood during the late Middle Ages (see Cissie Fairchilds, *Women in Early Modern Europe 1500–1700*, Pearson Longman, Harlow, 2007, pp. 15–18; and Elisabeth Gossmann, 'The Construction of Women's Difference', p. 200).

92 Bardsley, *Women's Roles in the Middle Ages*, p. 179.

93 Euan Cameron, *The European Reformation* (second edition), Oxford University Press, Oxford, 2012, pp. 11–17.

94 Charles Taylor, *A Secular Age*, Harvard University Press, Cambridge MA, 2007, pp. 77–79.

95 Euan Cameron, *The European Reformation*, p. 4.

96 William Monter, *Ritual, Myth and Magic in Early Modern Europe*, The Harvester Press, Brighton, 1983, pp. 8–9; Swanson, *Religion and Devotion in Europe c.1215-c.1515*, pp. 182–83.

97 Lionel Rothkrug, 'Popular Religion and Holy Shrines', in James Obelkevich (ed.), *Religion and the People 800–1700*, The University of North Carolina Press, Chapel Hill, 1979, pp. 49–51.

98 Monter, *Ritual, Myth and Magic in Early Modern Europe*, pp. 10–11.

99 Euan Cameron, *The European Reformation*, p. 14.

100 While in theory this means that even a non-Catholic baptism is valid, there are so many points of uncertainty raised as regards the diverse Protestant practices that the only way to be certain that a child is correctly baptised from the perspective of the Catholic Church is to have it done by the church.

101 Barbara A. Hanawalt, *Growing up in Medieval London*, Oxford University Press, Oxford, 1993, p. 44; Christopher W. Maslanka, *Christening, Women, Men, and Monsters: Images of Baptism in Middle English Hagiography and Romance*, PhD thesis, University of Wisconsin, Madison, 2012, p. 4.

102 John Myrc, *Medieval Instructions for Parish Priests*, translated by Edward Peacock, Early English Text Society, London, 1868 (first published about 1403); Hanawalt, *Growing up in Medieval London*, p. 44.

103 Swanson, *Religion and Devotion in Europe c.1215-c.1515*, p. 31.

104 Hanawalt, *Growing up in Medieval London*, p. 45.

105 Gonsalv K. Mainberger, 'Original Sin as a "Cultural Matrix" Today', in Christopher Boureux & Christoph Theobald (eds), *Original Sin: A Code of Fallibility*, SCM Press, London, 2004, pp. 99–107, 100.

106 Alexander of Hales similarly claimed that the 'penalty is unending, but

they [unbaptised infants] will not suffer on its account, for they are unaware of the higher goods of which they have been deprived' (Henri Rondet, *Original Sin: The Patristic and Theological Background*, Alba House, New York, 1972, pp. 176–79).

107 Stearns, *Childhood in World History*, pp. 60–61.

108 Philippe Ariès, *Centuries of Childhood*, translated by Robert Baldick, Jonathan Cape, London, 1973; Michel Foucault, *Surveiller et Punir: Naissance de la Prison* [*Discipline and Punish: The Birth of the Prison*], Gallimard, Paris, 1975. For a discussion of these and other scholars who explore this theme, including Lawrence Stone and Simon Schama, see Jeroen J. H. Dekker, Bernard Kruithof, Frank Simon & Bruno Vanobbergen, 'Discoveries of Childhood in History: An Introduction', *Paedagogica Historica: International Journal of the History of Education*, vol. 48, no. 1, 2012, pp. 1–9.

109 Monter, *Ritual, Myth and Magic in Early Modern Europe*, pp. 19–21; Swanson, *Religion and Devotion in Europe c.1215–c.1515*, pp. 199–200.

110 Julian of Norwich, *Showings*, translated and introduced by Edmund Colledge & James Walsh, Paulist Press, Mahwah, 1978, pp. 299–300.

111 Matthew Fox, *Original Blessing: A Primer in Creation Spirituality*, Jeremy P. Tarcher/Putnam, New York, 2000 [1983], p. 5. I am grateful to Julian Welch for his insightful translation of *ancilla animae*.

112 Meister Eckhart, *Selected Treatises and Sermons*, translated and introduced by James M. Clark & John V. Skinner, Fontana, 1963, pp. 149–50.

113 Hildegard of Bingen, *Scivias*, translated by Mother Columba Hart & Jane Bishop, introduced by Barbara J. Newman, Paulist Press, New York, 1990, p. 9.

114 Hildegard of Bingen, *Let There be Light: Based on the Visionary Spirituality of Hildegard of Bingen*, Ave Maria Press, Notre Dame, 1997, pp. 29, 31.

115 Hildegard of Bingen, *Let There be Light*, pp. 29, 90; Hildegard of Bingen, *Scivias*, p. 86.

116 Grace M. Jantzen, *Power, Gender and Christian Mysticism*, Cambridge University Press, Cambridge, 1995, pp. 227–28.

117 Jantzen, *Power, Gender and Christian Mysticism*, pp. 228, 232–35.

118 During Mechtild's lifetime, the Beguines were increasingly targeted by the church, and she became a Cistercian in 1270.

119 Caroline Walker Bynum, *Jesus as Mother: Studies in the Spirituality of the High Middle Ages*, University of California Press, Berkeley, 1984, pp. 228–33 (my emphasis).

120 Ibid. (my emphasis).

121 Julian of Norwich, *Enfolded in Love: Daily Readings with Julian of Norwich*, Darton, Longman, Todd, London, 1996.

122 Julian's account of the Fall is as notable for who is not named as for who is:

'Adam' represents men and women; with Eve kept out of the story, gender is not an issue and women cannot be blamed.

123 Julian of Norwich, *Showings*, pp. 302–04 (my emphasis).

124 Matthew Fox, *Whee! We, Wee All the Way Home: A Guide to Sensual Prophetic Spirituality*, Bear & Company, Sante Fe, 1981, p. 20.

125 Julian of Norwich, *Enfolded in Love*.

126 Julian of Norwich, *Showings*, pp. 329–30, 305.

127 Such was the diversity of the reform agenda and its regional context that many historians no longer speak of a single *Reformation* but variously named *reformations*. While the protest against Catholicism and its regional manifestations were diverse, it is remarkable the extent to which disparate groups and individuals shared a passionate commitment to a single concept of salvation that crossed immense regional and cultural divides. The argument that this makes it appropriate to speak of *the* Reformation is developed in Cameron, *The European Reformation*, and MacCulloch, *Reformation*.

128 It is not just a matter of biographical interest that Luther found 'justification by faith alone' through Bible study. Faith could be received only by the grace of God, but the fact that this grace was transmitted to the central figure of the early Reformation through the study of 'the Word' would profoundly shape the Reformation to come.

129 Roland Bainton, *Here I Stand: Martin Luther*, Lion Publishing, Tring, 1987 [1978], p. 65.

130 These reflections were published by Luther as the *Disputation against Scholastic Theology*. He later recalled that the scholastics might be 'fine and delicate wits', but 'they neither saw nor felt Adam's fall' (Martin Luther, *The Table Talk of Martin Luther*, translated and edited by William Hazlitt, H. G. Bohn, London, 1857, pp. 235–36).

131 Cameron, *The European Reformation*, pp. 101–03.

132 The pamphlet wars of the 1520s generated 6000 separate publications in German-speaking lands, and their mass production (literally millions were printed) meant that they could sell for the price of a few hours' work for an artisan; see Andrew Pettegree, *Reformation and the Culture of Persuasion*, Cambridge University Press, Cambridge, 2005, pp. 159–60.

133 Martin Luther, *On the Bondage of the Will: Written in Answer to the Diatribe of Erasmus on Free Will*, translated by Henry Cole, W. Simpkin & R. Marshall, London, 1823 [1525], p. 231.

134 MacCulloch, *Christianity*, p. 613; Michael A. Mullett, *Martin Luther*, Routledge, London, 2004, pp. 172–74, 254.

135 Luther, *The Table Talk of Martin Luther*, p. 287. *Table Talk* is not a collection of Luther's writings, but a collection of his sayings compiled by students who shared the Luther family home. They need to be used with care, but do

provide an irreplaceable picture of the man and his thought.

136 Luther, *On the Bondage of the Will*, pp. 230–31.

137 R. Devonshire Jones, *Erasmus and Luther*, Oxford University Press, London, 1968, p. 86.

138 Personal religious motives are notoriously difficult to access from written sources (hence their sometimes shabby treatment by historians), but it is clear that 'one did not become a first-generation reformer by habit, compulsion, or default'. However they are judged, these were people of conviction. As Euan Cameron argues, 'where any evidence exists, it suggests that the reformers reached their positions only after serious and earnest heart-searching' (Cameron, *The European Reformation*, p. 131). Andrew Pettegree's analysis and conclusion are similar (*Reformation and the Culture of Persuasion*, pp. 2–3).

139 Martin Luther, *Reformation of Law and Liberty*. My overall argument is based on the thesis of Euan Cameron, *The European Reformation*.

140 Carther Linberg, 'Luther's struggle with social-ethical issues', in Donald K. McKim (ed.), *The Cambridge Companion to Martin Luther*, Cambridge University Press, Cambridge, 2004, p. 157.

141 Hieko A. Oberman, *Luther: Man between God and the Devil*, translated by Eileen Walliser-Schwarzbart, Yale University Press, New Haven, 1989, pp. 272–74.

142 Ibid.

143 Convents could be forcibly closed when an area became Protestant. Women were not always eager to leave, as convents could be places of comparative freedom for women, as well as confinement (see Cissie Fairchilds, *Women in Early Modern Europe 1500–1700*, Pearson Longman, Harlow, 2007, p. 198).

144 Oberman, *Luther*, p. 282.

145 Ibid.

146 Ibid., p. 276.

147 The seventeenth-century Dominican biographer Heinrich Seuse Denifle argued that Luther's lust was one of the main causes of the Reformation. It was Luther's sexuality which led him to believe that original sin was insuperable, and lust led him to reinterpret scripture to legitimise it (Oberman, *Luther*, p. 275).

148 Ibid., pp. 282–84.

149 Erik Erikson even argued that Luther's frequent juvenile beatings help to explain the Reformation! See Stearns, *Childhood in World History*, p. 60.

150 . Oberman, *Luther*, p. 94.

151 Ibid., p. 283. Of music, he wrote: 'It has often revived me and relieved me of heavy burdens' (ibid., p. 310).

152 Ibid., pp. 275–76.

153 Linberg, 'Luther's struggle with social-ethical issues', pp. 170–71 (a minor revision to the translation has been made by the author); Fairchilds, *Women in Early Modern Europe 1500–1700*, pp. 196–202.

154 Linberg, 'Luther's struggle with social-ethical issues', pp. 173–74.

155 Luther, *The Table Talk of Martin Luther*, p. 259; MacCulloch, *Reformation*, p. 143.

156 Jane E. Strohl, 'Luther's Spiritual Journey', in McKim (ed.), *The Cambridge Companion to Martin Luther*, pp. 160–61.

157 Luther's single-minded focus on salvation, his immersion in a medieval world view and his sanctification of daily life meant that he deplored the destruction of sacred art, remained devoted to the Eucharist and was comparatively tolerant of traditional rites and rituals.

158 Strohl, 'Luther's Spiritual Journey', pp. 155–56.

159 Diarmaid MacCulloch prefers to talk of the 'farmers war' in order to give a better sense of the class that led the uprising (MacCulloch, *Christianity*, p. 624).

160 Martin Luther, 'A Sermon on Keeping Children in School (1530)', *Luther's Works*, vol. 46, Fortress Press, Philadelphia, 1967, pp. 213–57.

161 Luther, *The Table Talk of Martin Luther*, pp. 331–32.

162 Henri Blocher, *Original Sin: Illuminating the Riddle*, Wm B. Eerdmans, Grand Rapids, 1999, p. 15.

163 G. R. Potter, *Huldrych Zwingli*, St Martins Press, New York, 1977, p. 79.

164 Potter, *Huldrych Zwingli*, pp. 38, 18.

165 Although Zwingli's theological bias suggests sympathy for the Anabaptist attempt to restore the godly lifestyle of primitive Christianity, he was as appalled as Luther at what this implied for the concept of a universal church. His conviction that God's law must not only be preached but enforced led the Zurich Council to proclaim on 7 March 1526 that 'henceforth in this city, territory and neighbourhood no man, woman or maiden shall re-baptize another, and one who shall do so ... shall without appeal be put to death by drowning'. Some people were killed in this horrific manner, but most Anabaptists fled the persecution to begin what were often decades of wandering before asylum was secured (Potter, *Huldrych Zwingli*, p. 44).

166 The immediate cause of the Swiss civil war was the attempt to reduce five inner Catholic states to submission by economic blockade. Zwingli's death and Zurich's defeat, followed by the defeat of Protestant Berne later that month, ended this fight. Peace terms were reached in November 1531, whereby parishes, communities and territories could make their own decision to stay reformed or return to 'old, true, Christian beliefs' (Potter, *Huldrych Zwingli*, pp. 136–46).

167 John Calvin, *Institutes of the Christian Religion*, translated by John Allen, First American Edition, London, 1813, p. 280.

168 The original words of the Latin title were chosen deliberately: *institutio* referred not just to the structures but also to the teachings of the church, while *religio*, not a word in common use (precisely because every citizen had been assumed to be a member of the one faith), was borrowed from classical texts to delineate the public profession of faith from the true piety which led to salvation (see Mark Greengrass, *The French Reformation*, Basil Blackwell, Oxford, 1987, pp. 24–30).

169 An example of Calvin's approach to the Bible is his conviction that the author of Genesis 'was ordained to be a teacher of the unlearned and primitive, as well as the learned', meaning he 'could not achieve this goal without descending to … crude means of instruction'. Calvin was clear that the 'six days' of creation were simply a way of designating an extended period of time (see Alister E. McGrath, *Reformation Thought: An Introduction* [second edition], Blackwell, Oxford, 1995, pp. 232–34).

170 Calvin, *Institutes of the Christian Religion*, pp. 283–85; John Calvin, *Institutes of the Christian Religion, In Two Volumes*, Presbyterian Board of Christian Education, Philadelphia, 1936, p. 331.

171 Calvin, *Institutes of the Christian Religion*, pp. 30–32.

172 Calvin, *Institutes of the Christian Religion, In Two Volumes*, p. 274, 288–89.

173 Calvin, *Institutes of the Christian Religion*, pp. 284–85; Calvin, *Institutes of the Christian Religion, In Two Volumes*, pp. 275-76, 342–45.

174 Calvin even acknowledged what many of his followers still aggressively deny: that Christians might learn from people of other religions: 'If we believe that the spirit of God is the only fountain of truth, we shall neither reject nor despise the truth itself, wherever it shall appear, unless we wish to insult the spirit of God … And shall we esteem anything laudable or excellent, which we do not recognise as proceeding from God? Let us then be ashamed of such great ingratitude … let us not forget that these are most excellent gifts of the Divine Spirit, which for the common benefit of mankind he dispenses to whomsoever he pleases' (*Institutes of the Christian Religion*, pp. 309–311).

175 Because Calvin was determined to assert that sanctification is only 'from supernatural grace', his God could ultimately dwell 'only in the faithful'. It might have 'pleased the Lord that we should be assisted in physics, logic, mathematics, and other arts and sciences, by the labour and ministry of the impious', but Calvin left no room for doubt as to where eternal righteousness lay (Calvin, *Institutes of the Christian Religion*, pp. 311, 288–90).

176 Calvin, *Institutes of the Christian Religion, In Two Volumes*, p. 277.

177 Calvin, *Institutes of the Christian Religion, In Two Volumes*, pp. 334, 318,

324; Calvin, *Institutes of the Christian Religion*, p. 525.

178 Tony Lane, *A Concise History of Christian Thought*, T&T Clark, London, 2006, p. 176.

179 There were also positive dimensions to ecclesiastical interference. By 1544 the Consistory had admonished twenty-one men for violence against their spouses, a practice which was not only legal but still ethically acceptable in most of Europe (see Fairchilds, *Women in Early Modern Europe 1500– 1700*). Four women were also punished for the same offence!

180 William Monter, *Ritual, Myth and Magic in Early Modern Europe*, The Harvester Press, Brighton, 1983, p. 45.

181 While Calvin directly repudiated every claim that moderated the totality of the impact of original sin, his theological formula moderated the practical implications of the *Institutes'* anthropology on everyday life: 'amidst this corruption of nature there is some room for Divine grace, not to purify it [human nature], but internally to restrain its operation'. God 'by his providence restrains the perverseness of our nature from breaking out into external acts, but does not purify it from within'. In short, because of God's mercy to humanity, the Fall has not 'been followed by the total destruction of our [outer] nature'. It was because of this mercy that government and church could actively construct a godly society (Calvin, *Institutes of the Christian Religion, In Two Volumes*, p. 316; Calvin, *Institutes of the Christian Religion*, pp. 311–12).

182 Robert M. Kingdon & Robert D. Linder (eds), *Calvin and Calvinism: Sources of Democracy*, D. C. Heath and Company, Lexington, 1970, pp. 15–17; Winthrop S. Hudson, 'Calvin a Source of Resistance Theory, and Therefore of Democracy', in Kingdon & Linder (eds), *Calvin and Calvinism*, pp. 17, 22.

183 Kingdon & Linder (eds), *Calvin and Calvinism*.

184 Scotland executed about 1350 witches between 1560 and 1700, about two-thirds of them between 1639 and 1670 (Monter, *Ritual, Myth and Magic in Early Modern Europe*, pp. 53–57).

185 Hamlet's famous words – 'What a piece of work is a man: how noble in reason; how infinite in faculty; in form and moving how express and admirable; in action how like an angel; in apprehension how like a god; the beauty of the world, the paragon of animals' – do not initially suggest that Shakespeare was overly constrained by Calvinistic censure. However, it is important to remember that Hamlet concludes: 'And yet to me what is this quintessence of dust?' Shakespeare's sonnets are particularly concerned with how sexual pollution corrupts human nature, which is also a theme of *Hamlet*, *Measure for Measure* and *Timon*. Milton's *Paradise Lost* depicts Adam and Eve's life in Eden, until their fateful marital dispute, as one of steady growth toward perfection through ever-increasing knowledge and

experience (including pleasure in sex). The tragedy of the Fall was not that that this fundamental purpose of life changed, but that humanity lost the chance to develop without suffering, violence, despair and death. See E. M. W. Tillyard, *The Elizabethan World Picture*, Pelican Books, Harmondsworth, 1981 [1943], pp. 11–12; Thomas Kranidas (ed.), *New Essays on Paradise Lost*, University of California Press, Berkeley, 1969, pp. 99–100, 115–17; Patrick Collinson, 'England and International Calvinism 1558–1640', in Menna Prestwich (ed.), *International Calvinism 1541–1715*, Oxford University Press, Oxford, 1986, 197–223, 213.

186 Arminianism was named after a Dutch theologian, Jacob Hermanz, better known by his Latinised name, Arminius. It says much for the influence of Calvinist thought in England that Arminianism, which was already generally accepted by Lutherans (as it would be in the next century by no less a Protestant than John Wesley), was seen as popish largely because of its denial of predestination and its apparent compromise concerning the total destruction of human nature (Michael Heyd, 'Original Sin, the Struggle for Stability, and the Rise of Moral Individualism in Late Seventeenth-Century England', in Philip Benedict & Myron P. Gutman (eds), *Early Modern Europe: From Crisis to Stability*, University of Delaware, Newark, 2005, p. 199).

187 MacCulloch, *Christianity*, p. 631.

188 The Westminster Confession of Faith, chapter 6, sections 2, 4; Newell, *Listening to the Heartbeat of God*, p. 59. In what is sometimes called 'the confessional age' in Western Europe, all Reformed churches set out a statement of correct doctrine called a confession. In every one, original sin loomed large.

189 David Zaret, *The Use and Abuse of Textual Data*, in Hartmut Lehmann (ed.), *Weber's Protestant Ethic, Origins, Evidence, Context*, Cambridge University Press, Cambridge, 1993, pp. 245–272.

190 The emphasis is mine. The ninth article of the Church of England states that 'Original Sin standeth not in the following of Adam, (as the Pelagians do vainly talk;) but it is the fault and corruption of the Nature of every man, that naturally is ingendered of the off-spring of Adam; whereby man is very far gone from original righteousness, and is of his own nature inclined to evil, so that the flesh lusteth always contrary to the spirit; and therefore in every person born into this world, it deserveth God's wrath and condemnation. And this infection of nature doth remain, yea in them that are re-generated; whereby the lust of the flesh ... is not subject to the Law of God. And although there is no condemnation for them that believe and are baptized, yet the Apostle doth confess that concupiscence and lust hath of itself the nature of sin' (Articles of Religion, *The Book of Common Prayer*, SPCK, London, pp. 688–89).

191 Linda Colley, *Britons: Forging the Nation 1707–1837*, Yale University Press, New Haven, 1992, p. 28.

192 MacCulloch, *Reformation*, p. 485.

193 Christopher Hill, *Reformation to Industrial Revolution*, Penguin, Harmondsworth, 1969, pp. 109–10.

194 Alexandra Walsham, *The Reformation of the Landscape: Religion, Identity, and Memory in Early Modern Britain and Ireland*, Oxford University Press, Oxford, 2011, pp. 9–14, 111, 115.

195 Euan Cameron, *The European Reformation*, pp. 422–33.

196 Historians from both sides of this debate sometimes uncritically reproduce Reformation-era judgements about what is true Christianity. The eminent English social historian Christopher Hill believed that in 'the fifteenth to seventeenth centuries ... all over Europe, Christianity was going over to the offensive against paganism, trying, perhaps for the first time, to eliminate its hold on popular feelings'. Hill documents how the Protestant leaders attacked 'magic' of all kinds and beliefs in spirits, ghosts and witches – beliefs which he depicted as pagan on the basis that they originated in the pre-Christian era. But while there is no doubt that most Reformation activists generally saw Christianity in such terms, the people themselves would have seen no such tension between the two belief systems. It is important to remember that from the perspective of the peasants, it was the reformers' attack on local holy places and religious practices which was 'un-Christian'. As has been previously discussed, the fact that many practices and beliefs had ancient origins does not mean that they had not, through centuries of enculturation, become 'Christian' (Christopher Hill, *Reformation to Industrial Revolution*, pp. 115–16).

197 Monter, *Ritual, Myth and Magic in Early Modern Europe*, p. 46.

198 Iain McGilchrist, *The Master and his Emissary: The Divided Brain and the Making of the Modern Western World*, Yale University Press, New Haven, 2009, pp. 314–23.

199 Max Weber, *The Protestant Ethic and the Spirit of Capitalism*, translated by Talcott Parsons, Unwin University Books, London, 1965 [1930]. Weber's book was first published in Germany in 1904–05.

200 Guy Oakes, 'The Thing that Would not Die: Notes on Refutation', in Hartmut Lehmann (ed.), *Weber's Protestant Ethic, Origins, Evidence, Context*, Cambridge University Press, Cambridge, 1993, pp. 286–87.

201 Ibid.

202 Cameron, *The European Reformation*, p. 419.

203 Anthony Fletcher, *Growing Up in England: The Experience of Childhood 1600–1914*, Yale University Press, New Haven, 2010, p. 4.

204 Stephen Mintz, *Huck's Raft: A History of American Childhood*, Harvard University Press, Cambridge MA, 2004, pp. 17, 11.

205 Ibid., p. 16.

206 Ian A. McFarland, *In Adam's Fall: A Meditation on the Christian Doctrine of Original Sin*, Wiley-Blackwell, Chichester, 2010, p. lx.

207 Chloe Hooper, *The Tall Man*, Hamish Hamilton, Camberwell, 2008, p. 112.

208 Mintz, *Huck's Raft*, p. 25.

209 Ibid., pp. 13, 21.

210 Ibid., pp. 26–27. See also MacCulloch, *History of Christianity*, pp. 792–93.

211 Roger Cox, *Shaping Childhood: Themes of Uncertainty in the History of Adult–Child Relationships*, Routledge, London & New York, 1996, pp. 30–35.

212 Mintz, *Huck's Raft*, p. 31.

213 The Catholic reform movement of this period is commonly called 'the Counter-Reformation', but while this captures its responsive element it does not do justice to its independent commitment to renewal. The most straightforward way to describe the movement is simply 'the Catholic Reformation'. John O'Malley prefers the term, 'Early Modern Catholicism', as a way of 'acknowledging that the Catholic Church was subject to all the forces at play in the period and to some degree or other, agent for them' (*Trent and All That: Renaming Catholicism in the Early Modern Era*, Harvard University Press, Cambridge MA, 2002, pp. 2–10).

214 During the confusion and flux of the 1530s and early 1540s, it seemed that the Catholic and Protestant reform movements might become one. The evangelical Italian spirituality known as Valdesian theology, in which the Englishman Cardinal Reginald Pole was a leading figure, gained considerable influence in the papal court after the ascension of Pope Paul III in 1534. In 1541 a fellow Valdesian, Cardinal Contarini, gained papal approval to meet with representatives of the Protestant churches at Regensburg, where he and Luther's confidante, Philipp Melanchthon, came to a semi-accord in which agreement was reached on the major points of doctrinal difference concerning sin and salvation. But these tentative attempts to reach an understanding were angrily denounced by a group in the Curia led by Gian Pietro Caraffa, a future pope, who in 1542 succeeded in obtaining a papal bull that established the Roman Inquisition (one of whose functions was to usurp the role of formulating theological orthodoxy from the Sorbonne, which was considered to be too remote from papal control). The primary objective of the Inquisition was to construct a theological wall between the Catholic and Protestant understandings of the Christian faith. See Cameron, *The European Reformation*, pp. 136–37; O'Malley, *Trent and All That*, pp. 18, 136–42; and Robert Bireley, *The Refashioning of Catholicism 1450–1700*, Macmillan, London, 1999.

215 Opposing views were put at the Council of Trent. Cardinal Cajetan advanced the proposition that Christian infants must be able to be saved through their parents' faith, as God could not have intended that the coming of Jesus would have rendered salvation more difficult for some categories of person. But his views were censured and expunged from his collected works (see Neil Ormerod, *Grace and Disgrace: A Theology of Self-Esteem*, E. J. Dwyer, Sydney, 1992, p. 135). Trent made use of the same misquoted Biblical texts formerly employed by Augustine, even though the scholarship of Erasmus had established that Romans 5:12 had been mistranslated from the Greek in the Latin Vulgate (see Tatha Wiley, *Original Sin: Origins, Developments, Contemporary Meanings*, Paulist Press, New York, 2002, pp. 87–93; and James Allison, *The Joy of Being Wrong: Original Sin through Easter Eyes*, Crossroad, New York, 1998, pp. 280–82).

216 This position was set out in fifth canon of the council: 'The holy council confesses and perceived that in the baptized, concupiscence or a tendency to sin remains; since this is left for the struggle, it cannot harm those who do not give consent but, by the grace of God, offer strong resistance … This concupiscence the Apostle sometimes calls sin … but the holy council declares that the Catholic Church has never understood it to be called sin in the sense of being truly and properly such in those who have been regenerated, but in the sense that it is a result of sin and inclines to sin. If anyone holds a contrary view: let him be anathema.' (See Henri Rondet, *Original Sin: The Patristic and Theological Background*, 182.)

217 Uta Ranke-Heinemann, *Eunuchs for the Kingdom of Heaven: The Catholic Church and Sexuality*, Penguin, Harmondsworth, 1991, pp. 249–50.

218 The hostility the Protestants directed at the Jesuits related less to their theology (of which few would have known anything) than to their vow of obedience to the pope. In its revised statement of purpose of 1550, the Society of Jesus added 'defence of the faith' to the original aim of 'propagation of the faith', and after the death of their saintly founder they were often employed as foot soldiers in the papal cause. A positive focus was the Jesuits' establishment of schools, and they exerted enormous influence on Western culture through their unparalleled experiment in mass education. Many also became esteemed scholars in various disciplines, as well as highly influential theologians.

219 David L. Fleming, *Draw Me Into Your Friendship: A Literal Translation and a Contemporary Meaning of the Spiritual Exercises*, The Institute of Jesuit Sources, St Louis, 1996, pp. 10, 20, 50, 112.

220 Uta Ranke-Heinemann, *Eunuchs for the Kingdom of Heaven*, pp. 263–65.

221 MacCulloch, *Christianity*, p. 797.

222 O'Malley, *Trent and All That*, pp. 123–24.

223 Of all of the European countries in which the Catholic Church had been predominant before the Reformation, it was only in England, Scotland and the Scandinavian nations where it did not still have a major presence, and only in Europe's largest nation, France, did the Protestant cause seem all but defeated. Other countries with a significant Protestant presence in the sixteenth century, most notably Poland and Lithuania, also once again became overwhelmingly Catholic during the century that followed.

224 A. D. Wright, 'The Significance of the Council of Trent', *The Journal of Ecclesiastical History*, vol. 26, no. 4, 1975, pp. 357–58; Jonathan Israel, *Radical Enlightenment: Philosophy and the Making of Modernity 1650–1750*, Oxford University Press, Oxford, 2003, pp. 15–16.

225 The story of Domenico Scandella is told in detail by Lionel Rothkrug, 'Cheere and Worms: The Cosmos of a Sixteenth Century Miller', in James Obelkevich (ed.), *Religion and the People 800–1700*, University of North Carolina Press, Chapel Hill, 1979, pp. 87–168.

226 Leonardo Boff, *Good News to the Poor: A New Evangelization*, Burns and Oats, 1992, pp. 14–15.

227 David Hume, *A Treatise of Human Nature: Being an Attempt to Introduce the Experimental Method of Reasoning into Moral Subjects*, Fontana/Collins, 1978 [1739], p. 40.

228 James Petigru Boyce was the founder of the Southern Baptist Convention's first seminary. This quote is taken from his major work, *Abstract of Systematic Theology* (Founders Press, Cape Coral, 2006 [1858], pp. 249–251).

229 Francis Bacon, 'Of Atheism', in Francis Bacon, *The Essays or Counsels, Civil and Moral of Francis Ld. Verulam Viscount St Albans*, Read How You Want, Sydney, 2008, pp. 83–86; Francis Bacon, 'Of Goodness and Goodness of Nature', in Bacon, *The Essays or Counsels ...*, pp. 64–65; Aldous Huxley, *The Human Situation: Lectures at Santa Barbara 1959*, Harper and Row, New York, 1977, pp. 8–9.

230 John Murray (ed.), *The Autobiographies of Edward Gibbon*, London, 1896, p. 127; cited by Gertrude Himmelfarb, *The Roads to Modernity: The British, French, and American Enlightenments*, Vintage Books, New York, 2005, p. 40.

231 For a defence of the legitimacy of speaking of a single enlightenment, see Jonathan Israel, *Radical Enlightenment: Philosophy and the Making of Modernity 1650–1750*, Oxford University Press, Oxford, 2003, pp. v–vi.

232 Voltaire, 'Original Sin', in Voltaire, *A Philosophical Dictionary*, The University of Adelaide, 2014, http://ebooks.adelaide.edu.au/v/voltaire/dictionary/chapter353.html.

233 John Locke, 'The Reasonableness of Christianity', in John Locke, *The Selected Political Writings of John Locke*, edited by Paul E. Sigmund, W.W

Norton & Company, New York & London, 2005, pp. 209–10; W. M. Spellman, 'Locke and Original Sin', in Locke, *The Selected Political Writings of John Locke*, pp. 363–65; Michael Heyd, 'Original Sin, the Struggle for Stability, and the Rise of Moral Individualism in Late Seventeenth-Century England', in Philip Benedict & Myron P. Gutman (eds), *Early Modern Europe: From Crisis to Stability*, University of Delaware, Newark, 2005, p. 21; S. J. Barnett, *The Enlightenment and Religion: The Myths of Modernity*, Manchester University Press, Manchester, 2003.

234 See, for example, Steven Pinker, *The Blank Slate: The Modern Denial of Human Nature*, Allen Lane, London, 2002, p. 5.

235 See, for example, Pinker, *The Blank Slate*.

236 John Locke, 'Essays on the Law of Nature' in Locke, *The Selected Political Writings of John Locke*, p. 175.

237 John Locke, *An Essay Concerning Human Understanding*, Pennsylvania State University, Electronic Classics Series, Hazleton, 1999 [1690], pp. 46–48, 711–712; Simon Blackburn, 'Meet the Flintstones, Review of Steven Pinker, *The Blank Slate: The Modern Denial of Human Nature*', *New Republic*, 21 November 2002.

238 John Locke, 'Some Thoughts Concerning Education' (1690), in Philip J. Greven Jr., *Child-Rearing Concepts, 1628–1861*, Rutgers University, Itasca, 1973, pp. 18–41.

239 Locke, 'Some Thoughts Concerning Education' (1690), p. 36.

240 Locke, 'Some Thoughts Concerning Education' (1690), pp. 21–29, 39, 29.

241 Anthony Ashley Cooper, third Earl of Shaftesbury, *Characteristics of Men, Manners, Opinions, Times* (sixth edition), 1737 [1711], vol. II, p. 27, cited by Himmelfarb, *The Roads to Modernity*, p. 112.

242 Thomas Hobbes, *The Leviathan* (1660), Chapter XIII, 'The Natural Condition of Mankind as Concerning Their Felicity and Misery', ebooks.adelaide.edu.au/h/hobbes/thomas/h681.

243 Roger Trigg, *Ideas of Human Nature: An Historical Introduction*, Basil Blackwell, Oxford, 1988, pp. 59–61.

244 David Hume, *A Treatise of Human Nature*, p. 42.

245 Roger Trigg, *Ideas of Human Nature*, pp. 76–80.

246 Himmelfarb, *The Roads to Modernity*, pp. 34–35.

247 Himmelfarb, *The Roads to Modernity*, pp. 43–44.

248 Bruce Haddock, *A History of Political Thought: 1789 to the Present*, Polity Press, Cambridge, 2005, pp. 30–31.

249 Edmund Burke, *Reflections on the Revolution in France*, New York, 1961 [1790], p. 90, cited in Himmelfarb, *The Roads to Modernity*, p. 90.

250 Aldous Huxley, 'How Original Is Original Sin?' 1959 lecture, in Aldous Huxley, *The Human Situation*, p. 62.

251 Himmelfarb, *The Roads to Modernity*, pp. 150–56, 267.

252 Julian Offray de Lamettrie, 'Discourse on Happiness'; Himmelfarb, *The Roads to Modernity*, p. 171.

253 Jean-Jacques Rousseau, *Émile*, translated by Barbara Foxley, www.gutenberg.org/cache/epub/5427/pg5427.html, p. 5.

254 Rousseau, *Émile*, p. 5; Alan Jacobs, *Original Sin: A Cultural History*, Harper Collins, New York, 2009, p. 149 (my emphasis).

255 Roger Cox, *Shaping Childhood: Themes of Uncertainty in the History of Adult-Child Relationships*, Routledge, London & NY, 1996, p. 64.

256 Henry Chadwick, *The Early Church*, Penguin, Harmondsworth, 1983 [1967], p. 227.

257 Willem Firjhoff, 'Historian's Discovery of Childhood', *Paedagogica Historica: International Journal of the History of Education*, vol. 48, no. 1, 2012, pp. 11–29; Jean-Jacques Rousseau, *The Confessions*, edited by S. W. Orson, The Aldus Society, London, 1903, vol. 1, pp. 22–25, www2.hn.psu.edu/faculty/jmanis/rousseau/confessions.pdf.

258 Tim Blanning, *The Romantic Revolution*, Weidenfeld & Nicolson, London, 2010, pp. 22, 13–14, 59.

259 Immanuel Kant, *Religion Within the Limits of Reason Alone*, The Open Court Publishing Company, London, 1934, pp. 25–37. Kant even chose to cite the Latin Vulgate version of St Paul's letter to the Romans, which claimed that 'in Adam all have sinned' – the same translation used by Augustine – despite acknowledging that this was a mistranslation of the original Greek. The footnote acknowledging the mistranslation was inserted in the Berlin edition of his book.

260 Kant, *Religion Within the Limits of Reason Alone*, pp. 42–47 (emphasis original).

261 Blanning, *The Romantic Revolution*, pp. 84–86.

262 MacCulloch, *Christianity*, p. 750.

263 Wesley, *The Doctrine of Original Sin According to Scripture, Reason and Experience*, pp. 10–12; H. Shelton Smith, *Changing Conceptions of Original Sin: A Study in American Theology Since 1750*, Garland Publishing, New York & London, 1987 [1955], pp. 11–13; Wesley, 'Original Sin', Sermon 44, The United Methodist Church, http://new.gbgm-umc.org/umhistory/wesley/sermons/44. John Taylor (1694–1761) was a Presbyterian minister long based in Norwich, who in 1740 had published a widely read and highly influential text, *The Scripture-Doctrine of Original Sin Proposed to Free and Candid Examination*.

264 Wesley, *The Doctrine of Original Sin According to Scripture, Reason and Experience*, pp. 71–72, pp. 253–54.

265 John Wesley, 'A Word in Season or Advice to an Englishman' and

'Thoughts on the present scarcity of provisions 1773', in Wesley, *The Works of John Wesley*, vol. XI (fourth edition), John Mason, London, 1841, pp. 50–56, 173–75.

266 Garth Lean, *John Wesley, Anglican*, Blandford Press, London, 1964, pp. 52–55. Wesley even called the magazine he founded the Arminian magazine.

267 Wesley, 'Original Sin' (my emphasis).

268 Wesley, *The Works of John Wesley*, vol. XI, pp. 50–56, 363.

269 John Ferguson, *Pelagius: A Historical and Theological Study*, W. Heffer & Sons, Cambridge, 1956, p. 182.

270 Lean, *John Wesley, Anglican*, p. 45.

271 John Wesley, 'Sermon on the Education of Children' (c. 1783), in Philip J. Greven Jr., *Child-Rearing Concepts, 1628–1861*, p. 55.

272 Lean, *John Wesley, Anglican*, p. 61.

273 Ibid., p. 62; Himmelfarb, *The Roads to Modernity*, pp. 125–26.

274 Wesley believed that 'as sickness and diseases have created the necessity of medicines and physicians, so the disorders of our rational nature have introduced the necessity of education … Education … is, as far as it can, to supply the loss of original perfection' (John Wesley, 'A Plain Account of Kingswood School, 1781', in Wesley, *The Works of John Wesley*, vol. XIII, pp. 274–86.

275 Wesley, *The Doctrine of Original Sin According to Scripture, Reason and Experience*, pp. 239–240.

276 Wesley, 'Sermon on the Education of Children' (c. 1783), p. 54–58.

277 Ibid., p. 59.

278 Susanna Wesley, 'On the Education of Her Family' (1732), in Philip J. Greven Jr., *Child-Rearing Concepts, 1628–1861*, pp. 47–49.

279 Wesley, 'Sermon on the Education of Children' (c. 1783), pp. 60–62.

280 See G. M. Best, *Seven Sisters*, The New Room, Bristol, 2011.

281 Ibid., pp. 16–27.

282 Cox, *Shaping Childhood*, p. 103.

283 Himmelfarb, *The Roads to Modernity*, p. 120; Wesley, *The Works of John Wesley*, vol. XIII (fourth edition), pp. 252–53.

284 Jacobs, *Original Sin*, p. 86.

285 MacCulloch, *Christianity*, pp. 874–75.

286 Jacobs, *Original Sin*, p. 133.

287 Franklin recalled that: 'In 1739 arrived among us from Ireland the Reverend Mr. Whitefield, who had made himself remarkable there as an itinerant preacher. He was at first permitted to preach in some of our churches; but the clergy, taking a dislike to him, soon refus'd him their pulpits, and he was oblig'd to preach in the fields. an evening without hearing psalms

sung in different families of every street.' He observed that 'It was wonderful to see the change soon made in the manners of our inhabitants. From being thoughtless or indifferent about religion, it seem'd as if all the world were growing religious ...' (Benjamin Franklin, *The Autobiography of Benjamin Franklin, with introduction and notes edited by Charles W. Eliot*, The Electronic Classics Series, Hazleton, p. 97).

288 Cedric B. Cowing, *The Great Awakening and the American Revolution: Colonial Thought in the 18th Century*, University of Hawaii, Rand McNall, Chicago, 1971, pp. 50–51.

289 George M. Marsden, *Jonathan Edwards: A Life*, Yale University Press, New Haven & London, 2003, pp. 7–8; Kenneth Boa, *Augustine to Freud: What Theologians and Psychologists Tell Us About Human Nature (and Why it Matters)*, Broadman and Holman, Nashville, 2004, p. 27.

290 Edwards wrote of Taylor's work that 'no one book has done so much towards rooting out of these western parts of New England, the principles and scheme of religion maintained by our pious and excellent forefathers' (Marsden, *Jonathan Edwards*, p. 457).

291 Jonathan Edwards, *The Great Christian Doctrine of Original Sin Defended* (fourth edition), Boston 1784, pp. 14–17.

292 An example of Edwards' creative use of metaphor was his suggestion that 'Adam and all his posterity had coexisted' in a single tree, so that 'the hearts of all the branches of mankind, by the constitution of nature and the law of union, [were] ... affected just as the heart of Adam, their common root, was affected'. But ultimately Edwards' point came back to the fact that original sin was a teaching that had to be accepted as one of 'the sovereign constitutions of the supreme Author and Lord of all, who gives none account of any of his matters, and whose ways are past finding out' (Marsden, *Jonathan Edwards*, pp. 454–56).

293 Marsden, *Jonathan Edwards*, pp. 385, 449–52.

294 Jacobs, *Original Sin*, p. 142.

295 Smith, *Changing Conceptions of Original Sin*, pp. 6–8.

296 Douglas A. Sweeney, *Nathaniel Taylor, New Haven Theology, and the Legacy of Jonathan Edwards*, Oxford University Press, 2003, pp. 4–6, 80–82, 152, 112; Smith, *Changing Conceptions of Original Sin*, pp. 104–09, 125.

297 Charles G. Finney, *Systematic Theology*, The Master Christian Library Series, 1997, p. 296; Richard Kyle, *Evangelicalism: An Americanized Christianity*, Transaction Publishers, New Brunswick, 2006, pp. 36–38.

298 Philip J. Greven Jr., *Child-Rearing Concepts, 1628-1861*, pp. 128–33.

299 Horace Bushnell, 'Christian Nurture' (1867), in Philip J. Greven Jr., *Child-Rearing Concepts, 1628-1861*, pp. 138–46 (my emphasis).

300 Mintz, *Huck's Raft*, p. 82.

301 *The Theory of Moral Sentiments* was published in four editions before *The Wealth of Nations* was first published.

302 Adam Smith, *The Wealth of Nations*, edited and introduced by Andrew Skinner, Penguin, Harmondsworth, 1974 [1776], p. 26.

303 Smith, *The Theory of Moral Sentiments* (second edition), A.Miller, London and A. Kincaid and J. Bell, Edinburgh, 1761 [1759], pp. 47–48, 54–56.

304 Ibid., pp. 47–48.

305 Ibid., pp. 226–27.

306 Ibid., pp. 237–38.

307 Ibid., pp. 156–57, 222–23, 245–47, 162–63.

308 Ibid., pp. 97–101.

309 Ibid., pp. 287–88.

310 Ibid., 287–88.

311 Smith, *The Wealth of Nations*, pp. 118–19. While in *Moral Sentiments* the 'Invisible Hand' is presented as benefiting society, in *The Wealth of Nations*, it benefits individuals *and* society.

312 John Wesley, 'Original Sin': Sermon 44, The United Methodist Church website, http://new.gbgm-umc.org/umhistory/wesley/sermons/44.

313 Christopher Lasch, *The True and Only Heaven: Progress and its Critics*, W. W. Norton and Company, New York & London, 1991, pp. 52–53.

314 Himmelfarb, *The Roads to Modernity*, p. 35.

315 James Madison, 'The Federalist No. 51: The Structure of the Government Must Furnish the Proper Checks and Balances Between the Different Departments', *Independent Journal*, 6 February 1788.

316 Madison, 'The Federalist No. 51'; Bruce Haddock, *A History of Political Thought: 1789 to the Present*, Polity Press, Cambridge, 2005, pp. 15–18.

317 Pinker, *The Blank Slate*, pp. 297–98.

318 Himmelfarb, *The Roads to Modernity*, p. 151.

319 Barry Shain, 'Religious Conscience and Original Sin: An Exploration of America's Protestant Foundations', in David Womersley, editor, *Liberty and American Experience in the Eighteenth Century*, Amagi Books, Indianapolis, 2006, pp. 153–208, 195.

320 Ibid.

321 It is significant that God does not rate a single mention in the American constitution, that the famous adage 'In God We Trust' did not appear on US currency until 1864, and that it did not become the official motto of the United States until 1956, two years after Congress added the words 'under God' to the pledge of allegiance. But it is also true that comparatively low church attendance rates in the late eighteenth century, the later emergence of mass evangelicalism and the particularly unorthodox beliefs of men like Jefferson and George Washington (who never received the Eucharist and

preferred to speak of 'Providence' than God) do not mean that the Western Christian tradition did not shape the ideals of the new Republic. See Shain, 'Religious Conscience and Original Sin', p. 207; MacCulloch, *Christianity*, pp. 764–65; Richard Kyle, *Evangelicalism: An Americanized Christianity*, Transaction Publishers, New Brunswick, 2006, p. 132.

322 Daniel Walker Howe, 'Franklin, Edwards and the Problem of Human Nature', in Barbara B. Oberg & Harry S. Stout (eds), *Benjamin Franklin, Jonathan Edwards, and the Representation of American Culture*, Oxford University Press, New York, 1993, pp. 76–77.

323 Benjamin Franklin, *The Autobiography of Benjamin Franklin*, P. F. Collier & Son, New York, 1909, p. 92.

324 John Adams, *The Works of John Adams, Second President of the United States*, Little, Brown, Boston, 1850–1856, p. 408 (cited in H. Richard Niebuhr, *Theology, History and Culture: Major Unpublished Writings*, Yale University Press, New Haven & London, 1996, p. 184).

325 John P. Diggins, *The Lost Soul of American Politics: Virtue, Self-Interest, and the Foundations of Liberalism*, Basic Books, New York, 1984; Shain, 'Religious Conscience and Original Sin', p. 198.

326 Russell Kirk, *The Conservative Mind: From Burke to Eliot* (fifth revised edition), Henry Regnery Company, Chicago, 1972 [1953], pp. 78–80.

327 Pinker, *The Blank Slate*, pp. 297–98.

328 Thomas Paine, *Common Sense*, New York, 1992 [1791], p. 5, cited in Himmelfarb, *The Roads to Modernity*, p. 98.

329 Haddock, *A History of Political Thought*, pp. 14–15.

330 Shain, 'Religious Conscience and Original Sin', pp. 153–208.

331 Charles B. Sanford, *The Religious Life of Thomas Jefferson*, University of Virginia Press, Charlottesville, 1987, pp. 57–59.

332 Richard Reeves, *John Stuart Mill: Victorian Firebrand*, Atlantic Books, London, 2007, pp. 11–15.

333 John Stuart Mill, *Autobiography of John Stuart Mill*, (1873), The Floating Press, Auckland, 2009, 175.

334 J. S. Mill, *Three Essays on Religion*, cited in Reeves, *John Stuart Mill*, p. 477.

335 The original title of the book was *On the Origin of Species*.

336 One of *Origin*'s epitaphs was a quote from Francis Bacon's *Advancement of Learning*: 'let no man out of a weak conceit of sobriety, or an ill-applied moderation, think or maintain, that a man can search too far or be too well studied in the book of God's word, or the book of God's works ... but rather let men endeavour an endless progress or proficiency in both' (Charles Darwin, *The Origin of Species*, P. F. Collier and Son, New York, 1909, pp. 11–12).

337 What is often forgotten, however, is that original sin had never relied on a historical reading of Genesis. Advances in geological and Biblical history

meant that most English intellectuals by the mid-nineteenth century were already interpreting the story of the Fall as an allegory. In doing so, moreover, they were upholding a tradition which went back to Augustine himself. *The Origin of Species* might have accelerated the move away from Biblical literalism, but it did not initiate it. See John Hedley Brooke, 'Darwin and Victorian Christianity', in Jonathan Hodge & Gregory Radick (eds), *The Cambridge Companion to Darwin*, Cambridge University Press, Cambridge, 2003, p. 193.

338 Charles Darwin, *Autobiography* (1876), in Charles Darwin & Thomas Henry Huxley, *Autobiographies*, edited and introduced by Gavin de Beer, Oxford University Press, London, 1974, pp. 49–50.

339 Ibid., pp. 50–54.

340 Darwin, *The Origin of Species*, p. 404.

341 Charles Darwin, *The Descent of Man, and Selection in Relation to Sex*, in James D. Watson (ed.), *Darwin: The Indelible Stamp*, Running Press, Philadelphia, 2005, p. 612.

342 Diane B. Paul, 'Social Darwinism and Eugenics', in Hodge & Radick (eds), *The Cambridge Companion to Darwin*, pp. 217, 235.

343 Darwin, *The Descent of Man*, pp. 612–613.

344 Charles Darwin, *The Descent of Man and Selection in Relation to Sex*, vol. 2, D. Appleton and Company, New York, pp. 315, 327. Darwin did suggest that the fact that man had become 'superior to woman' had its downside: 'Woman seems to differ from man in mental disposition, chiefly in her greater tenderness and less selfishness ... [while] man is the rival of other men; he delights in competition, and this leads to ambition which passes too easily into selfishness. These latter qualities seem to be his natural and unfortunate birthright' (*The Descent of Man*, pp. 324–26).

345 Darwin, *The Descent of Man*, pp. 399–402.

346 Darwin, *Autobiography*, p. 85; James Dryburgh, 'Austral Reflections', in *Essays from Near and Far*, Walleah Press, North Hobart, 2014, pp. 19–20.

347 Charles Darwin, *The Voyage of the Beagle* (1845), in Watson (ed.), *Darwin: The Indelible Stamp*, pp. 292, 300.

348 Paul, 'Social Darwinism and Eugenics', p. 218.

349 Darwin firmly rejected the blank slate: 'I am inclined to agree with Francis Galton in believing that education and environment produce only a small effect on the mind of any one, and that most of our qualities are innate' (Darwin, *Autobiography*, p. 22).

350 Darwin, *The Descent of Man*, pp. 399–400.

351 Ibid.

352 Darwin's summary of why a man will generally choose to behave ethically is: 'If he acts for the good of others, he will receive the approbation of his

fellow-men and gain the love of those with whom he lives; and this latter gain undoubtedly is the highest pleasure on this earth. By degrees it will become intolerable to him to obey his sensuous passions rather than his higher impulses' (Darwin, *Autobiography*, p. 55).

353 In *The Principles of Sociology* (1876), Herbert Spencer argued: 'The saying that the savage has the mind of a child with the passions of a man ... possesses a deeper meaning than appears. There is a relationship between the two natures such that ... we may regard the coordination of them in the child as analogous to the coordination of the primitive mind' (see Hugh Cunningham, *The Children of the Poor: Representations of Childhood since the Seventeenth Century*, Blackwell, Oxford, 1992, p. 126). It was Spencer who coined the term 'survival of the fittest', which was used to justify unrestrained competition, especially in the United States. Darwin himself found little scientific benefit in Spencer's generalisations; see Darwin, *Autobiography*, p. 64.

354 Cunningham, *The Children of the Poor*, p. 129.

355 Mintz, *Huck's Raft*, pp. 190–91. Spock's own parenting manual would become a highly influential bestseller in the second half of the twentieth century.

356 Michael Ruse (ed.), *Philosophy after Darwin: Classic and Contemporary Readings*, Princeton University Press, Princeton, 2009, p. 8. Christian symbolism is perhaps further evident here: out of sacrifice and death came redemption; see Robert J. Richards, 'Natural Selection and its Moral Purpose', in Michael Ruse & Robert J. Richards (eds), *The Cambridge Companion to The 'Origin of Species'*, Cambridge University Press, New York, 2009, pp. 65–66.

357 Darwin, *The Descent of Man*, pp. 399–402.

358 According to Tim Blanning: 'The axiom of the Romantics was absolute inwardness' (Blanning, *The Romantics*, pp. 82–84).

359 This argument was expounded in detail and depth by Richard Webster in, *Why Freud Was Wrong: Sin, Science and Psychoanalysis* (The Orwell Press, Oxford, 2005). My own reflections have drawn heavily on his scholarship. The major weakness of Webster's insightful work is his failure to recognise original sin as a distinctively *Western* Christian tradition.

360 Kenneth Boa, *Augustine to Freud: What Theologians and Psychologists Tell Us About Human Nature (and Why It Matters)*, Broadman and Holman, Nashville, 2004, pp. 83–89.

361 Sigmund Freud, *The Future of an Illusion*, in Peter Gay (ed.), *The Freud Reader*, Vintage, London, 1995, pp. 670–77.

362 Sigmund Freud, 'Civilization and its Discontents' (1930), in Gay (ed.), *The Freud Reader*, pp. 749–50.

363 Freud, 'Civilization and its Discontents' (1930), pp. 754–55.

364 Sigmund Freud, 'Thoughts for the Times on War and Death' (1915), www. panarchy.org/freud/war.1915.html.

365 Freud, 'Civilization and its Discontents' (1930), p. 750.

366 Freud, 'Thoughts for the Times on War and Death'.

367 Freud, 'Civilization and its Discontents' (1930), pp. 749–50.

368 Ibid., p. 749

369 Carl Jung parted with Freud primarily over what he considered his mentor's obsession with sexuality. Jung believed that 'in the place of a jealous God whom he [Freud] had lost, he had substituted another compelling image, that of sexuality … The name alone had changed' (C. G. Jung, *Memories, Dreams, Reflections*, Flamingo, London, 1989, pp. 174–75).

370 Sigmund Freud, 'The Ego and the Id' (1923), in Peter Gay (ed.), *The Freud Reader*, pp. 652–53; Freud, 'Civilization and its Discontents' (1930), p. 756.

371 Webster, *Why Freud Was Wrong*, p. 313.

372 The similarities between the Catholic confessional and the psychoanalytic couch have long been noted. Both provided a private place where a person's darkest secrets could be safely revealed, and where they were expected to tell all. Those who assume that the Christian confessor was more reticent concerning human sexuality than the modern psychoanalyst are far from the mark. Far from denying the importance of human sexuality, for much of its history the church was obsessed by the intimate detail and complex variety of sexual practice. Freud's routine questioning of patients on when they had masturbated and their modes of intercourse and contraception was consistent with the tradition of confession. Moreover, the liberated Viennese was in no less doubt about the *harmful* effects of masturbation and *coitus interruptus* than was the church. But while the Catholic confessional has obvious similarities with psychoanalytic technique, perhaps the private soul-searching undertaken by zealous Protestants (who were often no less obsessed by sex) more closely foretells the Freudian way. In Freud's writing and in his deliberately distant therapeutic manner, there is a more of a sense of fostering the lonely individual confrontation with self than there is of replicating the role of the judgemental but ultimately forgiving mother church.

373 Freud, 'The Future of an Illusion', pp. 706, 713–14.

374 Shadia B. Drury, *Terror and Civilization: Christianity, Politics, and the Western Psyche*, Palgrave Macmillan, New York, 2004, pp. 101–02; Neil Ormerod, *Grace and Disgrace: A Theology of Self-Esteem, Society and History*, E. J. Dwyer, Sydney, 1992, pp. 148–49.

375 Sigmund Freud, 'An Autobiographical Study' (1925), in Peter Gay (ed.), *The Freud Reader*, pp. 508–09.

376 Freud, 'Some Psychical Consequences of the Anatomical Distinction Between the Sexes' (1925), pp. 670–77.

377 Freud, *The Future of an Illusion*, p. 702. Despite Freud's genuine conviction to the contrary, his conclusions cannot be legitimately described as scientific since there is no conceivable pattern of human behaviour that could falsify his theories. For a discussion of this, see John Maynard Smith, 'Science and Myth', in David L. Hull & Michael Ruse (eds), *The Philosophy of Biology*, Oxford University Press, Oxford, 1998, pp. 376–77.

378 David McClelland, *The Roots of Consciousness*, D. Van Nostrand Co., Princeton, 1964, pp. 127–28, cited in Webster, *Why Freud Was Wrong*, p. 321.

379 Ernest Gellner, *The Psychoanalytic Movement*, Paladin, London, 1985, p. 36, cited in Webster, *Why Freud Was Wrong*, p. 320.

380 Webster, *Why Freud Was Wrong*,p. 319.

381 Drury, *Terror and Civilization*, p. 101.

382 Peter Gay (ed.), *The Freud Reader*, pp. xiii–xiv.

383 Anthony Storr, *Freud*, Oxford University Press, Oxford, 1996, p. 128.

384 Webster, *Why Freud Was Wrong*, pp. 332–33.

385 Freud, 'Civilization and its Discontents' (1930), pp. 729–34, 772.

386 In 1946 Dr Benjamin Spock published his twenty-five-cent paperback, *The Common Sense Book of Baby and Child Care*. Stephen Mintz notes that 'Spock succeeded in translating Sigmund Freud's ideas into nonthreatening language that any parent could understand … Dr Spock's greatest talent was to make Freudian concepts – such as the latency period, Oedipal conflict, castration anxiety, and penis envy – seem like common sense.' There was to be, though, no let-up in responsibility for mothers. A basic premise of the psychoanalytically oriented child-rearing advice of the postwar era was that a mother's relationship with her children was the key to their psychological and emotional development (see Mintz, *Huck's Raft*, pp. 279–82).

387 Storr, *Freud*, pp. 2–3; Sigmund Freud, *The Interpretation of Dreams*, 1899.

388 Sigmund Freud, *Civilization, Society and Religion*, Penguin, Harmondsworth, 1985, pp. 345–47.

389 Ibid., pp. 350–62.

390 Andrew S. Finstuen, *Original Sin and Everyday Protestants: The Theology of Reinhold Niebuhr, Billy Graham and Paul Tillich in an Age of Anxiety*, The University of North Carolina Press, Chapel Hill, 2009, pp. 1–2.

391 Finstuen, *Original Sin and Everyday Protestants*, p. 4.

392 H. Shelton Smith, *Changing Conceptions of Original Sin: A Study in American Theology Since 1750*, Garland Publishing, New York & London, 1987 [1955], p. 211.

393 Reinhold Neibuhr, 'The Nature and Destiny of Man', in E. J. Tinsley, *Modern Theology: Reinhold Niebuhr*, Epworth Press, London, 1973, p. 52.

394 Reinhold Neibuhr, *Beyond Tragedy*, in Tinsley, *Modern Theology*, pp. 67–68.

395 Rienhold Niebuhr, *The Children of Light and the Children of Darkness: A Vindication of Democracy and a Critique of its Traditional Defence*, Charles Scribner's Sons, New York, 1944, pp. x–xii, 40–41.

396 Smith, *Changing Conceptions of Original Sin*, p. 217.

397 Finstuen, *Original Sin and Everyday Protestants*, pp. 63–66.

398 Barth published a commentary on the epistle to the Romans in 1919, signalling the start of his lifelong critique of what he saw to be the overly optimistic liberal assessment of the human condition.

399 Finstuen, *Original Sin and Everyday Protestants*, p. 127.

400 'Sinners in the Hands of an Angry God' was first preached by Jonathan Edwards on 5 July 1741. He preached it many times during the Great Awakening, and it became his most famous sermon. It was based on the apparently innocent text, 'Their foot shall slide in due time' (Deuteronomy 32:35).

401 Finstuen, *Original Sin and Everyday Protestants*, pp. 5, 140.

402 C. S. Lewis considered the Fall to be a myth about the rise of moral consciousness, and baldly stated that 'Anselm's legal doctrine as well as the doctrine of our physical presence in Adam's loins do no good to me'. Lewis observed that our view of the individual is not the Bible's, and that we therefore have limited capacity to grasp what it 'might mean to be "in Adam" or in Christ'. Our notion of separateness gets in the way, 'so the truth that is there is now lost to us, we are blind to it' (C. S. Lewis, *The Problem of Pain*, Fontana Books, New York, 1957 [1940], pp. 59–76.

403 Richard Kyle, *Evangelicalism: An Americanized Christianity*, Transaction Publishers, New Brunswick, 2006, pp. 221–23.

404 Interview with CNN, 14 November 2012, www.religion.blogs.cnn.com/2012/11/14; Franklin Graham, *The Name*, Nelson Books, Nashville, 2002, pp. 18–19, 45, 70–71.

405 Franklin, like so many American evangelicals, is a Christian Zionist, and believes in the notion of greater or Biblical Israel, and that the titanic struggles of the end times will be played out in a Middle Eastern conflict. America must support Israel to fulfil its divinely ordained duty (even though most Jews are ultimately destined to die). His analysis of the Palestinian issue begins and ends with his heretical interpretation of the Bible. See Graham, *The Name*, pp. 185, 191.

406 Wallis, *God's Politics*, pp. 142–43.

407 Lest Franklin Graham's dangerous cocktail of extremist politics and religion be considered only an American phenomenon, it is worth noting that

missions by him have been sponsored by mainstream churches across the Western world. Franklin's mission to Australia, for example, was organised and promoted by every major Protestant denomination in the country *and* the Catholic Church. Christians across the Western world have been reluctant to separate themselves from the 'success' (and the resources) associated with the American evangelists, even when this has come at the expense of orthodox Christian teaching and their own evangelical tradition.

408 Richard Roberts, 'Sin, Saga and Gender: The Fall and Original Sin in Modern Theology', in Paul Morris & Deborah Sawyer (eds), *A Walk in the Garden: Biblical, Iconographical and Literary Images of Eden*, JSOT Press, Sheffield, 1992, pp. 244–61, 248–51.

409 David Barrett & Todd Johnson, 'Annual Statistical Table on Global Mission: 2003', in *International Bulletin of Missionary Research*, vol. 27, no. 1, 2003; Allan Anderson, *An Introduction to Pentecostalism: Global Charismatic Christianity*, Cambridge University Press, Cambridge, 2010, pp. 1–5; Stephen Prothero, *God is Not One: The Eight Rival Religions that Run The World and Why Their Differences Matter*, Black Inc., Melbourne, 2011, pp. 91–93.

410 Anderson, *An Introduction to Pentecostalism*, pp. 228–33.

411 Neil Ormerod, *Grace and Disgrace: A Theology of Self-Esteem, Society and History*, E. J. Dwyer, Sydney, 1992, pp. 88–89; James O'Donnell, *Augustine: A New Biography*, Harper Perennial, New York, 2006, p. 13.

412 The Dutch theologian George Vandervelde noted in the 1970s that 'Roman Catholic publications on the subject of original sin have been issued in a constant stream', and recorded some seventy-odd works published between 1965 and 1975. Some of the new ideas were expressed in the innovative Dutch Catechism of 1966.

413 O'Donnell, *Augustine*, pp. 285–86.

414 There were instructions of a pastoral nature only in 1958, and throughout the 1950s it was emphasised that 'for the Catholic, original sin is a dogma of faith' (see Henri Rondet, *Original Sin: The Patristic and Theological Background*, Alba House, New York, 1972, pp. 179–84).

415 In 1794 the Synod of Pistoia had been condemned by Pius VI for having rejected as 'a Pelagian fable that place of suffering (which the faithful call the limbo of infants)', but he dared not canonise the pastorally popular concept, largely because it threatened the purity of the doctrine of original sin. Only in 1904 did Pope Pius X officially declare that babies who die without baptism 'go to Limbo, where they do not enjoy God, but neither do they suffer, because, having Original sin alone, they do not deserve Paradise, but neither do they merit Hell or Purgatory' (see Rondet, *Original Sin*, pp. 179–81).

416 J. Ratzinger & V. Messori, *The Ratzinger Report: An Exclusive Interview on the State of the Church*, Ignatius Press, San Francisco, 1985, cited in Daryl P. Domning & Monika K. Hellwig, *Original Selfishness: Original Sin and Evil in the Light of Evolution*, Ashgate, Aldershot, 2006, p. 4.

417 Ratzinger suggested that the doctrine of original sin referred to the fact that all human life is 'relational': we are all part of the first and every subsequent sin, not because guilt is transmitted to every person, but because we are not isolated and self-contained individuals (Joseph Ratzinger, *In the Beginning: A Catholic Understanding of the Story of Creation and the Fall*, William B. Eerdmans, Grand Rapids, 1995 (first published in German in 1986), pp. 70–74.

418 *Catechism of the Catholic Church* (second edition), St Pauls Publications, Strathfield, 2003, pp. 98–103.

419 Uta Ranke-Heinemann, *Eunuchs for the Kingdom of Heaven: The Catholic Church and Sexuality*, Penguin, Harmondsworth, 1991, pp. 298–99.

420 The audience was given on Wednesday 6 February 2013; the pope's resignation was announced the following Monday.

421 In his daily homily on 22 May 2013, Pope Francis stated: 'The Lord has redeemed all of us, all of us, with the Blood of Christ: all of us, not just Catholics. Everyone!'

422 Matthew Fox, *Original Blessing: A Primer in Creation Spirituality*, Jeremy P. Tarcher/Putnam, New York, 2000 [1983], pp. 6–7. Fox claims that Ratzinger 'misread the book': '... in point of fact, I do not deny original sin a modest place in our worldview, but I do decry its prominence in church teaching. I believe that ... original sin ideology is profoundly dangerous and deviant. Dangerous for our planet and therefore for our children to come. And deviant for our souls that strive for hope and promise and creative co-creation.' To be fair to Ratzinger, though, it must be admitted that the 'modest place' Fox allows for the doctrine of original sin is not at all obvious in his book!

423 Most of the new theology also avoids the subject of guilt. As Alistair McFadyen points out: '[W]hat is socially inherited and communicated, [and] passively received, cannot be guilt' (McFadyen, *Bound to Sin: Abuse, Holocaust and the Christian Doctrine of Sin*, Cambridge University Press, Cambridge, 2000, pp. 29–39).

424 Since the 1970s there have been many books exploring how original sin might be passed on through social structures and cultural means, and might speak to a universal human solidarity. It was the Jesuit theologian Teilhard de Chardin (1881–1955) who first popularised the idea that original sin was the 'universal law of imperfection', which is part of the evolutionary order of creation (although Teilhard was forced by Rome to retract his state-

ments in 1925). More recently, Michael Ruse believes has asserted that 'there is a perfect consilience between the Darwinian human and the Christian human.'. And for Patricia Williams, 'original sin is a doctrine about human origins and human nature.' (See Michael Ruse, *Darwinism and its Discontents*, Cambridge University Press, Cambridge, 2006, p. 279; Patricia Williams, *Doing Without Adam and Eve: Sociobiology and Original Sin*, Fortress Press, Minneapolis, 2001, pp. xXiii--xiv See also Patricia Williams, *Doing without Adam and Eve: Sociobiology and Original Sin*, Minneapolis: Fortress, 2001.) A number of other writers have pursued similar themes.: See, for example, Raymund Schwager, *Banished from Eden: Original Sin and Evolutionary Theory in the Drama of Salvation*, Gracewing, Leominster Herefordshire, 2006; Daryl P. Domning and & Monika K. Hellwig, *Original Selfishness: Original Sin and Evil in the Light of Evolution*, Ashgate, Aldershot, Hampshire, 2006, pp. 118--119; S. J. Reese, 'The Science of Sin: Original Sin after Evolution': A research report presented in partial fulfilment of the requirements for the diploma of Postgraduate Diploma of Arts in Religious Studies, Massey University, New Zealand, 2011.

425 Alan Grafen & Mark Ridley (eds), *Richard Dawkins: How a Scientist Changed the Way We Think*, Oxford University Press, Oxford, 2006, p. xi. This disappointing book contains over twenty essays which, almost without exception, contain not a single criticism of Dawkins or critically engage with his thought. A higher compliment to their mentor would have been for the editors to compile a collection that made a serious contribution to the debate sparked by Dawkins' ideas.

426 Dawkins freely acknowledges that *The Selfish Gene* packaged up *existing* ideas but makes the important point that 'expounding ideas that have hitherto appeared only in the technical literature ... requires insightful new twists of language and revealing metaphors. If you push novelty of language and metaphor far enough, you can end up with a new way of seeing' (Richard Dawkins, *The Selfish Gene*, Oxford University Press, Oxford, 2006 [1976], p. xvi).

427 Dawkins, *The Selfish Gene*, pp. 2, vii–ix.

428 Dawkins, *The Selfish Gene*, p. 4.

429 Dawkins, *The Selfish Gene*, p. 3.

430 Dawkins, *The Selfish Gene*, pp. 192–94.

431 Dawkins, *The Selfish Gene*, pp. 195–96.

432 For a fuller discussion of these issues, see Alister E. McGrath, *Dawkins' God: Genes, Memes, and the Meaning of Life*, Blackwell Publishing, Malden, Oxford and Carlton, 2005, pp. 128–134.

433 Dawkins recalls that, as a young scientist focused on animal behaviour, 'I became intrigued by Popper's vision of science as a two-stage process: first

the creative – almost artistic – dreaming up of a hypothesis of "model", followed by attempts to *falsify* predictions deduced from it' (Dawkins, *An Appetite for Wonder: The Making of a Scientist, A Memoir*, Transworld Publishers, London, 2013, pp. 184–85).

434 Darwin & Huxley, *Autobiographies*, p. 64.

435 Cited in Webster, *Why Freud Was Wrong*, p. lv.. See also Mary Midgley, 'Why Memes', in Hilary Rose & Steven Rose (eds), *Alas Poor Darwin: Arguments Against Evolutionary Psychology*, Vintage, London, 2001.

436 Dawkins, *An Appetite for Wonder*, pp. 278–80.

437 Richard Dawkins, 'Foreword', in Susan Blackmore, *The Meme Machine*, Oxford Univeristy Press, 1999, pp. vii–xviii.

438 Richard Dawkins, 'A Shameful Thought for the Day', *The Guardian*, 25 December 2010; Dawkins, *The Selfish Gene*, p. 330.

439 Dawkins, *An Appetite for Wonder*, pp. 139–40.

440 Dawkins, *The Selfish Gene*, pp. 200–01.

441 Dawkins, *The Selfish Gene*, pp. 198, 200–01.

442 In an endnote to the second edition of *The Selfish Gene*, Dawkins rejects the criticism that he is a dualist even as he restates an essentially dualist position: 'We, that is our brains, are separate and independent enough from our genes to rebel against them' (Dawkins, *The Selfish Gene*, p. 331-32). In *The God Delusion* (2006), Dawkins suggests there might be an innate predisposition to dualism: 'Native dualism and native teleology predispose us, given the right conditions, to religion, just as my moths' light-compass reaction predisposed them to inadvertent "suicide". Our innate dualism prepares us to believe in a "soul" which inhabits the body rather than being integrally part of the body' (Dawkins, *The God Delusion*, Bantam Press, London, 2006, p. 181).

443 Dawkins, *The Selfish Gene*, p. ix. See also Dorothy Nelkin, 'Less Selfish than Sacred? Genes and the Religious Impulse in Evolutionary Psychology', in Hilary Rose & Steven Rose (eds), *Alas Poor Darwin*.

444 Dawkins, *The Selfish Gene*, pp. 1, 267.

445 Dawkins, *The God Delusion*, pp. 165–66. The irony of Dawkins' understandable frustration with having metaphors such as 'selfish' taken literally is that his own critiques of religious stories fail to recognise that they are *also* allegories designed to open windows of understanding rather than to provide literal representations of reality. For example, Dawkins presents 'a typical origin myth from a group of Tasmanian aborigines' in his book for children as another example of how people have got it wrong, seemingly unaware that, in doing so, he is presenting a contemporary caricature of their creation story, which was never intended to be heard as 'history' in the way modern Westerners understand it (Richard Dawkins, *The Magic of*

Reality: How We Know What's Really True, Bantam Press, London, 2011, pp. 32–35).

446 Pinker, *The Blank Slate*, pp. 1–2. It is also noteworthy that Sigmund Freud does not rate a single mention in Pinker's review of twentieth-century psychology. And in a reference list of over nine hundred books, not one concerns the history of Christian thought or the church (with the single possible exception being a 1982 book called *Abusing Science: The Case Against Creationism*).

447 The term 'Standard Social Science Model (SSSM)' was coined by the evolutionary psychologists John Tooby and Leda Cosmides in 1992.

448 It also should be acknowledged that much of the focus on the environment in postwar social research reflected the mundane fact that education, housing, health, employment and income availability largely determine the life-opportunities available to disadvantaged people and are the influences most amenable to change.

449 Francis Collins, 'Foreword', in Ted Peters, *Playing God: Genetic Determinism and Human Freedom*, Routledge, New York & London, 1997, p. x. See also Barbara Herrnstein Smith, 'Sewing Up the Mind: The Claims of Evolutionary Psychology', in Hilary Rose & Steven Rose, *Alas, Poor Darwin: Arguments against Evolutionary Psychology*, Harmony Books, New York, 2000, p. 159.

450 The neuroscientist and philosopher Raymond Tallis believes the reason why 'Darwinitis' (the idea 'that we are defined by our origins') is widely supported despite the lack of scientific support for its claims is that we are captive to a language in which human behaviour is described in animalomorphic terms. It is worth remembering, however, that language reflects as well as shapes culture. Tallis has written a number of books on 'Darwinitis', the most recent of which is *Aping Mankind: Neuromania, Darwinitis and the Misrepresentation of Humanity* (Acumen, 2012).

451 Dawkins, *An Appetite for Wonder*, p. 144.

452 Richard Dawkins, *The Blind Watchmaker*, Penguin, London, 1991 [1986], p. xiv.

453 My thinking on this question was assisted by reading Ted Peters' *Playing God: Genetic Determinism and Human Freedom* (Routledge, New York & London, 1997).

454 Dawkins, *An Appetite for Wonder*, pp. 13–15.

455 Christian de Duve, *Genetics of Original Sin: The Impact of Natural Selection and the Future of Humanity*, Yale University Press, New Haven & London, 2010, pp. xxii, xxvii.

456 James Davies records a story which highlights how Western people have understood the fatal flaw of communism: 'There is a legend that some

second-generation Marxists in Moscow were debating whether to introduce private ownership of business enterprise into the Soviet Union. The arguments on the advantages of private versus public ownership grew so vigorous and persuasive that the issue was not at last settled until one man succinctly reviewed almost a half-century of Soviet social success and concluded, "You can't change human nature"' (James C. Davies, *Human Nature in Politics: The Dynamics of Political Behaviour*, John Wiley and Sons, New York, 1963, p. 1).

457 John Gray has described modern politics as 'a chapter in the history of religion' which is 'driven by the belief that humanity can be delivered from immemorial evils by the power of knowledge. In its most radical forms this belief underpinned the experiments in revolutionary utopianism [such as communism and Nazism] that defined the last two centuries' (John Gray, *Black Mass: Apocalyptic Religion and the Death of Utopia*, Allen Lane, London, 2007, pp. 1, 14).

458 David Noble has argued that the reason modern technologies are so often unrelated to meeting humanity's basic needs is because they 'have been aimed rather at the loftier goal of transcending such mortal concerns altogether'. Noble believes that the roots of the technological enterprise go back to the 'formation of Western consciousness, to the time when the useful arts first became implicated in the Christian project of redemption' and 'the worldly means of survival were ... turned toward the other-worldly end of salvation' (Noble, cited in Aidan Davison, 'Ruling the Future? Heretical Reflections on Technology and Other Secular Religions of Sustainability', *Worldviews*, vol. 12, 2008, pp. 146–62, 153–54.

459 Friedrich Nietzsche, *The Gay Science*, edited by B. Williams, Cambridge University Press, Cambridge, 2001, p. 69, cited in Julian Young, *A Philosophical Biography of Friedrich Nietzsche*, Cambridge University Press, Cambridge, 2010, pp. 443, 539; Richard Tarnas, *The Passion of the Western Mind*, Pimlico, London, 2010, pp. 370–71.

460 The bestselling book in the United States in 1953 and 1954 was *The Power of Positive Thinking* by the Reverend Norman Vincent Peale. Peale uncritically celebrated the American way of life and sought to mould not only positive thinking but *successful* and *prosperous* Christians who would fulfil their dreams. His three-step plan to prosperity was 'Prayerize', 'Picturize' and 'Actualize'. Peale's book is an example of a genre of bestselling twentieth-century self-help books, both Christian and secular, which emphasised the capacity of individuals to recreate themselves.

461 It is not suggested that Apple's logo was based on the creation story, just that this helps explain its cultural resonance. There are competing stories as to the origin of the symbol, in part because the original and larger logo

from the 1970s included Isaac Newton sitting under a tree. In a 2009 interview with *Creative Bits*, Rob Janoff, the man who drew the current logo, said there was no specific brief from Steve Jobs (who always remained publicly silent on the issue), and that the bite was there only to ensure that the now smaller fruit still looked like an apple and not a cherry. But the question is whether it is only the cultural association produced by the creation story which can explain why Janoff could assume (rightly) that a single bite would turn a nondescript small fruit into an apple.

462 Anselm of Canterbury, *Monologion, Proslogion, Debate with Gaunilo, and a Meditation on Human Redemption*, p. 143.

463 Blaise Pascal, *Pensées*, Section VII, 'Morality and Doctrine' (1660), cited in Wiley, *Original Sin*, p. 109.

464 Smith, *The Wealth of Nations*, p. 86.

465 The relationship between Marx's view of human nature and the Western tradition deserves a chapter of its own. While in Western Christianity the source of each person's alienation from his or her true nature (or what Marx called 'species being') is something each person is *born with* as a result of original sin, and while from a Marxist perspective it is a condition that people were *born into* as a result of the economic system, this distinction is not as pronounced as might be supposed. Both Marx and Augustine believed that alienation was the product of human history. The sociologist Philip Rieff has noted that the concept of alienation 'has its origin in the parable of the Fall of Man', and that 'there is a clear path from Old Testament to Marx, through St Paul, Augustine, Luther and Hegel' (Rieff, *The Triumph of the Therapeutic*, Chatto & Winduss, 1966, pp. 206–07; Roderick Martin, 'Sociology and Theology: Alienation and Original Sin', in Robin Gill (ed.), *Theology and Sociology: A Reader*, Cassell, London, 1996, pp. 113–14).

466 Alain de Botton, *Religion for Atheists*, Penguin, Camberwell, 2012, pp. 80–83, 180–81. Nor is de Botton the only atheist who sees value in original sin. As Theo Hobson has suggested, 'the key novelty of the newer atheism ... is its attentiveness to human frailty'. He points to the work of Douglas Murray, Andrew Brown, John Gray and Julian Baggins (see Theo Hobson, 'Richard Dawkins Has Lost: Meet the New New Atheists', *The Spectator*, 13 April 2013).

467 Roger Trigg, *Ideas of Human Nature: An Historical Introduction*, Basil Blackwell, Oxford, 1988, p. 101.

468 George Nash's influential history, *The Conservative Intellectual Movement in America Since 1945*, demonstrates how widely key thinkers in the movement drew on the doctrine of original sin to understand human behaviour. Bernard Iddings Bell claimed that 'exaggerated optimism about man' was 'the chief cause of our decay'. Russell Kirk's landmark text *The Conservative*

Mind stated that 'the saving of civilization is contingent upon the revival of something like the doctrine of original sin'. For Richard Weaver, no concept gave 'deeper insight into the enigma that is man' than original sin, describing evil as a 'subtle, pervasive, protean force'. Eliseo Vivas concurred: inside every man was 'brutality'. Peter Viereck, author of the influential *Conservatism Revisited*, believed that conservatism was 'the political secularization of the doctrine of original sin'. See George H. Nash, *The Conservative Intellectual Movement in America Since 1945*, Basic Books, New York, 1976, pp. 60–66.

469 For a discussion of the radical equalitarianism inherent to original sin, see H. Richard Niebuhr, 'The Idea of Original Sin in American Culture' (a talk given in 1949), in H. Richard Niebuhr, *Theology, History and Culture: Major Unpublished Writings*, Yale University Press, New Haven & London, 1996, pp. 174–91.

470 James C. Davies, *Human Nature in Politics: The Dynamics of Political Behaviour*, John Wiley and Sons, New York, 1963, pp. 49–50.

471 Shain, 'Religious Conscience and Original Sin', pp. 153–208, 189.

472 Roger Cox, *Shaping Childhood: Themes of Uncertainty in the History of Adult-Child Relationships*, Routledge, London & New York, 1996, p. 30.

473 Martin Luther King believed Niebuhr had 'refuted the false optimism characteristic of a great segment of Protestant liberalism'. He wrote that, before reading Niebuhr, he was convinced of the natural goodness of man; it was his study of Niebuhr in his final year at Crozer Theological Seminary that made him aware of the reality of sin on every level of man's existence and the need to avoid the dangers of a false idealism. However, King never abandoned his belief in the potential and the majesty of created human nature. He frequently referred back to Genesis, pointing out that there 'always remains enough of God's image for him [mankind] to turn his weak and sin-battered life toward the Great Physician, the curer of the ravages of sin'. See Martin Luther King, *Strength to Love*, Harper & Row, New York, 1963, pp. 123, 135–36; John J. Ansbro, *Martin Luther King, Jr.: The Making of a Mind*, Orbis Books, Maryknoll, New York, 1982, p. 151; Christopher Lasch, *The True and Only Heaven: Progress and its Critics*, W. W. Norton and Company, New York & London, 1991, pp. 389–91.

474 Jane Lampman, cited in Wallis, *God's Politics*, p. 150.

475 Calvin, *Institutes of the Christian Religion*, p. 280.

476 Milton, *Paradise Lost*, 1667, Book IX, 1–47, my emphasis. The relevant text in full is:

    '... I now must change
    Those notes to tragic; foul distrust, and breach
    Disloyal on the part of man, revolt,

And disobedience: on the part of heaven
Now alienated, distance and distaste,
Anger and just rebuke, and judgment given,
That brought in to this world a world of woe,
Sin and her shadow Death, and Misery
Death's harbinger ...'

477 *Gaudium et Spes*, 22:2, cited in Brother Roger, *Peace of Heart in All Things: Meditations for Each Day of the Year*, Harper Collins, London, 1996, p. 8.

478 Augustine, 'Marriage and Desire: Answer to the Two Letters of the Pelagians, Answer to Julian', in *Answer to the Pelagians II* (*The Works of St Augustine: A Translation for the 21st Century*, volume I/24), introduced, translated and with notes by Roland J. Teske, New City Press, New York, 1998, p. 428.

479 Most Biblical scholars agree that two creation accounts, originally separate, were joined to make up the first three chapters of Genesis. The story of Adam and Eve (Genesis 2:4 ff.), told in the language of folklore, is considered the older of the two accounts, dating between 1000 and 900 BCE; the account now placed first (Genesis 1:1–2:3) dates to the post-exilic theologians (c. 400 BCE); see Elaine Pagels, *Adam, Eve and the Serpent*, Random House, New York, 1988, pp. xxi–xxii.

480 This is the story cited by Jesus: 'Haven't you read ... that at the beginning the Creator made them male and female'(Genesis 1–2:3; Matthew 19:4).

481 The apple became identified with the forbidden fruit due to the easy Latin pun and/or mispronunciation of *malum* (apple) for *malus* (evil).

482 God's concern was that the human beings, having 'become like one of us, knowing good and evil', must not be allowed to become still more divine through achieving immortality by eating 'also from the tree of life' (Genesis 2:4–3).

483 Irenaeus (d. c. 202) believed that the Fall of Adam was a necessary stage in the childhood of humanity, because although 'it was possible for God Himself to have made man perfect from the first ... man could not receive this, being yet an infant'. The 'glory of God' was 'the human being fully alive', but a journey (a microcosm of that taken by humanity as a whole) was required to reach the divine destination. Irenaeus suggested that '[e]very human being needed to pass 'through all things' and acquire 'the knowledge of moral discipline' so he or she could learn 'from experience, what is the source of his deliverance' and 'always live in a state of gratitude to the Lord'. The reason this journey was necessary was because there was a difference between the image and the likeness of God. Humanity inherited the *image* of God by birth, and the *likeness* of God through growth facilitated by the Holy Spirit. A similar perspective was held by Clement of Alexandria (d. c. 220), who believed that Adam was not created perfect 'in

his creation, but [was] adapted to the reception of virtue'. Clement had to flee Alexandria after another imperial persecution broke out there, and his replacement as Bishop, Origen (d. 229), presented an even more positive view of human potential, so it is somewhat surprising that he was also the first of the Church Fathers to use the term 'original sin'. Origen justified infant baptism on the grounds that all babies 'are tainted with the stain of original sin which must be washed off by water and the spirit'. But Origen read Genesis 3 as an allegory which told of how all souls had been corrupted by a cosmic event, and it was only through baptism and rebirth that the soul could begin its ascent back to the transcendent realm from which it had originally descended. Over fifteen hundred years before Charles Darwin was born, Origen posed the question: 'What man of intelligence will believe that the first and the second and the third day, and the evening and the morning existed without the sun and moon and stars? ... I do not think anyone will doubt that these are figurative expressions which indicate certain mysteries through a semblance of history and not through actual events.' See Origen, *On First Principles*, translated by G. W. Butterworth, Harper & Row, New York, 1966, pp. 284–88; Wiley, *Original Sin*, pp. 46–48; MacCulloch, *Christianity*, p. 149; Charles Hill, *Making Sense of Faith: An Introduction to Theology*, E. J. Dwyer, Alexandria, 1995, p. 110; John Hick, *Evil and the God of Love*, Macmillan, London, 1977, pp. 211–17.

484 Another way of understanding these two streams of spirituality is to compare the contrasting emphasis within the Gospel of John (traditionally favoured by the Eastern Churches, Celts and mystics) and the so-called synoptic Gospels (Matthew, Mark and Luke). In the former, Jesus equates new birth in Christ with *seeing* the Kingdom of God, while in the synoptic Gospels the emphasis is on how to *enter* it. Thus, one tradition understands the Kingdom of God to be present *in* life, while the other places it *outside* or *beyond* the sinful world.

485 The first Church Father to write in Latin rather than Greek was Tertullian (d. 230), and in retrospect it seems no coincidence that he was also the first to suggest that human nature had been permanently corrupted by the sin of Adam. Tertullian believed that a propensity to sin was sown in each soul, and that this was passed on from parent to child. However, not even Tertullian believed that the *inclination* to sin was an actual sin that required forgiveness.

486 The universality of sin is a major Biblical theme, but its primal origins are not discussed. Indeed, Adam and Eve don't rate further mention in the Hebrew scriptures after Genesis. It is God's call to Abraham in Genesis 12 that begins the covenant history of Israel with which the scriptures are primarily concerned (Wiley, *Original Sin*, p. 32).

487 See Romans 5:12–21 and 1 Corinthians 15:21–2. The latter, although attributed to Paul, is unlikely to be have been written by him.

488 Plato believed that '[t]he soul is utterly superior to the body, and what gives each one of us his being is nothing else but his soul, whereas the body is nothing more than a shadow which keeps us company' (*Laws*, XII, 959), and those who developed his thought in the first centuries of the Common Era took this analysis to ever greater extremes. The Hebrew tradition knew nothing of an evil body, as opposed to a good spirit, but Greek thought came to see the higher mind (or spirit or soul) as alien to the lower physical side of humanity. It was this tradition which helped open early Christian thinkers to the possibility that there could be a corrupted, sinful body coexisting with a redeemable soul.

489 In the mid-second century, Justin Martyr argued that 'infants are born with wayward inclinations', but he did not link this tendency to the transgression of Adam, or suggest that it had undermined the capacity to choose good. Cyprian, the Bishop of Carthage (d. c. 250), believed that a baby should be baptised as soon as possible, because, 'being born physically according to Adam, he has contracted the contagion of the ancient death by his first birth'; that is, he did not see babies as having inherited *sin* but *mortality* (Justin Martyr, *The First Apology of Justin Martyr: Addressed to the Emperor Antoninus Pius*, Griffith Farran Browne & Co., London, 1889, pp. 58–61; Wiley, *Original Sin*, p. 42; Hill, *Making Sense of Faith*, p. 43; Pelikan, *The Christian Tradition*, vol. 1, p. 291).

490 Stoic philosophy claimed that people must do what they are bound to do – that is, follow their fate. Gnostic thinking was similarly deterministic. See Pelikan, *The Christian Tradition*, vol. 1, pp. 280–85; Drury, *Terror and Civilization*, p. 197.

491 John Hick, *Evil and the God of Love*, pp. 215–17; Rondet, *Original Sin*, pp. 38–48; Wiley, *Original Sin*, p. 40.

492 The Emperor Constantine was converted to Christianity in 312, but the process of Christianity becoming the religion of the Roman Empire was gradual and uneven, and was only finally fulfilled in the latter part of the century, when the establishment embraced the new faith and it became possible to realistically envisage the possibility of a Christian society.

493 Pagels, *Adam, Eve and the Serpent*, p. 39.

494 Ambrose's proof text was the much abused Psalm 51: 'behold I was brought forth in iniquity, and in sin did my mother conceive me.' His logic pointed towards the final destination of original sin: 'Even though [Jesus] assumed the natural substance of this very flesh, he [alone] was not conceived in iniquity nor born in sin' (Pelikan, *The Christian Tradition*, vol. 1, pp. 287–89).